Stanford University Press

Translating Literatures Translating Cultures

New Vistas and Approaches in Literary Studies

Edited by
Kurt Mueller-Vollmer and Michael Irmscher

STANFORD UNIVERSITY PRESS
STANFORD, CALIFORNIA
1998

Printed with the support of the
Alexander-von-Humboldt-Foundation.

Stanford University Press
Stanford, California

© 1998 Erich Schmidt Verlag GmbH & Co., Berlin
Originating publisher: Erich Schmidt Verlag GmbH & Co.

First published in the U.S.A. by Stanford University Press, 1998
Printed in Germany

Cloth ISBN 0-8047-3083-0
Paper ISBN 0-8047-3544-1

LC 60722

This book is printed on acid-free paper

Contents

Introduction IX

I. Translation Studies as Cultural History and Criticism

HARALD KITTEL
Inclusions and Exclusions:
The "Göttingen Approach" to Translation Studies and Inter-Literary History 3

ARMIN PAUL FRANK
Schattenkultur and Other Well-Kept Secrets:
From Historical Translation Studies to Literary Historiography 15

RAINER SCHULTE
Translation Studies:
A Dynamic Model for the Revitalization of the Humanities 31

LISELOTTE GUMPEL
Meaning and Metaphor: The World in Verbal Translation 47

II. Translating German Philosophy and Literature to the American Context

KURT MUELLER-VOLLMER
Translating Transcendentalism in New England:
The Genesis of a Literary Discourse 81

CYRUS HAMLIN
Transplanting German Idealism to American Culture:
F. H. Hedge, W. T. Harris, C. T. Brooks 107

ERNST BEHLER
Translating Nietzsche in the United States:
Critical Observations on *The Complete Works of Friedrich Nietzsche* 125

III. Translating Prose, Poetry, and Drama

HELGA ESSMANN
Weltliteratur Between Two Covers:
Forms and Functions of German Translation Anthologies 149

JOHN FELSTINER
Translating as Transference:
Paul Celan's Versions of Shakespeare, Dickinson, Mandelshtam, Apollinaire ... 165

BRIGITTE SCHULTZE
Highways, Byways, and Blind Alleys in Translating Drama:
Historical and Systematic Aspects of a Cultural Technique 177

THOMAS FREELAND
Heiner Müller's *Mommsen's Block* and the Languages of the Stage 197

Contributors 209

Index of Authors 211

IN MEMORY OF
ERNST **B**EHLER
1928 - 1997

Introduction

The essays in this volume originate from presentations at an international conference entitled "Translating Cultures—Translating Literatures," held at Stanford University on March 17 and 18, 1995. The meeting brought together European and North American scholars from different fields in the humanities who share an interest in the issues of translation pertaining to literary and cultural history. The purpose of this publication is twofold: to acquaint the North American reader and academic community with some prominent trends in translation studies presently pursued in Europe, notably at the "Center for Advanced Studies in Literary Translation" at the University of Göttingen, and to provide a forum for current research undertaken by American scholars in the field of literary translation and cultural transfer.

Although translation has always been a principal agent in the evolution of literate cultures, it has been accorded only scant and sporadic attention within the established academic disciplines. In Western history, for instance, the first major cultural transfer occurred with the translation of Greek authors by the Roman elite, and numerous other examples can be cited testifying to the eminent role translation has played: the influential career of the Vulgate Bible and its vernacular successors, spanning over a millennium and a half of cultural and political history; the transposition of Aristotle's works into Arabic and from Arabic into Latin in Spain during the Middle Ages, instigating the revival of the sciences; the large-scale translation program of the Humanists that helped launch the Renaissance and the rise of European national cultures; the translation endeavors encompassing European as well as non-European languages, inaugurated by the Romantic writers and since then a hallmark of the modern age. Nevertheless, translation as a subject matter in its own right did not become part of literary criticism and historiography when these disciplines, as part of the emerging nationalist cultural politics, became institutionalized at universities during the nineteenth century. To literary scholars who, following the model of nationalist historiography, took as their guiding principle the unfolding and cultural triumph of their respective national "spirit," anything that was owed to or even borrowed from other cultural traditions by way of translation could only be of subordinate, if any, importance at all.

This nationalist bias is still reflected today in the auxiliary status accorded to translation within literary studies. In institutions of higher learning, translation is usually relegated to the language departments as one of their less significant concerns. Yet the educational system, particularly colleges and universities, depends more than ever upon translations for their multicultural curricula. Oftentimes scholars who dismiss translation as a subject matter of serious academic concern, as Susan Bassnett has observed, "do at the same time teach a substantial number of translated texts to monolingual students."[1]

In Europe and elsewhere there has been a rapid growth of interest in translation as an area of scholarly and scientific research in the past few decades and a variety of approaches have been developed across national and institutional boundaries. The general term "translation studies" has been introduced in English to comprise different types of investigation concerned with "the problems raised by the production and description of translations."[2] This definition is flexible enough to allow for a broad spectrum of approaches and methodologies in three principal areas of translation studies, namely the theory and practice of translation, the evolution of translation models, and the history of translations in different cultural settings.

In the United States, however, the rise of translation studies has remained largely unnoticed in the humanities. Instead, the view of translation as mainly a didactic exercise still prevails, and the purpose of such studies is believed to lie in the elaboration of specific rules and guidelines governing the "correct" translation of utterances from one language to another. Moreover, the general reading public and its representatives still hold to the dogma of the "translator's invisibility," which defines a successful translation as one so transparent it appears not to be a translation and thus of foreign origin. Only recently has this paradigm been scrutinized and called into question.[3]

In European countries such as Austria, Germany, Great Britain, and Switzerland there are well-established academic centers and programs, dedicated both to the "science of translation" (*Übersetzungswissenschaft*) and to the training of professional translators and interpreters, which engender a lively international debate on a multitude of theoretical and practical issues. This in turn has gener-

---

[1] Susan Bassnett, *Translation Studies*, rev. ed. (London and New York: Routledge, 1991) 4.

[2] André Lefevere, "Translation Studies: The Goal of the Discipline," in James S. Holmes, José Lambert, and Raymond van den Broeck (eds), *Literature and Translation* (Louvain: Acco, 1978) 234.

[3] Lawrence Venuti, *The Translator's Invisibility: A History of Translation* (London and New York: Routledge, 1995).

Introduction

ated a great deal of specialized literature.[4] The proponents of the "science of translation" have utilized methodologies and ideas derived from a variety of disciplines, ranging from comparative literature and literary theory to linguistics, philosophy of language, hermeneutics, communication theory, semiotics, anthropology, sociology, and theology. As a result, translation has become a multi-dimensional phenomenon—the linguistic and textual aspect being just one among many—discussed in diverse conceptual frameworks. Yet despite the fact that the "science of translation" has become theoretically sophisticated and comprises diverging positions on a number of important issues, including what constitutes an acceptable definition of translation, it has remained, due to its implicit didactic orientation, a normative and prescriptive enterprise.[5]

During the past two decades, however, new schools of thought with agendas differing from that of the science of translation have emerged, notably in Belgium, Germany, Great Britain, Israel, and the Netherlands. Their endeavors, albeit not homogeneous, can best be characterized by the term "descriptive," or more accurately "historical descriptive translation studies," wherein practitioners share the perception of translation as primarily a cultural and historical phenomenon that warrants exploration. This new viewpoint challenges several traditional assumptions in translation theory and practice: the normative conception of translation which privileges the original text as an absolute point of reference, the representational theory of language designed to account for translating "meanings" successfully from one language to another, and the postulate of reliable categories for detecting "equivalences" between the source and the target document. On the basis of this critique, a number of scholars in Israel, notably Even-Zohar and Gideon Toury, have developed an approach which has come to be known as polysystem theory. They argue that the principal focus of translation research should lie on the rendered text and its place and function within the receiving literary system. Accordingly, the source language text is considered significant only to the extent that it would cast additional light on the translated text. For prac-

---

[4] See for example the essays and bibliographic information in the volume *Translation Studies: An Interdiscipline*, ed. Mary Snell-Hornby, Franz Pöchhacker, and Klaus Kaindl (Amsterdam/Philadelphia: John Benjamins Publishing, 1992), and the literature that is discussed in Werner Koller's widely used textbook, *Einführung in die Übersetzungswissenschaft*, 4th ed. (1979; Heidelberg: Quelle and Meyer, 1992). Also indicative of the emerging status of translation studies as an "interdiscipline" is the multi-volume international encyclopedia, *Übersetzung–Translation–Traduction*, a work in progress edited by A.P. Frank, N. Greiner, T. Hermans et al. and to be published by Walter de Gruyter (Berlin-New York).

[5] Koller in his *Einführung in die Übersetzungswissenschaft* defines the discipline as the non-prescriptive "science of translation processes and of translations," but has to admit that one of its major problems is to establish a meaningful relationship between its theoretical and practical components (12–13). Yet it is precisely the normative orientation of this "science" that joins the two.

titioners of the polysystemic approach, therefore, translations count as facts only within the literary system of the target language.[6] The ideas of these Israeli theorists were adopted and expanded by a group of Dutch and Belgian scholars in the 1970s and 1980s, among them Theo Hermans, José Lambert, and Raymond van den Broeck, whose work has been widely discussed.[7]

In line with the descriptive orientation polysystem theory advocated, the interdisciplinary Center for Advanced Studies in Literary Translation (*Sonderforschungsbereich 309 "Die literarische Übersetzung"*), established at the University of Göttingen in 1985, has taken translation studies in yet a new direction. Recognizing the often ignored fact that translation is not merely a linguistic affair but essentially constitutes a complex practice of cultural transfer, the Center has explored this dimension through a variety of individual case studies and large-scale empirical investigations, with an emphasis on the processes of Anglo-German literary and cultural transfer during the eighteenth, nineteenth, and twentieth centuries.[8] Based on this body of research, a model of translation studies was developed which combines a cultural historical outlook with rigorously applied philological and hermeneutic methods.

Broadly speaking, the "Göttingen approach" can be characterized as transfer-oriented and thus distinct from polysystem theory. Unlike the latter, which focuses primarily on the translated text within the target literary system, the Göttingen school considers both source language text and target language text in their respective environments. This is indeed necessary if one is to study the processes of literary and cultural transfer in their specific historical settings. One of the crucial issues raised by the Göttingen scholars, then, is the question of the particular linguistic, literary, and cultural factors that have guided historical processes of cultural transfer among different nations. Four of the essays in this volume provide first-hand insight into the issues that are associated with the

---

[6] See Gideon Toury, *Descriptive Translation Studies and Beyond* (Amsterdam, Philadelphia: John Benjamins Publishing Company, 1995).

[7] A concise treatment of this development can be found in Edwin Gentzler's study *Contemporary Translation Theories* (London and New York: Routledge, 1993), chapter V: "Polysystem Theory and Translation Studies," 105–143. José Lambert has recently published a detailed insider's account of the impact this approach has had on translation studies worldwide, particularly in Belgium and the Netherlands. See his "Translation, System and Research: The Contribution of Polysystem Studies to Translation Studies," *TTR* (*Traduction, Terminologie, Rédaction*) 8.1 (1995): 105–152.

[8] The results of the Center's research appear in two publication series, the *Göttinger Beiträge zur Internationalen Übersetzungsforschung* (since 1987) and the *Forum Modernes Theater* (since 1988). A list of these publications is included in Harald Kittel's contribution to this volume (pp. 11–13).

Introduction

Göttingen approach, a concise summary of which can be found in a number of programmatic treatises by Armin Paul Frank, the speaker of the Center.[9]

The first part of the present volume is centered around the formation of the new discipline of translation studies and some key issues it has raised. The Göttingen Center is represented with two contributions. Harald Kittel provides a concise history of the Center and its philosophy as it relates to other schools of translation studies; moreover, he shows how the Center's various projects are interconnected with problems of cultural and literary history. Participants in these cooperative endeavors were from different philologies, representing Arabic, Chinese, English (American and British), German, Romance, Scandinavian, and Slavic Studies. The existence and organization of such a Center for Advanced Studies within an academic institution, established exclusively for the pursuit of long-term interdisciplinary research projects in the humanities,[10] may be of particular interest to readers in North America where comparable centers virtually do not exist and where scholars in the liberal arts, unlike members of the scientific community, usually conduct research in isolation of one another. Humanistic projects of this kind thus find their limitations in what the individual is capable of achieving in a relatively short period of time. The Göttingen Center, on the other hand, has allowed senior and junior faculty, post-doctoral and graduate students of various departments to collaborate in significant long-term research.

In his essay Armin Paul Frank not only utilizes the transfer-oriented Göttingen approach to disclose the "shadow culture" of translations in literary histories, but also demonstrates how the methods of descriptive translation studies may be successfully applied to our understanding of non-translated literature and ultimately to the writing of literary history. To illustrate this point, he discusses the various techniques by which the colonial and post-colonial authors in North America established their literary and cultural identity vis-à-vis the powerful influ-

---

[9] See for example A. P. Frank, "Towards a Cultural History of Literary Translation" in which he summarizes the work of the Center, critically contrasting it to current tendencies in translation and comparative literary studies. The essay can be found in *Geschichte, System, Literarische Übersetzung / Histories, Systems, Literary Translations*, ed. Harald Kittel, *Göttinger Beiträge zur Internationalen Übersetzungsforschung*, vol. 5 (Berlin: Erich Schmidt Verlag, 1992) 369–387.

[10] Such *Sonderforschungsbereiche*, or "Centers for Advanced Studies," are generally designed to operate for a twelve-year period during which the project is evaluated every third year by its sponsor, the *Deutsche Forschungsgemeinschaft* (the German Research Foundation). In 1997, upon the expiration of the translation research center, a new *Sonderforschungsbereich* entitled *Internationalität Nationaler Literaturen* (Center for Advanced Research on the Internationality of National Literatures) was established at the University of Göttingen. Its mission builds on the achievements of its predecessor which revealed the intercultural dimension of national literatures.

ences of British literary culture. His case study indicates how translation research becomes instrumental in reconstructing the way in which literary history has inscribed itself into the texts. Seen from this angle, literary historiography accompanied by descriptive translation studies can be understood as essentially philological, Frank argues, insofar as philology is the discipline that studies a culture in all of its aspects as they become manifest in and through its language.

Based on his experience at the Center for Translation Studies at the University of Texas, Dallas, Rainer Schulte discusses how translation studies are changing "the way we think about the function of interpretation in the arts and humanities," and outlines new models for interdisciplinary work. He identifies the significance of practical translation studies in terms of reorienting readers toward the verbal fabric of texts and redefining the function of hermeneutic practices in the humanities. Since translation encounters what is foreign in a given work, Schulte notes, it necessarily involves interpretation. Bacon's essay "Of Studies" serves as one example to show how the procedures used in translation help to explicate historically distant texts. Moreover, translation studies assist us in establishing the meaning of expressions by giving an account of their situational settings. The essay concludes with concrete proposals for developing translation criticism as a branch of literary studies and for incorporating the practice of translation into the liberal arts curriculum as a way to encourage students to interact with foreign cultures.

Liselotte Gumpel undertakes a comprehensive and fundamental critique of established conceptions of the metaphor and of poetic language that carries important consequences for the theory and practice of translation. Her own non-Aristotelian view of the matter develops out of a strong criticism of Western linguistic and poetic theories from antiquity to the contemporary French philosopher Derrida, as well as her contrastive examination of relevant linguistic phenomena in English and German. Her basic thesis is that languages do not represent "reality" but rather translate "worlds into words." Building on insights of Wilhelm von Humboldt, Ernst Cassirer, and in particular the Polish phenomenologist Roman Ingarden, Gumpel argues that the split between meaning and metaphor in traditional theories is untenable. Metaphor cannot be defined by its alleged content or form but solely by its function. In its purest state it becomes constitutive of lyric poetry.

The second part of this volume deals with different historical moments and aspects of interaction between German and American culture. Kurt Mueller-Vollmer investigates the role translations from classical and Romantic German literature have played in the formation of the literary and philosophical discourse of New England Transcendentalism in the first half of the nineteenth century.

Introduction

Whereas scholars in translation studies often presume the facility of the target language to readily incorporate foreign works, Mueller-Vollmer questions this assumption by focusing on the discursive aspect of translatory processes. Problems arise when the target language lacks a corresponding discourse, as was the case in New England with regard to German Romanticism and Idealism during the period in question. His essay clarifies the complex relationship between translation, cultural transfer, and the formation of the new cultural discourse of American Transcendentalism.

Cyrus Hamlin portrays the entrance of German philosophical and literary thought into the American tradition by tracing significant phases in the complex process whereby the intellectual culture of German Idealism and Romanticism was transmitted to America during the nineteenth century. He investigates three figures who served as important mediators and translators: Frederic Henry Hedge, the "Praeceptor Germanicus" of the Transcendentalist movement, William Torrey Harris, the prime mover among the so-called Saint Louis Hegelians, and Charles Timothy Brooks, who enjoyed an exceptionally prolific career as a translator of German prose and poetry. Although the achievements of these men are now largely forgotten, Hamlin puts forth a convincing case as to their historical importance as mediators of classical German culture in North America. Intriguing are the observations he makes on Emerson's translation of Hölderlin's invective (the famous *Scheltrede*) against the Germans in the novel *Hyperion*, included in one of Emerson's articles published in the Transcendentalist journal *The Dial* in 1843. These could be expanded if we consider yet another appearance of the German poet among the Transcendentalists in Margaret Fuller's essay "Bettine Brentano and Her Friend Günderode," published a year earlier in the same journal.[11]

Ernst Behler reports on the monumental task of producing an historical and critical American edition of Nietzsche's complete works in a new translation which employs a uniform terminology. This undertaking clearly involves much more than simply compiling individually translated texts or reproducing the German Nietzsche edition by Colli and Montinari in the English language.[12] One of the objectives of the American edition is to account for the complex editorial situation of Nietzsche's original oeuvre and to present his published texts along with the corresponding notes, fragments, and often unpublished versions not included in previous editions. Underlying this effort is the aim to document

---

[11] The essay includes a number of translations from the correspondence between the two women. In one letter by Günderode to Bettina von Brentano there is mention of a visit to Hölderlin. See *The Portable Margaret Fuller*, ed. Mary Kelley (New York: Penguin Books, 1994) 46–47.

[12] Friedrich Nietzsche, *Werke: Kritische Gesamtausgabe*, ed. Giorgio Colli and Mazzino Montinari (Berlin: de Gruyter, 1967–).

Nietzsche's ever evolving thought process with its "multiplicity of perspectives" and constant "shifting from position to counter position." Thus the challenge the team of editors and translators faces is to develop a consistent, coherent edition which nonetheless preserves the characteristic heterogeneity and flux of Nietzsche's thought, thereby counteracting tendencies toward unifying exegeses.

The third part of this volume is devoted to problems of literary translation in different genres and cultural contexts. Helga Eßmann from the Göttingen Center assesses the place that literary anthologies have occupied in German culture. She identifies over 3,000 literary anthologies published in Germany since the early nineteenth century, and concludes that these have constituted "the most important medium" for acquainting the German reading public with the works and ideas of foreign literatures during the last two centuries. While literary anthologies vary extensively in form, their functions on the other hand do not; they can be accurately described and classified, as Eßmann evinces. Her presentation finally points in the direction of a typology of literary anthologies which calls for similar investigations into other national literatures.

In his essay on Paul Celan, John Felstiner explores the poet's practice as a translator and his renderings of selected poems by American, British, French, and Russian authors with the intention of shedding new light on the formation of Celan's own poetic discourse. There exists, as Felstiner convincingly demonstrates, a close relation between the poet's own and his translated verses. Felstiner deliberately employs the term transference (*Übertragung*) rather than translation (*Übersetzung*) because it more accurately characterizes Celan's treatment of the aesthetic materials he rendered into German from other languages. Celan's versions carry their own poetic stamp and, while maintaining the structure and meter of the original, often disclose startling changes, thus revealing, as Felstiner aptly puts it, that what is "lost in translation" also releases something to be gained by it. Translation for Celan was not a subordinate activity, but rather an essential part of his literary endeavors and a formative element in his poetic discourse.

Brigitte Schultze, who participated in research at the Göttingen Center, scrutinizes the "cultural techniques" involved in the translational transfer of drama from one language and culture to another. She takes as her starting point the dual nature of the dramatic work, namely as a literary document and as a performance, each embedded in their respective traditions. The translation of dramatic texts therefore requires the simultaneous transfer of these two different forms of communication into the target language. Schultze rejects the normative approach of the science of translation (*Übersetzungswissenschaft*) since it disregards important historical, literary, and cultural aspects of the drama. Following the descriptive, historical orientation of the Göttingen Center, she views theatrical translation

Introduction

as an intercultural exchange with specific historical and typological dimensions. Drawing examples from different national literatures, Schultze elaborates on the concept of "theatrical potential," directing the reader's attention to the complex and essentially open medium of communication which drama embodies.

Thomas Freeland's essay concentrates on the relationship between text and performance, an issue already raised by Schultze. At the conference a group of students from the Stanford Department of Drama offered under Freeland's direction a performance of his own translation and stage adaptation of Heiner Müller's poem *Mommsens Block*. In his essay (which includes photographs from the actual production) Freeland relates and reflects upon the complex process at work in the discovery and unfolding of the different kinds of theatrical potential contained in Müller's text, a process which began with its translation into English and culminated in a multimedia performance on an American stage. His description of the multiple elements of transfer and translation that constituted the theatrical performance adds a fitting conclusion to this volume.

The Stanford Symposium and this ensuing volume grew out of a collaborative project undertaken by faculty at Stanford University and at the Georg-August Universität Göttingen in Germany. The project, entitled "The Making of New World Literatures—Contacts, Transfer, New Beginnings: New Vistas and Methods in Literary History," was sponsored by the Alexander von Humboldt Foundation as part of the program for transatlantic cooperation (TRANSCOOP) between Germany and the United States in the fields of the humanities and social sciences. In this joint venture Armin Paul Frank was responsible for examining the responses of American authors to British literature inscribed in their works over a period of 150 years, thus laying the foundation for an American literary tradition, while Kurt Mueller-Vollmer was to explore the contributions to American national literature which the New England Transcendentalists made by inventing a new literary and cultural discourse from their encounter with German Romanticism and Idealism. This particular project and the approaches and the methodology devised by its participants issued from the challenges they encountered through their work in translation studies.

The editors of this volume and the project participants are grateful to the Alexander von Humboldt Foundation and to Stanford University for having made this venture possible. Our thanks go to the former Dean of Humanities and Sciences, John Etchemendy, and to the Departments of Asian Languages and Literatures, Comparative Literature, Drama, English, French and Italian, German Studies, and the Graduate Program in Humanities for their financial support, and to the Humanities Center for lending us its facilities. We are especially grateful to our colleague George Dekker, Associate Dean of Graduate Policy, whose office not only supplied the remaining matching funds without which the conference would not have materialized, but who also generously agreed to chair its opening session. We are indebted for additional sponsorship to the office of the German Consulate General in San Francisco, the Siemens-Rolm Corporation of Cupertino, and the Health Outcomes Group of Palo Alto. Last but not least the editors and contributors of this volume owe their thanks to Jenifer Nogaki for her assistance in preparing the manuscript for publication.

Stanford University, October 1997   Kurt Mueller-Vollmer, Michael Irmscher

Part I

Translation Studies as Cultural History and Criticism

Harald Kittel

Inclusions and Exclusions: The "Göttingen Approach" to Translation Studies and Inter-Literary History

I

Translations are media of interlingual exchange and of intercultural contact, communication and transfer. Through the centuries, they have played a significant, though rarely acknowledged, part in the cultural histories of many nations. Literary translations, whether identified as such or not, have frequently contributed to the repertories of autochthonous texts, thereby enhancing not just 'national' literatures but entire cultures. In some instances, individual translations have been appreciated as significant achievements in their own right, and have consequently been adopted into the literary canons of the host cultures: for instance, the *German Shakespeare*, or the *Russian Heine*. As a rule, however, literature in translation tends to be overlooked or underestimated despite its ubiquity and cultural relevance. It forms part of the complex phenomenon for which we have coined the term *Schattenkultur* (shadow culture).

As a case in point, generations of historiographers of German literature have notably failed to take note of the vast body of translations into German since the Enlightenment, let alone consider it as an integral part of German literature and its history—*pace* Shakespeare. And even today, as examination of printed histories of other national literatures will prove, in most countries the historical and systematic exploration of literary translation has hardly advanced beyond the state described by Levý back in 1963, when he claimed that no national literature had systematically explored the history of its translations, despite the fact that literary historiography would remain incomplete until the largest of all the *genres* had been duly recognized.[1] There still is an urgent need for stock-taking and systematic

---

[1] "... noch keine Literatur [hat] die Geschichte ihrer Übersetzungen systematisch bearbeitet obwohl die Literaturgeschichte ohne eine literaturhistorische Würdigung dieser zahlenmäßig stärksten Gattung unvollkommen ist." Jiří Levý, *Die Literarische Übersetzung: Theorie einer Kunstgattung* (Frankfurt/M.: Athenäum, 1969) 160.

inquiry if we wish to obtain a better understanding of the growth and formation of European and American literatures, and of cultures in general. The literary histories—like the political histories—of the European countries and of the Americas are closely interwoven in many tangible ways, though hitherto unperceived, which transcend language barriers and cultural diversity. Hence, to persistently ignore the active role literary translations have played in the formation of national literary cultures is, in view of the overwhelming evidence to the contrary, a particularly irritating form of intellectual myopia. While cultural chauvinism among historians of national literatures has a great deal to answer for (in Germany as well as elsewhere), it is not the only—though it is perhaps the most obvious—reason for this widespread failing and its consequences.

Traditionally, a number of academic disciplines such as theology, philosophy, classics, and more recently, linguistics and literary studies, including comparative literature, have taken an interest in translation and related phenomena. Their presuppositions, aims, purposes, and methods differ, and—inevitably—so do their results. Research efforts, whether guided by purely academic, institutional, didactic, or practical and professional concerns, have both broadened and intensified in recent years. While concentrating on distinct areas of translation, these studies are not automatically invalidated by their limited range and focus, either by the absence of a common methodology, or by the apparent heterogeneity of their results. What may render them seemingly incompatible rather than complementary is the failure, on the part of some of the protagonists involved, to accept that in keeping with the type of text concerned, and the motivation and aims of their inquiries, research methods as well as results may—indeed they sometimes must—differ. Although some theorists boldly refer to their specific approach as *translation science*, translation studies as an academic discipline in its own right—with a universally recognized, comprehensive methodology—have not yet established themselves, nor has their object—translation—been unequivocally defined. This generalization holds true despite the fact that universities and colleges in many countries offer special courses on translation, including literary translation, at different levels.

Studies in literary translation are usually of limited scope, focusing on individual texts and isolated phenomena, and rarely on an entire period, a body of texts, or multiple translations produced in time by different translators in different places. Few attempts have been made at comprehensive, systematic research—for obvious reasons. In the area of literary translation, investigations that are at once extensive and intensive can hardly be carried out single-handedly by individual scholars working within the confines of their traditional academic disciplines. Instead, cooperation and interdisciplinary approaches encompassing as many languages, literatures and cultures as possible appear most promising. This is one of the premises on which the "Center for the Study of Literary Translation" (*Sonderforschungsbereich* 309 "Die Literarische Übersetzung") was founded at Göttingen University in 1985.

Obviously, the task of systematically and comprehensively exploring the history of literary translation into German in its entirety exceeds the powers of individual researchers. Yet, even a large research team, such as the one assembled at the Göttingen Center, could not possibly hope to complete this task within the space of twelve years—the life-span of a *Sonderforschungsbereich*. Instead, in keeping with their distinct areas of scholarly competence and personal interests, the members of the research team decided from the start to explore selected areas and aspects of literary translation into German dating from the early eighteenth century. It is their main objective to make inroads into this vast yet scarcely explored corpus of literature in German, cast some light on an as yet largely obscure network of inter-cultural transactions and contacts, and in the process contribute to the scholarly discourse on this important area of cultural history.

II

Interdisciplinary research at the Göttingen *Sonderforschungsbereich* is, in principle, historical, descriptive, and transfer oriented. Its objectives and, to some extent, the methods of inquiry employed, differ not only from traditional approaches but also from approaches more recently favored by some scholars working in the field of literary translation studies.

Explicitly or implicitly, many traditional studies are source-text oriented and prescriptive, sharing the premise that a translation should be the *equivalent* of or *equivalent* to its source text by *adequately* reproducing its meaning, its form and meaning, its structure, or its effect (or whatever individual theorists may consider to be the essence of literature). Given its essentially subjective, ahistorical, and unsystematic character this premise is unsuited for the purposes of historical research[2]:

- It is subjective because it invariably reduces the meaning (etc.) of a literary text to the translation critic's personal conception of it; this is tantamount to arbitrarily judging a translator's interpretation (his cognitive efforts being mainly

---

[2] I am not concerned here with the prescriptive approaches to translation commonly practiced by teachers at translation schools, linguists and literary scholars alike, for perfectly good and intelligible reasons. They are entirely justified if the individuals involved in the pursuit of their didactic aims (for instance, in the training of translators and interpreters) should place emphasis on how to translate *properly*. The aims of historical descriptive research are very different.

production oriented) by the critic's own interpretation including its implicit critical objectives;
- It is ahistorical because as a rule the postulate of *equivalent* (or *adequate*) translation fails to take into account the cognitive aims and conditions prevailing in different places and cultural epochs, and it ignores the fact that the fundamental notions of translating literature well and correctly have changed in the course of history. In any case, there are numerous areas of *equivalence*, as in denotative meaning, sound, and grammatical structure, none being more dubious than the notion of *equivalence of effect*.
- It is frequently unsystematic in a double sense: first, source-oriented approaches do not sufficiently take seriously the differences between the language systems concerned, the respective literary conventions, and the distinct intellectual and material characteristics of the cultures involved; secondly, only too often do they rely on somewhat incidental, isolated analyses.

In contrast, practitioners of an approach which is at once historical-descriptive and decidedly target oriented prefer to consider literary translations more or less exclusively within the phenomenological and/or functional *systemic* contexts—linguistic, literary, and otherwise—provided by the receptor culture. Theo Hermans, a prominent advocate of this approach, has programmatically stressed the importance of accounting "in functional terms for the textual strategies that determine the way a given translation looks," i.e., of ascertaining "translational norms and ... the various constraints and assumptions ... that may have influenced the method of translating and the ensuing product." It is indeed one of the central tasks facing historical translation studies to account "for the way translations function in the receptor (or target) literature", to explain "the impact the translation has on its new environment, i.e., the acceptance or rejection of a given translation (or ... a number of translations) by the target system." Furthermore, it is necessary "to go beyond isolated occurrences of texts and to take into consideration larger wholes (collective norms, audience expectations, period codes, synchronic and diachronic cross-sections of the literary system or parts of it, interrelations with surrounding literary or non-literary systems, etc.) in order to provide a broad contextual framework for individual phenomena." Particular instances indeed ought to be related to substantial corpora in order "to discover possible large-scale and long-term patterns and trends." And yet, this exclusive focusing on target-side concerns severely limits the potential of the historical-descriptive approach, allowing it to reveal only part of the wider and rather more complex total picture.

Hermans has argued that "from the point of view of the target literature, all translation implies a degree of manipulation of the source text for a certain purpose." But does not any translation, whether viewed from the source or the target side, involve a "manipulation of the source text," deliberate or incidental? Can this manipulation be ascertained without due consideration being given to the source text and its original network of relationships and functions? Of course one might choose to be pedantic and claim that the source text as such (A) is not being manipulated at all by the act of translation; on the contrary, it stays intact. At the same time, a second text (B) which has been produced in a different language inevitably differs from (A) both in appearance and, perhaps, in intended purpose, if not in actual function. The crux of the matter is that something new has been created in transit from (A) to (B) which is neither exclusively a source nor a target side phenomenon; it cannot be described satisfactorily or defined solely in their respective terms, nor can it be reduced to their respective limited concerns without incurring some loss. Translation does indeed represent "a crucial instance of what happens at the interface between different linguistic, literary and cultural codes,"[3] as Hermans states. Yet, neither a specifically target-side consideration, nor an exclusive source-side consideration would do justice to this phenomenon. By necessity, it involves both sides as well as the ultimate enigma: the historical figure of the translator, the vicissitudes of the translation process, and the dynamics of transfer. What happens to the translated text in the context of the receptor culture is merely one aspect of the complex phenomenon of interlingual, interliterary and intercultural transfer.[4]

Faced with the sometimes labyrinthine phenomena of literary translation, the members of the Göttingen *Sonderforschungsbereich* have either devised their own philological-historical modes and methods of inquiry, or have adapted familiar ones to their specific requirements. Thus, research on literary translation carried out within the organizational framework of the Center has a characteristic, though by no means uniform, profile. These are some of the central objectives of the Göttingen team:

- To systematically explore as comprehensively as possible the history of literary translation—particularly into German—since the beginning of the eighteenth century within its diverse, including institutional, contexts, thereby rendering this vast yet scarcely explored corpus of literature in German and its complex network of inter-cultural transactions and contacts available to national and international scholarship. It is hoped that this will initiate a fruitful discourse across linguistic, cultural, geographical, academic and ideological boundaries.

- To examine, categorize, assess and, if possible, explain the linguistic, semantic and hermeneutic differences between source and target texts, and to ascertain

---

[3] Theo Hermans (ed.), *The Manipulation of Literature. Studies in Literary Translation* (London & Sydney: Croom Helm, 1985) 11–14.

[4] This issue will be taken up by Armin Paul Frank's inquiry "*Schattenkultur* and Other Well-Kept Secrets," in this volume pp. 15–30.

linguistic, literary and generally cultural enhancements by translations, wherever there is evidence on the target side. While the methods and results of contrastive linguistics are particularly useful in this context, systematic (or pragmatic) language differences, though essential, are an insufficient criterion for describing and analyzing literary translations.

- Obviously, the notions of *proper* or *correct* translation have changed in the course of time. These changes, which do not necessarily coincide with the notion of *progress*, have to be taken into account when considering individual translations within their historical contexts. As a consequence of its philological-historical orientation the Göttingen project also has to take note of historical instances of *prescriptive* conceptions without itself claiming to offer *definitive* solutions to age-old questions.

Hence, this is the fundamental tenet from which our inquiries proceed: literary translations, as well as statements on such translations, have to be examined with a view of the wider context of the historical period in which they were produced, including national, political, ideological, cultural, literary, linguistic and biographical considerations. The central questions to be asked by a student of translation are closely linked: *what* was *when*, *how, why,* and *by whom* translated, and *why* was it translated *in a particular way* ? The answers, in turn, are contingent upon the contextual—source as well as target related—and procedural complexities.

During our investigations of the phenomena of literary and cultural transfer specifically associated with drama and theater translation, we became increasingly aware of the important part played by institutional factors. Therefore, in addition to our initial premises, the three most important types of activities associated with translation and the roles played by the protagonists involved had to be defined in such a manner as to render them relevant for all the *Ringprojekte*:

1. The activity of the translator (or of that group of individuals who participate in giving a translation its final shape, for example, an intervening assistant publisher) is contingent upon the fact that, in order to be acceptable, if not perfect, a literary translation has to deviate in some respects from its source text. In other words, even if the translator intends to create nothing but equivalencies, he also produces differences.

2. The activity of the target-side reader is contingent upon the fact that he can read and appreciate a translation from a language unfamiliar to him only as a text written in his own language and, as it were, in the contexts of the target literature and/or of translated literature. The latter only applies if he is conscious of the fact that he is presented with a translation, and if his familiarity with at least one other pair of languages and literatures has furnished him with some insight into the business of translating literature, thus providing him with some understanding of translation culture.

3. Unlike the reader who is only familiar with the target language, the translation critic and the historian of translations (not to mention the connoisseur/*Kenner*, i.e., the reader who has a knowledge of both the target as well as the source language) are able to appreciate translation as a transaction between source language, literature and culture, and target language, literature and culture, respectively. However, in the context of philological-historical translation studies it is also essential to take into account the activity of the reader solely familiar with the target language. After all, it is for him that most translations were produced, and not for bilingual readers.

III

Since its conception in 1985, several dozen scholars specializing in different national philologies—Arabic, Chinese, English and North American, Finno-Hungarian, German, Romance, Scandinavian, and Slavic—have cooperated in the Göttingen research program.

During the program's initial phase (1985–87) research focused primarily on bilateral historical probes, dealing with topics such as intermediate translations (mainly of English texts translated into German via French during the eighteenth century); on multiple translations or comets' tails (German translations mainly of American short-stories, of Polish plays and of British and Swedish novels); and on translating an entire oeuvre (Strindberg, Dickens) into German.

In the second phase (1988–90) integrative, interdisciplinary comparative projects were developed, studying, for instance, individual translators translating from more than one source language and literature, or examining the genre-related contributions made by translations from various literatures. In an effort to support and balance the findings by the projects based on individual national literatures and philologies, the historical and systematic conditions for the reception of translations into German were simultaneously investigated. These and other areas of observation produced results which, in their aggregate, provide strong evidence for the formation of a translation culture in the German-speaking countries.

Since 1988 comparative issues and, hence, interdisciplinary cooperation within the *Sonderforschungsbereich* have become increasingly dominant. These developments were anticipated by the interdisciplinary project "Drama and Theater as a Translation Problem," which was started in 1987. Since 1991 this model of interdisciplinary cooperation within the organizational framework of so-called *Ringprojekte*, involving several national philologies at once, has been established throughout the *Sonderforschungsbereich*. It provides the organizational basis for grappling with the complexities of translation culture in Germany—and possibly elsewhere—conceived of as the actualization (rendering available) of world literature by means of translating and in translations.

The research program for 1991–1993 addressed the following four areas of interdisciplinary research involving specific phenomena of *otherness* and problems of comprehension which result from the traffic between different languages, literatures and cultures:

1. Anthologies of Translated Literature: Establishing World Literature
2. Literary Translation as a Medium for Experiencing Otherness
3. Translated Fictional Prose of the Nineteenth and Twentieth Centuries: Coping with Innovative Presentations of Narrative Perspective
4. Drama and Theater as Translation Problems (Focusing on the Traditions and Conventions of Eighteenth and Nineteenth-Century Comedy)

During the present final three-year phase of the Center's existence it is intended to bring together the results of 12 years' research and to conclude the work of our Center which, from its inception, has had as its main objective the drafting of an outline history of translation culture in the German-speaking countries during the nineteenth and twentieth centuries. Two areas of research appear particularly suited for such a synthesis:

1. Two interdisciplinary projects deal with translation history as reflected in twentieth-century anthologies of poetry translated into German, and with so-called *series* of literary fiction in translation, respectively. Both media are instrumental in, and symptomatic of, inter-cultural transmission and communication by translation as well as the formation of literary repertoires in German-speaking countries.
2. Two projects approach translation history by focusing on the forms, conditions and effects of alterity in literary translation. More specifically: a number of sub-projects investigate the poetics and rhetoric of alterity of European and non-European origin, as manifest in translations and re-translations into German since the seventeenth century. Another group of projects continues to investigate the experience of alterity as manifested in drama and theater. The translatorial handling of comicality and laughter within the contexts of regional and national conventions and traditions is one area of inquiry. Another focal point is the role played by institutions in drama translation, in the adaptation of theatre texts and, ultimately, in the forming of non-German theatre repertoires on German-language stages, in particular at the *Burgtheater* in Vienna, and during the most prosperous years of the Gothaer *Hoftheater*.

While the present paper attempts to characterize research at the Göttingen "Center for the Study of Literary Translation" in terms of internal logic and in comparison with other positions currently taken in translation studies, Brigitte

The "Göttingen Approach" to Translation Studies

Schultze and Helga Eßmann both summarize research carried out in two of the Center's interdisciplinary projects: the one on theater and drama translation is being directed by Brigitte Schultze, Fritz Paul and Horst Turk; the other, on anthologies of literature in translation, was initiated by Armin Paul Frank, and is being directed by Helga Essmann and Birgit Bödeker. By drawing on some of the Center's findings and contributions to the current debate on literary translation, Armin Paul Frank explores ways in which principles and methods of the historical study of literary translations might be extended to enrich the study of literary history.

Publications of the Göttingen Center for Translation Studies

The *Sonderforschungsbereich* has organized numerous conferences and workshops with participants from different countries. Also, a printed series was started for the publication of the Center's research results and conference proceedings: *Göttinger Beiträge zur Internationalen Übersetzungsforschung*. Berlin: Erich Schmidt Verlag. The following volumes have been published so far:

Vol. 1: *Die literarische Übersetzung: Fallstudien zu ihrer Literaturgeschichte*. Ed. Brigitte Schultze, Intro. Armin Paul Frank (1987).

Vol. 2: *Die literarische Übersetzung: Stand und Perspektiven ihrer Erforschung*. Ed. Harald Kittel, Intro. Armin Paul Frank (1988).

Vol. 3: *Der lange Schatten kurzer Geschichten: Amerikanische Kurzprosa in deutschen Übersetzungen*. Ed. Armin Paul Frank (1989).

Vol. 4: *Interculturality and the Historical Study of Literary Translations*. Ed. Harald Kittel and Armin Paul Frank (1991).

Vol. 5: *Geschichte, System, Literarische Übersetzung / Histories, Systems, Literary Translations*. Ed. Harald Kittel (1992).

Vol. 6: *Die literarische Übersetzung als Medium der Fremderfahrung*. Ed. Fred Lönker (1992).

Vol. 7: *Übersetzer im Spannungsfeld verschiedener Sprachen und Literaturen*. Ed. Erika K. Hulpke and Fritz Paul (1994).

Vol. 8 (1/2): *Übersetzen, Verstehen, Brücken bauen: Geisteswissenschaftliches und literarisches Übersetzen im internationalen Kulturaustausch*. Ed. Armin Paul Frank, Kurt-Jürgen Maaß, Fritz Paul, and Horst Turk (1993).

Vol. 9: *International Anthologies of Literature in Translation*. Ed. Harald Kittel (1995).

Vol. 10: *Literaturkanon – Medienereignis – Kultureller Text: Formen interkultureller Kommunikation und Übersetzung*. Ed. Andreas Poltermann (1995).

Vol. 11: *Weltliteratur in deutschen Versanthologien des 19. Jahrhunderts*. Ed. Helga Eßmann and Udo Schöning (1996).

Vol. 12: *Übersetzung als Repräsentation fremder Kulturen*. Ed. Doris Bachmann-Medick (1997).

Vol. 13: *Weltliteratur in deutschen Versanthologien des 20. Jahrhunderts*. Ed. Birgit Bödeker and Helga Eßmann (1997).

Vol. 14: *Fremdheit als Problem und Programm: Die literarische Übersetzung zwischen Tradition und Moderne*. Ed. Willi Huntemann und Lutz Rühling (1996).

Vol. 15: *Kulturelle Identität: Deutsch-indische Kulturkontakte in Literatur, Religion und Politik*. Ed. Anil Bhatti and Horst Turk (1997).

The drama project has published the results of its work in a different series, *Forum Modernes Theater*, published by Gunter Narr Verlag, Tübingen.

Vol. 1: *Soziale und theatralische Konventionen als Problem der Dramenübersetzung*. Ed. Erika Fischer-Lichte, Fritz Paul, Brigitte Schultze and Horst Turk (1988).

Vol. 4: *Literatur und Theater: Traditionen und Konventionen als Problem der Dramenübersetzung*. Ed. Brigitte Schultze, Erika Fischer-Lichte, Fritz Paul and Horst Turk (1990).

Vol. 7: *Probleme der Dramenübersetzung 1960–1988: Eine Bibliographie*. Ed. Fritz Paul and Brigitte Schultze (1991).

Vol. 11: *Europäische Komödie im übersetzerischen Transfer*. Ed. Fritz Paul, Wolfgang Ranke and Brigitte Schultze (1993).

Vol. 16: *Komödie und Tragödie – übersetzt und bearbeitet*. Ed. Ulrike Jekutsch, Fritz Paul, Brigitte Schultze and Horst Turk (1994).

Vol. 19: TOTZEVA, Sophia. *Das theatrale Potential des dramatischen Textes* (1995).

Vol. 21: *Theaterinstitution und Kulturtransfer*. Ed. Bärbel Fritz, Brigitte Schultze, and Horst Turk (1997).

Apart from publishing numerous articles in international journals, individual members of the center have produced monographs and bibliographies on the subject of literary translation. For instance:

MARTENS, Klaus. *Die ausgewanderte "Evangeline": Longfellows epische Idylle im übersetzerischen Transfer*. Paderborn: Schöningh, 1989.

CZENNIA, Bärbel. *Figurenrede als Übersetzungsproblem. Untersucht am Romanwerk von Charles Dickens und ausgewählten deutschen Übersetzungen*. Frankfurt/M. etc.: Peter Lang, 1990.

GÖSKE, Daniel. *Herman Melville in deutscher Sprache.* Frankfurt/M. etc.: Peter Lang, 1990.

GRAEBER, Wilhelm, ed. *Französische Übersetzervorreden des 18. Jahrhunderts.* Frankfurt/M. etc.: Peter Lang, 1990.

LEMMERMEIER, Doris, and Brigitte Schultze, eds. *Polnisch-deutsche Dramenübersetzuung 1830-1988: Grundzüge und Bibliographie.* Mainz: Liber Verlag, 1990.

KECK, Thomas. *Der deutsche Baudelaire.* 2 vols. Heidelberg: Carl Winter Universitätsverlag, 1991.

LOSSAU, Norberet. *Die deutschen Petöfi-Übersetzungen: Ungarische Realienbezeichnungen im sprachlich-kulturellen Vergleich.* Frankfurt/M. etc.: Peter Lang, 1993.

ARMIN PAUL FRANK

Schattenkultur and Other Well-Kept Secrets: From Historical Translation Studies to Literary Historiography

I

From a retrospective point of view, the emancipation of the vernacular literatures was one of the most significant achievements of the men and women who wrote during the period of the European Renaissances.[1] It is one of the paradoxes of literary history that incipient national traits began to emerge while trans-national values still prevailed: values, first, of a classical heritage regarded as a canon for all moderns, later of canons based on a common human nature, specifically, in the self-styled Age of Reason, on the common rationality of all men (women included: the most outspoken rationalists, in the British and Anglo-American milieus, spoke out, most resolutely, for women's rights). The poetological discourse characteristic of the objective of cultivating the modern languages in the image of the Ancients or of Reason is that of the prescriptive-productive "l'art poétique."

Again retrospectively considered, unsuspected new areas for poetological study and speculation were opened when the prescriptive-productive mode was supplemented and finally replaced by the descriptive historical-philological mode, as part of the reversal of orientation that now goes under the misnomer of "Romanticism," with its insistence on the differentiation of the universal Parnassus and with its emphasis on specificity and the concomitant invention of "original genius": that of a nation, of an historical period, of an individual writer, of a single work. One of the important new areas thus opened was that of literary history, whose practice continues to be dominated by the organic—in fact, monadic—nationalism of *Volk, Zeit, Umwelt*, which Herder had learned from Lowth, and later

---

[1] The plural is intended to indicate the striking differences between the Romance languages whose speakers had some reasons to claim that they were reviving their very own patrimony whereas the "classical heritage" applies to the non-Romance languages only in an indirect, "metaphorical" manner.

practitioners from the socialized ideas of Herder. The rival paradigm of contacts and transfer among nations, sketched by Goethe under the term Weltliteratur, was immunized, for purposes of literary historiography, by mistaking "world literature" for a value term, supposedly signifying "a world league" of *literati* playing at a higher level of performance than "continental," "national," and "regional leagues."[2]

II

As far as translation studies are concerned, strong bids for a similar shift from the prescriptive-productive orientation of Eugene A. Nida's "science of translating," and of all his willing and unavowed followers with their respective interests in contrastive or textual linguistics, to several historically descriptive research approaches developed at such centers as Tel Aviv, Leuven, and Göttingen, have opened up promising new perspectives in this branch of literary study as well. In fact, the term "historically descriptive," for the more recent translation research, serves to contrast these newer approaches with those that can justly be subsumed under "science of translating." From a descriptive point of view, these newer approaches should probably be differentiated by recognizing the more systemic, target-based orientation of the Tel Aviv and Leuven Schools, who have obviously learned a great deal from Itamar Even-Zohar[3], and the transfer-oriented hermeneutic and philological practice of those members of the Göttingen Center who regard philology as the study of a culture in and through its language and literature, or languages and literatures, as the case may be.

The very term "science of translating" implies that its proponents, in their different ways, look at translation from the perspective of the practicing translator. Their interest in extant translations is hardly ever historical in the sense of an interest in the contributions which translations of classical legal texts have made to the development of law in Europe, or translations of literary works to a country's translation and literary cultures. As long as proponents of the "science of translating" believe that they deal with nothing but a mediating skill, and that the "best" contemporary practice, by-passing the accumulated experience of literary studies, can be immediately transposed into teachable lessons, a difference between the translator's knowledge and ignorance and the researcher's knowledge and ignorance tends to become a contrast in perspective.[4]

---

[2] Without the sporting metaphor, cf. JORDAN.
[3] Cf. LAMBERT 106 et passim.
[4] Training manuals for translators are, as a rule, remarkably unhistorical.

"Schattenkultur" and Other Well-Kept Secrets

A person at his desk about to produce what never existed before—a new text in the target language called a translation of X—knows, as a matter of course, what a translation researcher who wants to do a good job does not know but needs to find out: the precise version, in whatever form it is before him—manuscript or galley proof or newspaper or anthology or cheap paperback or definitive edition or acting version, etc.; the aids to translating—dictionaries, grammars, stylistics, encyclopedias, special studies, etc.—on his desk or on his shelves; his ideas about what makes for good and correct translating; his or his contemporaries' estimate and understanding of the text, its author, its cultural milieu; and, if working under contract, the conditions and time frame agreed upon. What the translator does not (yet) know, and much of what he will never know, but what any translation researcher worth his salt will have scoured out in preparation for his own work is the precise text of the translation and the place it has been accorded in the respective translation culture: the contemporaneous reviews it may have received; the use it may have afforded later translators or authors of untranslated literature; the fame it may enjoy on the part of anthologists, translation instructors, historians, and other more or less competent reviewers; and the literary and cultural studies of which it may have been made an object.

A competent translation scholar will not rest content with what the translators said they were or are doing or what they are said to do in some theory. Findings about a translator's performance cannot hope to be indisputable unless they are based on a comparison between the precise version of the source text (or text versions) on his desk and the text he produced, word by word, comma by comma, blank by blank. If, for instance, some words or sentences or paragraphs or even a whole chapter should be missing, this need not indicate anything about the translator's principles, intentions, or down-right sloppiness. Perhaps they are missing in the very source text which that particular translator used, or the blanks are in a previous translation, not infrequently written in a third language, which he took for a model because it was imbued with a special authority such as emanating from the writer's (careless) authorization, the prestige of a third literary or translation culture, or some form of censorship (including the editorial enforcing of political correctness). None of these cases has been made up; all of them have been identified in extant translation studies. Inquiries of this kind lead deep into *Schattenkultur* (shadow culture).

One might be tempted to assume that translators had less leeway after international copyright protection, or that they handled prestige genres with greater care than others. Neither assumption would in any way be covered by textual facts established by careful translation researchers. The roles which magazine and anthology versions, pirated printings, uncorrected proofs and similar fugitive media played, and continue to play, in interliterary exchange can hardly be overestimated. This is, one might say, where literary life is throbbing between nations. It is difficult to see how anyone might disagree in principle. Hasn't, after all, Goethe introduced the term *Weltliteratur*, world literature, precisely to draw attention to literary trade across national boundaries, in the form of translations, magazines, etc., with a concomitant gain of not only prestige for, but also understanding of, one's own literature, by seeing it through the eyes of a foreign translator or commentator? Indeed, without the internationally oriented though, as a rule, disregarded middlemen maintaining what may be called the "analectic network," Kant's fame might well have been buried with him at Königsberg, Wordsworth is likely to have remained an eminence strictly of the Cumberland Hills, and Stevens might just as well have set up house in a boat off Key West. But if so, why is it that literary histories, surveys, editions know so little of this life, of this real history of contacts and transfer, and even less, it would seem, the more recent they are? The vital part of literary life is under a shadow.

Descriptive historical translation studies have begun to lighten this shadow country. The most useful among them are those which are descriptive in the strict sense of the word: those which consider all actual translation shifts and which try to account for them in reasonable ways. Translation criticism of the kind which marks down peculiarities of extant translations insofar as they do not conform to the critic's idea of what makes for correct and good translating does not make much historical or cultural sense. What does is to try to account for them in translational, literary, scientific, or cultural preferences of the period in question: preferences, not necessarily norms. Explanations may be grounded in any aspect that has a bearing on an act of translation: source side conditions, target side considerations, the transfer itself, intermediate translations in third languages, and many more.[5]

A case in point are the translation shifts apparently made for the sake of explication. They need not always be accounted for by the translator's sense that the intended target audience lacks information about the source culture or literature which must be supplied in order to make the translation intelligible. Inserted explanations can also be encountered in cases when a deficiency on the part of the target audience cannot reasonably be posited, either because the cultural information is a regular part of education or because the type of hermetic text—the "modernist" poem, say, consistent in its local discontinuities—is well known from indigenous production in the target literature as well. If—as is more frequent than theory seems to admit—such translations are studded with explanatory expansions, these shifts can be explained in several ways: The individual translator may have been right about the need to make characteristic shifts in order to accom-

---

[5] For a survey, cf. FRANK/SCHULTZE.

modate target-side exigencies; he may have been in error about target-side exigencies or may have purposely flouted them; or his allegiance was less to the target audience than to his sense of the translator's duty in general: the duty of an interpreter to make his "message" as intelligible as possible, irrespective of a given target culture. This sense of duty—wherever it exists—is grounded in a general ethos of translating as a special mediating skill.

The emphasis that has so far been placed on so-called explicatory translation shifts was made in the interest of a more general argument. As a matter of historical fact, shifts—even considerable ones—have been more numerous, at all times, than a translation critic staring at the Big Serpent that goes by the name of *belles infidèles* would believe. These shifts are made for a variety of reasons, especially so in what we now call literary texts, both in verse and in prose. Again, they are motivated by much more than target side considerations. One motive seems to be competition among individual translators, as when opposite stylistic choices were made in the writing of near-contemporaneous translations.[6] Another is located in the nature of a poem, or literary work in the narrow sense, however differently it may have been conceived at various times, and in the concomitant mode of "translation" recommended for it. An idea of the special status of poetic, i.e., literary, "translation" can be gained by approaching the question from two directions, an historically early and a contemporary point of view.

In early British discourse on translation, there are indications that literary "translation" kept quite different company from that of Scriptural and "technical" translation. It is evident that absolute correctness of a translation is a matter of eternal life and death, for the faithful, when it comes to the translation of Holy Writings; moreover, it is only consistent for early European translation theory to focus on Bible translation.[7] It is also evident that mundane transactions, insofar as they rely on translation, need at least the facts to come across correctly, if not necessarily the *ordo verborum* which, as St. Jerome well knew, makes for the mystery of Sacred Writ.[8] The correct translation of both matters of faith and matters of fact is possible, it would seem, because in both cases there is an "outside" support of one kind or another on which to rely. For the religious translator, it is—to put it in an abbreviated form—his denomination's canonical interpretation of the respective Biblical canon or his hard-bought conviction that the Word of God, as he understands it, gainsays the canonical interpretation. The translator of mundane texts has at least two kinds of support: for one, the shared experience of the experts in a given kind of transaction—say, a mercantile one—in

---

[6] For a detailed historical study cf. WETZEL-SAHM.

[7] For the English domain, cf. AMOS.

[8] Cf. HIERONYMUS 1.

its mechanics so that it is possible to satisfactorily complete the transaction once the facts have come across correctly, and, secondly, the shared knowledge about, or, at least, empirical ascertainability of, a given set of circumstances which precedes all possible texts in any language and against which the correctness of a translation can be tested as long as the circumstances prevail—the *interlingual konstante Größe*, in Werner Koller's serviceable term.[9]

There is some evidence that literary "translation" kept different company in Renaissance thought. Thus, Jürgen von Stackelberg has suggested that in early modern French literature it was more closely associated with poetic methods of "imitating" the ancients than with scriptural (and, for that matter, "technical") translation and hence was regarded rather as a literary than a translational technique.[10] A similar distinction was made by Sir John Denham in Britain in the early seventeenth century when he insisted that he had not intended in his poetic "translations" to act as *fides interpres* because he did not deal in "matters of Faith nor in matters of Fact."[11] He felt that there was not yet a name for his kind of free literary treatment of his source texts. Some languages, however, do have one: *Nachdichtung* in German (in the sense of free poetic treatment of poetry originally written in some other language) or *anuvād* and *rupantar* in some Indian languages.[12] Denham might have considered the multi-purpose Renaissance literary term "imitation." For when John Dryden later tried to rein in such "libertine ways" of rendering poetry, he did so by locating the proper procedures of interlingual paraphrase this side of imitation.[13] Yet it has been shown that his own literary translations contain passages that cannot but be classified as extreme forms of imitation—*Nachdichtung*.[14]

Dryden's is a prominent case of a writer whose translation guidelines run counter to some of his own practices. And though later translators may have been tricked into a narrow practice as long as Dryden's guidelines remained canonical, there is sufficient evidence that many others continued to practice *imitation* (*Nachdichtung*), that is the production of *versions* rather than translations in the sense codified primarily by translators of religious texts, such as Eugene A. Nida, whose several theoretical books have defined *translation* for much of contemporary thought on the matter.

---

[9] Cf. KOLLER 115.
[10] Private communication.
[11] Cf. DENHAM 64–65.
[12] For the Indian, cf. GANESHAN 794.
[13] Cf. DRYDEN 68.
[14] Cf. AMOS 157; less apodictically, SLOMAN 8–10 et passim.

"Schattenkultur" and Other Well-Kept Secrets

The reason many modern "translators" not only of highly structured poetry but also of purportedly easy short stories inevitably continue to practice something like imitation lies in the peculiar structure which literary works of any complexity exhibit. This structural specificity has usually been recognized by those critics, aestheticians, and philosophers who developed their views of the nature of literature in opposition to the neo-classical form-content dualism.[15] From the point of view of literary "translation," it may be said that (1) to the extent that a literary work is "invention" and "disposition," in the sense of Renaissance rhetoric, or "fiction," in the sense of not referring to anything like Koller's coherent interlingual (i.e., extralingual) constant, a *Nachdichter* cannot rely on what is "factually correct." Despite Melville's parade of cetology, for instance, a translator of *Moby Dick* would do his readers poor service to correct any error which Melville might have made in his description of whaling because Melville hasn't described whaling but has used, among other things, whaling in order to project an "imaginative world" in which "factual errors" may be—and, indeed, in *Moby Dick*, are—imaginatively meaningful.

(2) It follows that every single element of a work's *ordo verborum* contributes to the "imaginative world" or "opined reality" of the work in question, as it is internally structured and as it is made to respond to other works and types of text which may or may not be part of the author's oeuvre. It seems evident that a reader hardly ever grasps a work's entire "potential of meaning" thus defined, and a translator, to the extent that he is, first and foremost, a reader, will be similarly handicapped except perhaps when confronted by an extremely short and truly simple work—if such a thing exists. Much less can a translator rewrite a literary work of any complexity in a way which makes the same potential accessible to the target reader—the linguistic, literary, cultural, natural, and historical differences are insurmountable obstacles. Of course, if in literature there had also been a truly soul-searching (and not only originality-searching) sequence of interpretations culminating in an orthodox, canonical one, an analogy between the "correctness" of scriptural and literary *translation* would be possible to establish. As things are in the literary domain, translators cannot but be *Nachdichter* who are lucky if they can inscribe their own interpretation into the target text, less lucky if the differences between source and target sides make it necessary for them to rewrite significant passages in order to at least come close to their interpretations, and downright unhappy if they fall short even of this compromise. One kind of *imitation* which a translation scholar trained in observing and interpreting translation shifts can easily find under the label translation is the reduction of even modestly

---

[15] One might think of "Romantic" organicism, Hegel's dialectical relationship of content and form or Wellek-Warren's structural solution.

complex texts to one literary level—in novels and stories usually the *plot*—so that large-scale omissions, striking changes, and slight additions make of many non-English versions of Poe's epistemological tale "Murders in the Rue Morgue" the "original" detective story it is purported to be. Only by giving fairly close attention to a consistent rendering of certain terms without resorting to variation (one of the most virulent shift-producing resources of the imitator) has Hans Wollschläger been able to make the epistemological aspect of the text readable in German.[16] The saddest, but certainly not rarest, case consists in the *Nachdichter* having produced such a variety and contrariety of shifts that they do not make any coherent sense.

III

A literary "translation" resounds with many voices, some loud and clear, some muffled and indistinct, and some noticeable by their studied avoidance. The privileged voice, one would hope, is that of the source text. Other voices can also be distinguished: those of one or more earlier translations into the target language, and voices of intermediate translations in a third language. One can, on occasion, hear echoes of voices of target-side writers, of non-translated literature whose words, phrases, or cadences a translator tried to catch. When a translation scholar has learned how to listen, he can also hear the voices of prescriptive stylists or of literary critics and commentators, and in some cases those of makers of dictionaries, or, for that matter, of Baedekers. Again, it is not likely that they are the ones on the researcher's desk but, frequently, so-called "outdated" ones at an earlier translator's hand.

This "hum and buzz," as Lionel Trilling might have put it, of a culture talking back and forth with both one or several other cultures and with its own former selves is what a translation scholar has to recover, recapture, re-activate. The term *shadow culture*, invented by Harald Kittel, is the visual equivalent.

Writers of non-translated literature are by and large in the same boat. The term *non-translated literature*, incidentally, seems preferable to "original literature," for a number of reasons. There is, first, a sense in which a literary work that has not been translated even once is incomplete, that it has not become "world literature" in any sense of the word. And, second, the works commonly called "original" deserve this attribute only by a kind of scholarly license. Poets who have reflected on their relationship with the past have stated as a matter of course that, in their poems, they converse with earlier writers, that they invite the voices of dead poets,

---

[16] Cf. POE; dazu FRANK/STEYER.

their ancestors, to speak through them. Poets steal. Mature poets acknowledge this. "Original" poets keep the matter hushed. That's the entire difference. Every work, every writer's *œuvre*, is a choir, so to speak, of all the voices, fragmentary or continuous, dissimulated and undisguised, adopted, adapted, and avoided, from past or contemporaneous writings—literary, philosophical, scientific, journalistic, etc.—in the writer's own language and in other languages, untranslated and translated, as they echo and re-echo in his lines and paragraphs and chapters and books. Specialists in a particular writer, at least some of them, do know. They will show how James Fenimore Cooper turned Walter Scott to his own account; they will identify the place Johann Wolfgang von Goethe has in Ralph Waldo Emerson; they will record the popularity which August von Kotzebue enjoyed with late eighteenth- and early nineteenth-century playwrights in both Britain and America. Literary historians know—or at least show—less and less of international literary connections. In 1917, *The Cambridge History of American Literature* found 33 occasions to refer to Scott, 14 to Goethe, and two to Kotzebue, on some fifteen hundred pages. The index to the 1500-page *Literary History of the United States* of 1974 has six entries for Scott, five for Goethe, and none for Kotzebue. In 1988, the count for the 1200-page *Columbia Literary History of the United States* was Goethe, one, Scott and Kotzebue, zero. Neither is there a single reference to Scott within the 900 pages of the *Columbia History of the American Novel* of 1991. A deep shadow has fallen over what Anglo-American writers really did when they wrote in response to Scott, Goethe, Kotzebue, and many another foreign writer. Contemporary literary historiography has a tendency to be narrowly national—and not only in the United States of America. It remains to be seen whether the new Cambridge History of American Literature will reverse the trend.

To tell half the truth is to tell a complete falsehood. A literary historian's task—not to say, his sacred task—is to unforget the whole truth about literature. The Stanford-Göttingen Transcoop project is intended to take a few steps towards this end, for the literature of British America and the USA.

IV

One of the first steps is to give unpleasant facts known to specialists—and, apparently, to specialists only—their full historical due. There has always been a common cross-Atlantic book market. Surveyors of the Anglo-American book market have shown that it was dominated by British products almost to the end of the nineteenth century, just as British reading of Anglo-American authors was never negligible.[17] The consequences for the Anglo-American reading culture are evident and inevitable: it was predominantly British in its habits and tastes. Writers resident in the early United States who calibrated their work for the majority tastes of their countrymen wrote, in effect, by British standards. Writers insisting on writing distinctively American literature were, for a long time, something like literary foreigners in their own country. This is one of the complexities that characterize the literature of a former settlement colony. A literature originating under such conditions cannot but be a chronologically second literature in the very same literary language in which the literature of the former imperial power has been written for some centuries. And representatives of the first literature in English, angered perhaps by the loss of the North-American colonies, tried to keep up their domination at least in cultural matters by bandying about opinions such as the following: "The literary independence of the Americans is far from being so complete as the political, for as yet they possess no national literature, and invariably regard ours as appertaining also to them." Thus writes *The* [London] *Athenaeum* for February, 1831, apparently afraid that Americans would walk away not only with British territorial possessions, but British literature to boot.[18]

It was customary on both sides of the Atlantic to debate literary independence as though it were of the same nature as political independence, as though it were something to either declare or deny. This link must be broken in the interest of a proper understanding of Anglo-American literary history, both colonial and postcolonial. To declare political independence is an act of will. One can gain it by fighting a war, if need be. Once a country is recognized as a separate subject under international law, the liberation movement has obtained independence in the sense of sovereignty. This is one matter. Another is the linguistic, literary, and cultural aspect. A former settlement colony—a colony made up primarily of immigrants and their descendants who use, or learn to use, the same language and, if they read, read, or learn to read, the same books as the people of the former imperial power—simply cannot avoid having their language and literature intricately bound up with that of the other country. It just doesn't work to declare a language or literature independent. The very recurrence of proclamations and programs to this effect during the decades of the Early Republic testifies to this fact. First among several, Noah Webster saw this clearly in the 1790s when he predicted that it would not take long before the American language was as dif-

---

[17] Cf. HART and HUBBELL for significant details of Anglo-American reading; SPENGEMANN (125–28) summarizes research on British reading of Anglo-American authors.
[18] Cf. RULAND 235.

ferent from English as German was from Dutch, Danish, or Swedish.[19] That was wishful thinking along the lines of a model then emerging in Germany which saw national identity as a combination of linguistic and literary separateness, usually with ethnic overtones. The stubborn post-colonial fact, for which there is no model, is that Anglo-American writers had to invent their literary identities (the plural is essential) in an inescapable relationship to the first literature in English, the literature of Britain.

What were writers resident in the United States of America doing when they were not writing programs and proclamations? Some adopted a British model and wrote their novel or poem or play or sketch or essay in keeping with British canons—a wise decision if one wanted to live by one's pen in a country whose literary market was dominated by British fare. Cooper did so in his first attempt, *Precaution* of 1820, by retelling and elaborating on a Jane Austen novel in the Amelia Opie tone.[20] In writing a would-be popular novel, he employed a method similar to that of those translators who combine in their own translation features of two or more preceding ones.

This is, of course, no way of giving an American identity to a literary work. Cooper went on to try to achieve this end by a method which other writers before and after him applied, by adapting a British model to an American setting and American circumstances. There is, however, nothing distinctively American in such a strategy at a time when British writers, also guided by an associationist poetics, were in the habit of giving a local habitation and, often a local name as well to their own compositions. In writing about Monument Mountain and the Illinois prairies, Bryant followed approximately the same aesthetic principles as Wordsworth in writing about the valley of the River Wye or Derwent Water; and Loch Lomond and the Scottish Highlands play a part in Scott for fairly similar aesthetic reasons as Lake Glimmerglass and the Highlands of the Hudson do in Cooper. In fact, in writing *The Spy* in 1821, with some carry-over from *Precaution*, Cooper for the most part transferred the model of Scott's historical romances about border warfare in unsuccessful rebellions against the House of Hanover to his description of fictitious incidents in the successful American revolution against the same Monarchy, picturesque and patriotic incidents set on the neutral ground to the north and northeast of New York City. As George Dekker argued, Cooper employed much the same literary machinery as Scott had before him.[21] To be sure, certain differences of detail do exist. Mr. Harper alias General

---

[19] Cf. MENCKEN 9–10; SIMPSON 52–90.

[20] On the Cooper-Austen nexus, cf. HASTINGS; on Cooper's use of Opie, cf. WALLACE, esp. 68–72.

[21] Cf. DEKKER, 22–24; cf. also GICZKOWSKI, esp. 55–62; for a different view, cf. WALLACE, esp. 89–116.

George Washington plays much more of a fairy-godmother to Harvey Birch and Frances Wharton than the Chevalier did to Edward Waverley. It is likewise true that, while Scott's disguise artist, Rob Roy Campbell McGregor, is a closely pressed Highland chieftain, his counterpart in *The Spy*, Harvey Birch, is as closely pressed but otherwise a simple peddler. Moreover, while Scott's romantic heroines are not very much more than alluring presences who stand next to waterfalls and pour down liquid strains in Gaelic, Frances Wharton sneaks out of the military camp and climbs a high mountain all by her lone self (and in her low slippers, mind you) in an attempt to help her brother Henry and Harvey Birch. Yet despite such differences of detail, the Cooper of *The Spy* is, indeed, an American Scott.

In writing his second historical romance, *The Pioneers* of 1823, Cooper is an un-Scottish American. Here, his main theme is the complexity of feeling that makes the reconciliation of former civil war enemies so difficult; and to the extent that the American revolution divided the loyalty of residents in British America, it was indeed a civil war. Reconciliation is also tacked on to the end of Scott's romances of the Stuart uprisings, *Waverley* and *Rob Roy*. If one takes these two and combines them with *Guy Mannering*, the earliest and most extensive of Scott's romantic treatments of the theme of the disinherited, which is also part of the fabric of *The Pioneers*, one has what might be called the "Waverley correlative": that set of Scott romances in relation to which this particular one of Cooper's historical romances is his *deviating response*—un-Scottish not only in subject and setting, but in many purely literary traits as well. This is not the occasion for a detailed comparison.[22] All that can be done here is to indicate the range of literary strategies by which Cooper, in *writing against a British correlative*, in practicing what Ezra Pound most pertinently called "criticism in new composition," invented an American historical romance which in turn served as inspiration for later Anglo-American, Anglo-Canadian, and Spanish-American writers.[23]

Some of Cooper's deviations in *The Pioneers* were indeed made to accommodate Scott to *American circumstances*, for instance the ones previously mentioned, resulting from fictionalizing a successful revolution as distinct from an unsuccessful uprising. Some were made for *artistic reasons*. As already suggested, Cooper is the more careful artist in integrating the theme of reconciliation. And sometimes, as in this case, the artistic considerations shade over into *moral and intellectual ones*. Cooper—again to mention just a single point—is more realistic than Scott in paying attention to the hurt pride and the fears and suspicions that make the reconciliation of former civil war parties such a delicate and protracted affair. In

---

[22] I have argued the case in detail, see FRANK, "Writing Literary Independence."
[23] Cf. POUND 75.

this moral and psychological interest as well as in other respects, such as developing a more complex character for his heroine by setting her off from Scott's, we suddenly recognize that Cooper is closer to a later, and greater, American writer, Hawthorne, than he is to Scott—to Hawthorne who, in 1850, wrote *The Scarlet Letter* largely as a deviating response to another Scott romance, *The Heart of Midlothian*.

Methods derived from an historical analysis of literary translations can indeed be transposed in order to serve a transfer-oriented, international history of Anglo-American literature. In so doing, one can distinguish basically three methods which American writers, colonial and post-colonial ones, employed *vis à vis* British literature—the critical literature for them. The strategies are (1) to adopt a British model, or two, and to follow it, or them, closely (in German: *nachschreiben*), to use the matter of X and write in his manner, to write in keeping with British canons, to write an affirmative response; (2) to adapt a British model to American circumstances (in German: *umschreiben*), to rewrite a British work in keeping with American facts, to write a naturalizing response (as the translational term is); and (3) to avoid a British model, to take a British work not as a model but as a point of departure and write against it (in German: *gegenschreiben*), to write a deviating response that will alienate the British correlative, that will make it over into something foreign. The first method evidently does not qualify to produce an Anglo-American literary identity. The second has frequently been recommended by writers of the Early Republic as an excellent strategy; it is not really an unqualified success. The third, it would seem, is. It helps the historian to identify different American qualities individually inscribed as deviating responses to British works, responses which can be shown to embody artistic, moral, and intellectual motives as well as Americanistic ones. And if one analyzes roughly parallel cases—for instance, Cooper and Hawthorne responding, each in his personal way, to different Scott romances—one can also discover common traits of more than one American writer. It would surely be erroneous to regard only common traits as signs of literary Americanness; the individual responses themselves point to differently interpreted and differently crafted literary Americannesses. And it would also be erroneous to assume that the adoption, adaption, and alienation of British models were the only strategies employed by Anglo-American writers. Since, under post-colonial conditions, Anglo-American literary identities amount to non-British identities, it would seem to be a good idea to look to a third literature as a hitherto overlooked but promising model. A good number of American writers did precisely this during significant decades of the nineteenth century, at least. They looked to Germany. And I look to Kurt Mueller-Vollmer's investigation[24] which elucidates this process of cultural transfer.

Works Cited

AMOS, Flora Ross. *Early Theories of Translation*. New York: Columbia UP, 1920.

BERCOVITCH, Sacvan, gen. ed. *The Cambridge History of American Literature*. Vol. 1, 1590–1820. Cambridge, Engl.: Cambridge UP, 1994.

DEKKER, George. *James Fenimore Cooper: The Novelist*. London: Routledge, 1967.

DENHAM, Sir John. "'The Preface,' The Destruction of Troy (1656)." T.R. Steiner. *English Translation Theory, 1650–1800* (Part II: The Documents). Approaches to Translation Studies 2. Assen/Amsterdam: Van Gorcum, 1975. 64–65.

DRYDEN, John. "'Preface,' Ovid's Epistles (1680)." Steiner (cf. above, DENHAM) 68–72.

ELLIOTT, Emory, gen. ed. *Columbia Literary History of the United States*. New York: Columbia UP, 1988.

—. *The Columbia History of the American Novel*. New York: Columbia UP, 1991.

FRANK, Armin Paul, and Brigitte SCHULTZE. "Normen in historisch–deskriptiven Übersetzungsstudien." *Die literarische Übersetzung: Stand und Perspektiven ihrer Erforschung*. Ed. Harald Kittel. Göttinger Beiträge zur Internationalen Übersetzungsforschung 2. Berlin: Schmidt, 1988. 96–121.

FRANK, Armin Paul, and Stefan STEYER. "Die Dupinade, oder: Die übersetzerische Quintuplikation eines meisterhaften Amateurdetektivs und deren bemerkenswerte Folgen." *Die literarische Übersetzung—Der lange Schatten kurzer Geschichten: Amerikanische Kurzprosa in deutschen Übersetzungen*. Ed. A. P. Frank. Göttinger Beiträge zur Internationalen Übersetzungsforschung 3. Berlin: Schmidt, 1989. 119–33.

FRANK, Armin Paul. "Writing Literary Independence: The Case of Cooper—the 'American Scott' and the un-Scottish American." *Comparative Literature Studies* 34.1 (1997) [in press].

GANESHAN, Vridhagiri. "Literarisches Übersetzen in einer multi-lingualen Gesellschaft: Ansichten eines indischen Germanisten." *Übersetzen, Verstehen, Brücken bauen: Geisteswissenschaftliches und literarisches Übersetzen im inter-*

---

[24] MUELLER-VOLLMER, "Translating Transcendentalism in New England: The Genesis of a Literary Discourse," in this volume pp. 81–106.

nationalen Kulturaustausch. Ed. A. P. Frank et al. Göttinger Beiträge zur Internationalen Übersetzungsforschung 8.2 Berlin: Schmidt, 1993. 793–800.

GICZKOWSKI, William. "Cooper and Hawthorne: American Innovators in the Tradition of Sir Walter Scott." Diss. Stanford University, 1971.

HART, James D. *The Popular Book: A History of America's Literary Taste*. New York: Oxford UP, 1950.

HASTINGS, G.E. "How Cooper Became a Novelist." *American Literature* 12.1 (March 1940): 29–51.

HIERONYMUS (St. Jerome). "Brief an Pammachius." Transl. Wolfgang Buchwald. *Das Problem des Übersetzens*. Ed. Hans Joachim Störig. 2nd ed. Darmstadt: Wissenschaftliche Buchgesellschaft, 1973. 1–13.

HUBBELL, Jay B. *Who Are the Major American Writers? A Study of the Changing Literary Canon*. Durham, N.C.: Duke UP, 1972.

JORDAN, Lothar. "Welche Grenzen? Reflexionen zu einem konstitutiven Element komparatistischer Forschung." *Nationale Grenzen und internationaler Austausch: Studien zum Kultur- und Wissenschaftstransfer in Europa*. Ed. Lothar Jordan & Bernd Kortländer. Tübingen: Niemeyer, 1995. 34–49.

KOLLER, Werner. *Einführung in die Übersetzungswissenschaft*. Heidelberg: Quelle & Meyer, 1979.

LAMBERT, José. "Translations, Systems and Research: The Contribution of Polysystem Studies to Translation Studies." *TTR* [Traduction, Terminologie, Rédaction] 8.1 (1995): 105–52.

MENCKEN, H.L. *The American Language: An Inquiry into the Development of English in the United States*. 4th ed., corrected, enlarged, and rewritten. New York: Knopf, 1962.

POE, Edgar Allan. "Die Morde in der Rue Morgue." Transl. Hans Wollschläger. *Das Gesamte Werk*. Ed. Kuno Schuhmann & Hans Dieter Müller. Vol. 1. Olten: Walter, 1966. 723–77.

POUND, Ezra. "Date Line" (1934). *Literary Essays of Ezra Pound*. Ed. T.S. Eliot. London: Faber, 1954. 74–87.

RULAND, Richard, ed. *The Native Muse: Theories of American Literature from Bradford to Whitman*. New York: Dutton, 1976.

SIMPSON, David. *The Politics of American English, 1776–1850*. New York: Oxford UP, 1986.

SLOMAN, Judith. *Dryden: The Poetics of Translation*. Prepared for Publication by Anne McWhir. Toronto: U of Toronto P, 1985.

SPENGEMANN, William C. *A Mirror for Americanists: Reflections on the Idea of American Literature*. Hanover, N.H.: UP of New England, 1989.

SPILLER, Robert E., et al., eds. *Literary History of the United States: History*. 4th ed., revised. New York: Macmillan, 1974.

TRENT, William P., et al., eds. *The Cambridge History of American Literature*. 3 vols. New York: Macmillan, 1917.

WALLACE, James D. *Early Cooper and His Audience*. New York: Columbia UP, 1986.

WETZEL-SAHM, Birgit. "Das Übersetzertrio Busch-Lange-Jacobi im Kometenschweif 'Journalism in Tennessee.'" *Die literarische Übersetzung—Der lange Schatten kurzer Geschichten: Amerikanische Kurzprosa in deutschen Übersetzungen*. Ed. A.P. Frank. Göttinger Beiträge zur Internationalen Übersetzungsforschung 3. Berlin: Schmidt, 1989. 203–08.

RAINER SCHULTE

Translation Studies:
A Dynamic Model for the Revitalization of the Humanities

> The foreigner allows you
> to be yourself by making
> a foreigner of you.
> *Edmond Jabès*

The emerging field of Translation Studies has produced some major paradigm shifts in the way we think about the function of interpretation in the arts and humanities. The methodologies derived from the art and craft of translation furnish tools that are modifying the interpretive approaches to literary and artistic texts; these methodologies have also been responsible for changing the field of textual scholarship and for creating a new theory of editing. Furthermore, they revitalize the procedures and practices of scholarly research that can be applied as a model for the development of interdisciplinary studies. Moreover, translation studies initiate new directions of scholarly and intellectual inquiry that will lead to innovative publications in the realm of literary and cultural criticism.[1]

Research Methodologies Based in Translation Thinking

How can we best characterize the work we do in the humanities? We constantly interpret: we interpret literary and artistic texts, we interpret ideas and concepts, and we interpret human situations. Almost all activities in the humanities are built in one form or another on principles of interpretation.

We seek entrances into texts so that we may enlarge our understanding of the intricate structures that interact in works and intensify the aesthetic experience. George Steiner tells us in *After Babel: Aspects of Language and Translation* that all acts of communication are acts of translation. When we consider the act of interpretation, we can say that we interact with the text, we establish a dialogue with

---

[1] For a selection of recent publications as well as complete citations for subsequent footnotes, see the bibliography at the end of this article.

the text, we communicate with the text. Thus, all acts of interpretation initiate an act of translation. Octavio Paz clarifies that idea for us. He says: when we interpret a text, especially one from a previous century, we must translate that text into our own sensibility of the twentieth century.[2]

To enter into a meaningful relationship with a text, we are aided by the research methods we employ to open up avenues of thinking about a particular work. The most urgent question that needs to be asked is: What kind of research has to be pursued in order to do justice to the text?

Jabès talks about the foreigner who lets you be yourself and at the same time makes you a foreigner to yourself. Whatever we encounter in terms of texts, whether they be written, visual, or musical texts, and whether the written texts come from contemporary authors or whether they originate in past centuries or other languages, all these texts are foreign to us, and we have to decipher their foreignness in order to find entrance into them and interpret them. That foreignness postulates the enactment of two mental processes: it must be identified as the foreign within the parameters of its own context, juxtaposed with our own intellectual environment in comparison to which it becomes foreign, and then translated into the possibilities of our own sensibility. Thus, we look at that which is familiar to us through the eyes of the foreign in the other text and begin to experience ourselves as foreigners.

No interpretive act seems possible without an act of translation. And in some art forms, the work can be experienced only through the medium of the interpreter/performer. Hardly anyone will have direct access to a musical piece, since most of us cannot read the language of scores. The musical piece becomes reality to us only through the interpretive perspectives of the performing musicians.

It is easy to understand that a work of music comes to life through the interpretive imprint of the performer. Yet, the same applies to all other forms of interpretive recreation. The interpreter, and in this case, the translator, becomes visible in the act of translating.

At the same time, every author, painter, or composer has enacted a particular perspective or vision in his or her work, the materialization of which also depends on the possibilities and strictures of the respective medium. In the realm of language, a translator has to cope not only with the vision that an author wanted to create in a work but also with the reality that each language in itself is a way of seeing. Paz correctly reminds us that the sun the Aztecs worship is quite different from the sun that the Egyptians worship.[3] Thus, the translator constantly reconstructs the foreign in a given text: first to understand that foreignness and then to

---

[2] HONIG, *The Poet's Other Voice* 162.
[3] PAZ, "Translation: Literature and Letters" 153.

transplant that foreignness into the target language, for instance contemporary English.

Once again, I underline the idea that each language is a way of seeing. That dictum applies not only to foreign languages but also to texts that were created at different times in the history of our culture. Literary criticism tells us that, for example, Francis Bacon's essay "Of Studies" was and is an important and powerful essay. When we read that essay for the first time today, that power is not immediately accessible to us; therefore, we must initiate a process of research, interpretation, and translation that is similar to the process when we transplant a text from a foreign language into our own. The first passage of that essay reads: "Studies serve for delight, for ornament, and for ability. Their chief use for delight is in privateness and retiring; for ornament, is in discourse, and for ability, is in the judgment and disposition of business."[4]

The introduction of the Bacon essay enlarges the parameters of translation workshop activities: a translation within the same language to investigate the appropriate research methods that lead to an understanding and ultimately to a translation of a work into our contemporary sensibility. At all times, the question must be asked: How can the power of that essay be reenacted through the possibilities of our language today?

And here we recognize an important research procedure that is derived from translation thinking. When we translate a text from another language, we must first explore the connotations and associations that words have in the context of the source language. When we encounter the word "Feuer" in German and immediately begin to think in terms of the English word "fire," we have already endangered the situational thinking inherent in the context of the source language. Anything that might be foreign around that word in the other language has been lost. In their linguistic and cultural traditions, "Feuer" and "fire" project two different magnetic fields of connotations.

Consequently, the research that needs to be enacted with respect to the Bacon essay is similar to the research that is involved in the exploration of a word or words in the foreign language. In Bacon's case, we have to think in terms of the perspectives of thinking that were generated by the magnetic field of words such as "delight, ornament, ability" in the sixteenth century. A first step toward an understanding will be the use of the dictionary within the same language, which in the case of Bacon translates into the *Oxford English Dictionary*. For a foreign language text, the monolingual dictionary initiates any serious attempt at transplanting a work into another language.

---

[4] Francis Bacon, *The Essayes or Counsels Civill and Morall of Francis Bacon* (New York: E.P. Dutton & Co., 1900) 214.

Rainer Schulte

A brief example in the poem "Nantucket" by William Carlos Williams can further illustrate this research procedure.

Nantucket

Flowers through the window
lavender and yellow

changed by white curtains—
Smell of cleanliness—

Sunshine of late afternoon—
On the glass tray

a glass pitcher, the tumbler
turned down, by which

a key is lying—And the
immaculate white bed[5]

Despite its apparent simplicity, "Nantucket" is a complex poem populated with ambiguities and nuances that become, in the end, focused into a singular question of feeling about this place in Nantucket. Scholars have, from time to time, taken on this poem and endeavored to explain it. One critic, who did not allow himself to become immersed in the whole poem, found a unique way of explaining it. He took as his point of departure what he considered the pivotal, central image: the tumbler. The tumbler, he went on to say, is, of course, an acrobat. And because the tumbler is "turned down," or denied, in the poem, the critic went on to establish his idea that "Nantucket" was a poem about the Puritan ethic, which was typically New England: severe, colorless, lifeless. Part of the problem lies in the critic's failure to interact with the words of the poem both individually and jointly; he did not use situational thinking and therefore interpreted the poem with prejudice by committing what I call "the primary prejudice." Take the word tumbler, for example. The critic chose to interpret the word as a synonym for acrobat, which indeed it is; but a quick trip to the dictionary (the ultimate and necessary travel guide) shows the word has a much greater potential of meaning. Tumbler is also a synonym for a drinking glass. As a practical concern, Williams could not have used the word glass because it already appears twice: once in the same line as "a glass pitcher," and once in the line before it as "the glass tray." It would have been impossible for the poet to choose the word a third time, so he chose the obvious synonym, tumbler. More importantly, however, a tumbler is "[in a lock] any locking or checking part, which, when lifted or released by the action of a key or the like, allows the bolt to move." If we project ourselves into the situational context, then the tumbler takes on another possibility: "The

---

[5] Williams Carlos Williams, *Selected Poems*, ed. Charles Tomlinson (New York: New Directions, 1985) 72.

tumbler turned down" becomes a locked lock. Moreover, the next line reveals a key, and certainly keys go with locks, and the potential exists for the key to open the lock. Except for one thing: "a key is lying." If the key is lying, then it might be a false key, unable to open this lock. What the critic failed to take into consideration is that in this case the poet had not used the word "tumbler" in its most common primary definition. A quick look at the dictionary would have told him that the word "tumbler" appears with eleven different definitions.

What this example shows is that the critic failed to engage in research that was intricately related to the need encountered in the situations of the text. As translators relate every word in the translated text to the semantic connotations of the word in the original text, they also use the situations in the original text to determine what kind of research has to be initiated in order to do justice to a full understanding of a text. Thus, the situational thinking that informs all sensitive attempts at translating a text also generates meaningful directions for research developments that should be considered essential to all literary and humanistic investigations.

This kind of research fosters associative thinking, which is the basic foundation of all translation thinking and, above all, interdisciplinary thinking. When we translate, we associate the word with its visual situation—we translate the word into its visual field of meaning; we associate one word with another, one situation with another, one way of seeing with another way of seeing. But more importantly, in the act of interpretation within the same text the reader/interpreter must continuously link the directions of thinking inherent in the magnetic field of a word with those in the text that project similar directions of thinking in other words.

Paz writes in the second line of his poem "Wind from All Compass Points," "The mountains are of bone and of snow."[6] In this case the reader will have to think through the connotations of "bone" as something that is "hard, old, and enduring." That direction of thinking fits into the overall aesthetic orientation of the entire poem. Paz does not describe the bone, but uses the quality of "boneness" to convey a certain atmosphere. Similarly, a few lines later Paz exclaims: "Bells motors radios." On the surface these words don't seem to have very much in common. However, when we consider what each of these words suggests, we find that they all produce noise. Again, that direction of thinking falls in line with the progression of the poem.

In this sense, the practice of translation encourages and refines the practice of continuously drawing associations within the same text, which then can lead to a

---

[6] Octavio Paz, "Wind From All Compass Points," trans. Paul Blackburn, *Mundus Artium: A Journal of International Literature and the Arts* 3 (Winter 1969): 51.

coherent interpretation of the text as a whole. In other words, the reader must at all times visualize the word in its situational existence before any meaningful interpretation can be initiated.

Translation is not simply the translation of words, but rather the translation of situations. Meaningful interpretations are the visualizations of words and the situations they project. The translator consistently considers the word as a sign toward something, as a sign beyond itself toward a situation that is in the process of being built.

The insight we derive from translation thinking as it relates to translation research can be formulated in the following manner: no technique without need. In other words, translation fosters an attitude of research that springs from the necessity of the moment in the text. Each word creates its own procedure for research exploration, first as an isolated phenomenon and then as a magnetic field in relation to another magnetic field. Herein lies an essential contribution of translation thinking to the renovation of the way research should be implemented in the realm of literature and the humanities: not research for the sake of doing research, but research guided by the necessity of the moment in the text, the word in the text, the situation in the text, or the perspective brought to the interpretation of the text. Perhaps a comparison with musical thinking can illustrate this procedure in a different way. Generally pianists are taught to play certain exercises every day, which turns out to be a somewhat mechanical act. However, what makes more sense would be to identify a particular difficult situation in the score itself and then design an exercise that would help the pianist to overcome that difficulty in a short time. Here again, the notion of "no technique without need" comes into focus. If we transfer that same thinking to the act of translation, the research methods to be initiated in order to solve problems within a given text should follow a similar progression of thinking toward meaningful ways of doing research. In short, translation research responds to the necessity of the situation in the text, and the act of translation reshapes our approach to and our thinking about a text.

Interpretation and Reading

Research into the internal movement of a word and how this movement relates from one word to the next, from one situation to the next, redirects and expands our way of thinking about the act of reading and interpretation. The translator, perhaps less certain than a critic, cannot support the assumption that there is such a thing as the definitive interpretation of a text. The basic dynamic inherent in any translation attempt is the linking of something with something else. The original German notion of "über-setzen" (to carry across) comes into focus here. The emotional and cultural landscapes on both sides of the river are incongruous; they are built on different premises and cultural traditions. Therefore, possible links have to be discovered in order for any communication to take place. Politically speaking, we have often thought in terms of conquering the other side of the river. Remnants of that kind of thinking are still reflected in the expression—frequently used by critics and scholars—to "attack" a text in order to interpret it. However, translators use a different vocabulary: they explore texts and establish a dialogue with the text, and, therefore, the question of "what does a text mean" is replaced by "how does a text come to mean something" when the translator establishes an interpretive perspective to a given text.

Translators can learn a great deal from the practice of deconstructing a text. A translator constantly engages in de-constructing words, in finding out what the magnetic field of a word might be, but the translator must at all times be concerned about the reintegration of the parts into the wholeness of the text. The translator always sees the necessity of moving inside a word in a constant relationship to other words within the context of a text. Therefore, the notion of deconstruction can only be a means toward a "reconstruction" of the aesthetic totality of the text. The danger and the damage that can be caused by non-textual interpretations—with the emphasis only on the exploration and deconstruction of single words—can be further illustrated by the episode attributed to the critic F.O. Matthiessen. He explicated the phrase "soiled fish of the sea," which appears in certain editions of Herman Melville's *White Jacket*, and published this critical assessment of the "soiled fish":

> Hardly anyone but Melville could have created the shudder that results from calling this frightening vagueness some "soiled fish of the sea." The unexpected linking of the medium of cleanliness with filth could only have sprung from an imagination that apprehended the terrors of the deep, of the immaterial deep as well as the physical.

However, the scholar John Nichol showed in 1949 that "soiled" was actually a typesetting slip-up for "coiled." No one knows whether the events are related, but within a year of Nichol's article Matthiessen committed suicide.[7]

Accepting the fact that there is no definitive interpretation of a given text, that there are a multiplicity of possible interpretations depending on the interpretive perspective that the critic/translator brings to the literary work, an important way to approach the interpretation of a translated work, especially a poem, is through the application of multiple translations. Here again, we know that no single

---

[7] Joan Oleck, "Versions of Vision," *Michigan Today* 23 (1991): 6–7.

translation will ever match the full impact of the original version. So what can multiple translations of a single poem achieve that goes beyond the insights provided by one translation? Whenever a word in the source language is translated by a variety of corresponding words in English, we are pretty safe in assuming that there is something going on in the original—the poet has created an environment of directed ambiguity. Each translator, in turn, has brought his or her interpretive perspective to that moment of ambiguity and has filled that space of ambiguity with a particular way of thinking through it, which is reflected in the different choice of words materialized in the translations. The reader is then confronted with several different translations that engage him or her to delineate the subtle nuances expressed through each choice. The thinking out of these nuances links the reader back to the situation in the text each time. Thus, even though no one translation fully transplants the power of the original, the study of multiple translations continuously reconnects the reader with the internal progression of the poem. The reader becomes an active participant in thinking through the poem and not looking at the poem as an object somewhere in the distance that can be defined and placed into the strictures of one definitive interpretation. The reader moves inside the text and recreates its internal flow.

Rainer Maria Rilke's famous poem "The Panther" has been rendered into English by several translators.[8] The first line of the poem reads: "Sein Blick ist vom Vorübergehen der Stäbe...." The word "Blick" is rendered by "glance," "gaze," "vision," "seeing," and "sight." If one examines the different nuances of meaning inherent in these words, it becomes clear that at that moment the original seems to project some kind of poetic insight. Furthermore, a closer look at the original word shows that "Blick" combines in itself two movements of thinking: the activity of directing the eyes toward something and the taking in of what the eyes see. For that double activity, there is no corresponding word in English. This probably explains the translators' divergence in their interpretation of the word. They could only catch one of the movements of the word. I mentioned that translation thinking has also been reflected in the way scholars look at the editing of present and past texts. The practitioners of textual scholarship no longer support the idea that there is a single original state of a text. Even Biblical scholars have difficulties in accepting the certainty of one original text. The work of art is considered to be more like a process than a product. Shakespeare might have written several versions of one of his plays. Marianne Moore published her poem "Poetry" in several different versions with varying lines. Thus, the multiple versions provide the reader with the opportunity to

---

[8] Rainer SCHULTE (ed.), *Comparative Perspectives* 193–211.

participate in the creative process of a given text, which certainly will increase the enjoyment of the aesthetic experience.

Translation Criticism and Publishing

Literary criticism, and to a certain extent art criticism, has been dominated in the past few years by application of canon-oriented methodologies to the interpretation of texts, whether it be feminist criticism, deconstructionist criticism, or post-modernist criticism. In many instances, the products of these kinds of criticism have become not only unreadable but also inaccessible to students and instructors alike, not to speak of the educated general reader. Criticism no longer seems to have the function of opening entrances into a literary work. The language that is being used by critics and scholars increasingly obscures rather than illuminates an understanding of the complex structures inherent in an artistic creation. One should remember that criticism comes after the creation of a work and that, in general, critics are not the ones who create the new ideas. In the humanities, that dilemma has greatly confused the general public and has contributed to the low esteem in which the humanities are held in our current culture.

An area of criticism that has been completely neglected both in the realm of newspapers and journals and in the academy is translation criticism. Very few intelligent reviews of English translations of foreign authors can be identified. In most cases, the same jargon-like expressions are used in reviews to characterize a translated book, if it is reviewed at all. Here is a wide-open field that should be of great concern to both instructors and students of literature and languages. It could provide an avenue for graduate students who are involved in the art and craft of translation to produce stimulating articles for publication in journals. In addition, critical evaluations of existing and new translations would constitute a major contribution to the study of literature, in both its national and international dimensions.

The students who should most ideally become involved in the activity of writing translation criticism would be those who have participated in both creative writing and translation workshops. Criticism dealing with translations must deal with a close comparative study of the original and its translation. Through such a comparative study—prepared by those who are familiar with the original language and also trained in the pulse of the contemporary English languages—the successes and failures of transplanting situations from another language into English will further intensify the dialogue with a given text. The reader will once again be brought more deeply into the text, into the differences that exist between a foreign language and culture and our own language, and the critic/scholar will help the reader to gain a better understanding of the language and cultural context within which a particular work came into existence. An entirely new area of scholarship is just about to make its way into the general flow of literary criticism. Once again, translation criticism would be anchored in the immediacy of the text rather than in some abstract theoretical structures that are imposed on a given literary text or texts.

Translation criticism should also address the problems of literary and cultural transfer via the avenue of anthologies. No major critical evaluation has taken place with respect to the quality of translations that are represented in anthologies. The critical judgment should cover not only the quality of translations but also the quality of texts that have been chosen for inclusion in anthologies. Unfortunately, in the past few years the considerations guiding selections in anthologies have been dogmatically political rather than aesthetic.

Expansion of International Perspectives

At a time when the world is becoming more and more globally connected, literary criticism seems to become more and more local—in a sense, restricted to criticism that is written *only* in English, although ironically many of the subject matters are anchored in foreign cultures. A cursory survey of bibliographies of master's theses and Ph.D. dissertations seems to confirm this isolationist tendency. We have established that each language is a way of seeing the world, of interpreting the world in a different way. That also applies to the formulation of critical approaches to texts and ideas. Translation Studies should play a major role in expanding the horizons of graduate research. The practice of multiple translations shows us that even within the same language there are various—and often strongly divergent—ways of interpreting situations in a text. When we look at texts through the eyes of another language by taking into consideration the critical methodologies that have been developed by scholars in other languages, new and often unexpected interpretive perspectives surface. However, since very few graduate students are equipped to read foreign texts fluently in more than one language, it falls within the realm of Translation Studies to promote the translation of dissertations, scholarly monographs, and critical and scholarly essays from other countries. It is amazing how very few important critical essays written in other languages find their way into English via translations. It is entirely conceivable that an anthology of critical and scholarly essays and articles translated from a foreign language with a critical essayistic introduction that would place these essays in their cultural and historical environment could easily become an exciting project for dissertations.

Another revitalization of dissertations should be the implementation of translation dissertations. Students would translate contemporary authors from other literatures and accompany these translations with an elaborate scholarly apparatus and a comprehensive critical essayistic section. In the essay part, the student would address the importance of the writer or writers in the context of national and international visibility, then discuss the importance of the work itself, and finally reconstruct through the means of critical language the process that went into the making of such a translation. The reconstruction of the creative process could be documented by adding the various drafts that a translator prepared to arrive at a final version, which would also provide the reader with an insight into the decisions that the translator implemented to find solutions for specific problems from one language into another. This kind of thinking brings a major reorientation to the study of literature and the humanities. The reader, interpreter, or translator anchors all of his or her interpretive approaches in the actuality of the moments in the text. All theoretical considerations grow from the practice and not vice versa. That change in attitude or approach seems to be essential in order to redirect and revitalize the study of literature and the humanities in the academy. In short, translation promotes the merging of the creative with the critical, the practice with the theory. The paradigm shift that becomes clear in this context is the shift from a content-oriented way of interpretation to a process-oriented exploration of texts and situations. Once again, translation reconnects interpretation and research in a meaningful way.

Translation and Interdisciplinary Studies

In the past few years, there has been a repeated call for interdisciplinary studies in colleges and universities.[9] The paradigm of many disciplines has come under serious scrutiny, since the parameters of these disciplines no longer meet the needs of our contemporary world. Thomas Kuhn tells us that when paradigms lose their initial power and vitality, they will be replaced by new paradigms that create their own energy and boundaries. Since disciplines were originally built on the notion of paradigms, we can assume that certain disciplines have exhausted themselves and have become stagnant in their research methods and the way they approach the solution of problems.

---

[9] See Rainer SCHULTE, "The Act of Translation."

One of the outstanding characteristics of translation studies is the integrative power of translation thinking. The practice of translation is built on an associative mode of thinking. The translator always links one word to another, and one should not forget that words are signposts not to themselves but to situations that lie behind words. The translator constantly navigates between word and situation. Sensitivity to the constant flow between word and situation as well as the decision-making process on the translator's part not to violate the basic boundaries of that situation are inherently interdisciplinary ways of going about studying a subject matter. Furthermore, translation is a problem-solving activity that considers the word not as an isolated phenomenon but always in association with something else: the visualization of a situation. Interdisciplinary thinking is the relentless effort to adjust thinking (which is expressed through words) to the refined necessities of a situation. By becoming sensitive to the needs of the situation, one can initiate the solution of the problem. Translation and interdisciplinary activities are anchored in *situational* thinking. The translator makes decisions within the dynamics of a text; thinking grows out of the needs of a text and is not imposed on the text by outside considerations. Once a translator has fully visualized the situation in the foreign text, the process of transplanting it into the new linguistic environment of another language begins. Interdisciplinary thinking follows a similar pattern: it establishes channels of interaction between a situation and all the possible ramifications of associations within that situation in order to start a decision-making process.

The translator must establish an association between a given situation in a text and the words that are to recreate that situation in the new language. In that sense, the translator constantly tries to balance word with situation. If the translator encounters the word "la casa" in a novel, then the most likely immediate translation would be "the house." To the English reader, the word "house" evokes certain connotations that might be incongruous with the situation in the novel, since the plot of the narrative has been placed into the jungle of a South American country. At that point, the translator must visualize the actual appearance of such a "casa" in the environment of a jungle. The transplantation of "casa" into "house" turns out to be the least convincing solution, since the appearance of such a "casa" is more like a "hut" or "shack." Before a solution for translating this word can be found, the translator must engage in an act of visualization through which the most convincing connection between word and situation can be enacted.

Critics of translations who believe in the dictionary correspondences of words from one language into another often attack translators because they have used words in the new language that do not correspond precisely to their dictionary meaning. If the word "lamb" as it appears in the Bible is transplanted by "seal" in Eskimo, then this could easily be identified as a lexical mistake. However, the translator might have had to establish a necessary association between the word "lamb" and the new situation of the Eskimo language in which the word "seal" creates an emotional reaction similar to that of "lamb" in the Bible.

Moreover, in the German language, the word "schwarz" (black) is also used—in a slightly derogatory sense—to indicate that someone belongs to the Catholic faith. If the word in this particular context is transferred into English with "black," the result would be a total misrepresentation of the situation in the original.

The necessity to link word to situation can also be illustrated within the same language. The first sentence in Francis Bacon's essay "Of Studies" reads: "Studies serve for delight, for ornament, and ability." Even though the words "studies," "delight," "ornament," and "ability" are written the same way today, their semantic, cultural, and psychological associations have drastically changed in subsequent times. Thus, the reader, in a manner similar to the translator, must first explore each word in the context of its given period before the interpretation of that text can take place. The situation behind the words must be reconstructed before any serious translation into the sensibility of the twentieth-century reader can occur.

All these examples reconfirm the notions that research springs from the necessity of each situation encountered in the text and that translation is indeed the transferal of situations and not of words. The translator identifies the problem in the text and then designs the procedures of research that might lead to feasible solutions in harmony with the needs of the situation.

Conclusion

All literature and humanities programs, especially on the graduate level, should incorporate translation workshops into their curriculum. Just as creative writing courses have in many instances revitalized the energy of English departments, translation courses can create different attitudes toward the reading of literary texts. The primary function of translation workshops is certainly not to produce professional literary translators. Where would they go to make a living after they have completed degree programs in literary translation? Hardly any literary translator in the United States can support himself or herself by translating literary works. As a matter of fact, the job opportunities for literary translators have been declining over the past decade. Recent statistics seem to confirm that dilemma: Germany and France each publish between seven and eight thousand translations each year. In comparison, only about 1800 translations of literary works make their way into American English, and that figure might even be considered a little high. Germany produces about four thousand book translations from English alone into German every year.

What translation workshops can achieve is a reorientation in the interaction with foreign cultures through their literary works. Students have to step outside of their own linguistic and cultural frame and enter into patterns of thought and perception that are different from those they have learned in their own culture. By stepping outside of their own language, they discover the foreignness in their culture and perceive patterns by which they approach the interpretation of the world around them. It is this constant flow from the one to the other that heightens our awareness of other-ness and activates a mental alertness to the fact that no two cultures perceive the same phenomena in the same way—as no two people see the same things in the same situation.

The paradigm shift that has been generated by translation thinking is anchored in a shift from a content-oriented paradigm to a process-oriented way of looking at the world. The practice of translation, and more specifically the reconstruction of the translation process, must be considered the means by which a process-oriented model of instruction can be achieved in the arts and humanities.

Selected Bibliography

ARROWSMITH, William and Roger SHATTUCK, eds. *The Craft and Context of Translation*. Austin: University of Texas Press, 1961.

BARNSTONE, Willis. "ABCs of Translation." *Translation Review* 2 (1978): 35–36.

BIGUENET, John and Rainer SCHULTE, eds. *The Craft of Translation*. Chicago: University of Chicago Press, 1989.

FELSTINER, John. *Translating Neruda: The Way to Macchu Picchu*. Stanford: Stanford University Press, 1980.

GADAMER, Hans Georg. *Truth and Method*. Trans. and ed. Garrett Barden and John Cumming. New York: Crossroad Publishing, 1984.

HONIG, Edwin. *The Poet's Other Voice: Conversations on Literary Translation*. Amherst: University of Massachusetts Press, 1985.

HUNG, Eva. "When They See Red: One Approach to Translation Criticism." *Translation Review* 48/49 (1995): 56–60.

KLINE, Nancy. "Writing As Translation: The Great Between." *Translation Review* 36/37 (1991): 4–11.

MAIER, Carol. "Teaching Literature Through Translation: A Proposal and Three Examples." *Translation Review* 46 (1994): 10–13.

MAIER, Carol. "Translation as Performance: Three Notes." *Translation Review* 15 (1984): 5–8.

MILLER, Elizabeth Gamble. "Retracing the Translation Process: Hugo Lindo's *Only The Voice*." *Translation Review* 7 (1981): 32–40.

PAZ, Octavio. "Translation: Literature and Letters." Trans. Irene del Corral. Rainer Schulte and John Biguenet, eds. *Theories of Translation: An Anthology of Essays from Dryden to Derrida*. Chicago: University of Chicago Press, 1992. 152–62.

RAFFEL, Burton. *The Forked Tongue: A Study of the Translation Process*. The Hague: Mouton, 1971.

RIMER, Thomas J. "Translation: Strategies for Context." *Translation Review* 10 (1982): 9–12.

SCHULTE, Rainer. "The Act of Translation: From Interpretation to Interdisciplinary Thinking." *Translation Review* 4 (1979): 3–8.

—. "Translation and Literary Criticism." *Translation Review* 9 (1982): 1–4.

—. "Translation and Research." *Translation Review* 16 (1984): 1–3.

—. "Literary Translation: Toward an Esthetic of Complexity." *Translation Review* 14 (1984): 1–3.

—. "Translation and Reading." *Translation Review* 18 (1985): 1–2.

—. "The Study of Translation: Re-creative Dynamics in Literature and the Humanities." *Mid-American Review* IX.2 (1989): 69–80.

— and John BIGUENET, eds. *Theories of Translation: An Anthology of Essays from Dryden to Derrida*. Chicago: University of Chicago Press, 1992.

—, ed. *Comparative Perspectives: Anthology of Multiple Translations*. New York: American Heritage Custom Publishing, 1994.

STEINER, George. *After Babel: Aspects of Language and Translation*. London: Oxford University Press, 1975.

ZDANYS, Jonas. "Teaching Translation: Some Notes Toward a Course Structure." *Translation Review* 23 (1987): 9–11.

LISELOTTE GUMPEL

Meaning and Metaphor: The World in Verbal Translation

Introduction

The topic of translation is as central to my study here as it was to my presentation at the Stanford Symposium of 1995 on which it is based. I continue, however, to give the concept a wider interpretation. That is why the reference to "verbal translation" in my title does not reflect a tautology, as it may appear to do at first glance. Translation is not meant to be taken in its current, narrow sense by merely pointing to an interlingual exchange of meaning. What I stress instead is how this verbal medium known as language—always concreted in *a* language—becomes the ontological mediator between domains as it "translates" *worlds* perceived directly into the forms of *words*.

To make my point, I begin Section One with "Some Basic Ontological Considerations." These will reveal that the entire human universe consists of a "Reality Remade" (Nelson Goodman), since limited faculties are called upon to "translate" an *extramental* or "noumenal" state (Kant) into a sphere palatable to finite beings. Going from there, it did not take a thinker such as F. Nietzsche long to label the state of human existence "metaphor": *translation* has evolved into a form of *transference,* in keeping with the etymological root of (Greek) "meta-ferein," which suggests loosely that something is being "carried across," from one entity to another.

Translation, and indeed, a transference of sorts, thus turn out to be at the very core of the human condition. In that type of ontological setting, language becomes a Reality Remade that is also *twice removed* from any *extramental* realm. Between these two domains is located the *extralinguistic* reality humans perceive first, before they express themselves about it in the words of their language. Since the first of these realities remains too inscrutable for human consumption, it is primarily in assessing the relation between the latter two that critics become confused, particularly when attempting to distinguish meaning from metaphor *in* language because they always seek the determinants *outside* of language.

For the majority of critics, *reference* in language is *representational* of the reality surrounding it; *logic* becomes superimposed on *language* in order to make one realm accountable for the other. In addition, there exists that preoccupation with what linguists term "motivation." The aim here is to seek out certain transparencies that reflect various "diachronic" *stages* of the original contact between language and its extralinguistic environment. Yet beyond that surface linger the "synchronic" language *states* (de Saussure) that alone guide native competence and are thus of far greater importance. The synchronic plane defies all logic because its origin is pure speech activity. Here language not only *remakes* its own reality but in the process "recycles" its own entities, thus creating a veritable labyrinth of apparent "homonyms."

Undeterred by these facts, critics continue to claim that when linguistic reference breaks down in representation, a mode of "transference" has taken over, causing "metaphor" to replace (ordinary, literal) "meaning." Then the explicit contents are said to display an *anomaly* which nonetheless may be bridged by some inherent point of *analogy*. Yet the most concrete evidence of the fact that such a theory does not work is that this kind of metaphor constantly *disappears* as it turns back into meaning, simply because the normalizing powers of language have flattened the presumed oddity into an everyday designation, a commonplace. A meaning that has undergone this metamorphosis critics call *dead metaphor*. Ironically, the term itself constitutes a dead metaphor, since "death" is logically out of bounds for abstract entities such as meanings that fail to undergo the physiological demise of living organisms. But who still thinks of decomposing bodies when uttering this term!

The next step is to identify the major contingent of critics involved. That I do in Section Two dealing with the "Standard Assumptions" of so-called *neo-Aristotelians*. Their ideas do indeed go back to those of Aristotle, who defined metaphor as the "strange term"—Greek "allotrios"—beneath whose surface still lurks some sustainable analogy, much as "death" may stand for "disappearance" in the context of the elusive metaphor. In one way or another, the notion of *deviance* as a trait of metaphor caught on. Still today philosophers look to "category-mistakes" of logical type-trespassing while linguists focus on violated "selectional rules" of incongruous content, with no one taking the trouble to define the norms and/or categories which *language* rather than logic is supposed to be subverting. When no more synonyms are left for designating deviance, metaphor becomes described with metaphor: Latin rhetoric sought its transference in a series of "leaps" or "jumps," modern thinkers (M. Beardsley) prefer "twists" and turns. Another contingent I call the "Fregeans" (after G. Frege) split "sense" from "reference" and make metaphor "non-denoting" since it does not seem to *say* explicitly what it *means* implicitly.

Meaning and Metaphor: The World in Verbal Translation

However, when I proceed towards my own theory of *non-Aristotelian* semantics in the final two sections, I shall demonstrate—among other things—that any extant word meaning with a validated content *must* embody both sense and reference. The issue of distinguishing meaning from metaphor is, in the first place, not one of *content* as such but rather the mode of *contextualization*. To stress that point, I adhere in my illustration to the same four words—"Hawk and Dove," "Bull and Bear." Are they meaning or metaphor? Are they live or dead metaphors when they refer literally to the animals any competent speaker associates with their contents, or when, in recycled English, they include people in certain types of contexts? Is this a rhetorical question of "To be or not to be" for meaning and metaphor? Given my non-Aristotelian semantics, I will answer in the negative.

I. Language in a Language: Some Basic Ontological Considerations

The term "language" may come in many guises but I mean it to embody a *speech community* whose members share the forms of words. In that respect this kind of language differs from the "Languages of Art" Nelson Goodman treated, for example, in his exploration of the "Reality Remade" by the aesthetic media and the *visual* rather than *verbal* icons on which they relied.[1] To be sure, the concept of "language" when deployed in the singular, minus any articles, remains an abstraction, hence a realm made tangible only when concreted in *a* given language, as I shall have ample opportunity to demonstrate. What unites all extant languages in principle, however, is their mode of "translating" *worlds* into *words* through speech activity. That is their fundamental identity of Remaking Reality, no matter how diverse their particular inventory of semantic values.

On that basis, then, language consists of one domain that may undergo the scrutiny of the "ontological considerations" I shall subject it to for purposes of determining its unique state of being. As already indicated in the introduction, in the widest sense all of the human universe amounts to a "language" of sorts, remade as it is by human faculties when brought into finite immanence. Kant's transcendental divide depended on that fact when, in the eighteenth century, he saw fit to distinguish the impenetrable extramental reality as "noumenon" from its "ideal" or intramental opposite, the "phenomenon," that humans receive filtered through their senses.[2] Although the latter sphere amounts to a vulnerable state

---

[1] Nelson Goodman, *Language of Art: An Approach To a Theory of Symbols* (Indianapolis, New York: The Bobbs-Merrill Company, 1968); "Reality Remade" covers section I (pp. 3–44).

[2] See Immanuel Kant, *Kritik der reinen Vernunft*, in *Immanuel Kants Werke*, ed. Ernst Cassirer, vol. III (Berlin: Bruno Cassirer, 1913) 212–224.

obtained from the mere transmission of finite capabilities, it was envisaged by Kant as something positive, since it projected the human mind as an active force "constituting" a world of its own making. He posited three major faculties (*Vermögen*) capable of generating the basic constitutive domains: theoretical reason (*Vernunft*) yielded "nature" in exploration of the natural sciences; "practical" reason was held accountable for the kind of moral freedom which, guided by the pure intention of a "categorical imperative," led to committing the truly good deed; and aesthetic "judgment" became the unique foundation of the spontaneously generated work of art.[3]

Admirable as Kant's triadic division remained, it manifested one major omission, and that concerned the domain of *language,* grounded as it is exclusively in acts of meaning.[4] Many issues revolving around the distinction between meaning and metaphor in language might have been solved had this oversight been recognized, perhaps by some of Kant's immediate successors in the nineteenth century who belonged to the school of Philosophical Idealism. Since that did not occur, I turn instead to another thinker of that century, whose theory in this particular context remains more relevant for my topic, and that is Friedrich Nietzsche. Iconoclast that he was, Nietzsche at first appeared to condemn the reality humans remake for themselves, labeling it an "extramoral lie" devoid of genuine truth, even if no real mendaciousness may accompany an ontological condition.[5] Not surprisingly, he re-invokes also a Kantian concept here when asserting that humans will never get to know any extramental "thing-in-itself" (*Ding an sich*).[6]

Nietzsche then radicalizes the condition surrounding his extramoral lie: no mere *translation* of some extramental state, it represents a form of "transference" or "Übertragung" by carrying something across from one dubious realm to

---

[3] See Kant's table for the three ontological division of nature, art, and moral freedom in his Third Critique on aesthetic judgment: Kant, *Kritik der praktischen Vernunft; Erste Einleitung in die Kritik der Urteilskraft,* in *Immanuel Kants Werke,* ed. Ernst Cassirer, vol. V (Berlin: Bruno Cassirer, 1914) 267 (from the second edition of 1793).

[4] See Liselotte Gumpel, "Language, the Missing Constitutive Domain: The Contribution of Roman Ingarden's Phenomenology to Immanuel Kant's Critical Philosophy," in Adam Wegrzecki (ed.), *Roman Ingarden, filozofia naszego czasu* (Kraków: Oficyna Cracovia, 1995) 261–282.

[5] Friedrich Nietzsche, "Über Wahrheit und Lüge im außermoralischen Sinn," in *Nietzsches Werke in zwei Bänden,* vol. II (Salzburg: Das Bergland Buch, n.d.) 1079–1092. Title in Maximilian A. Mugge's English translation reads, "On Truth and Falsity in Their Extramoral Sense"; see Warren Shibles (ed.), *Essays on Metaphor* (Whitewater, Wisconsin: The Language Press, 1972) 1–14. Yet Nietzsche clearly used "Lüge" to mean "lie" explicitly—if extramorally—as I have translated it.

[6] Nietzsche, ("Über Wahrheit und Lüge" 1082), on the "thing-in-itself" as pure, acausal truth, as taken from Kant's "Ding an sich" in the First Critique (note 2, pp. 214, 221–222).

another. Both the English and German terms are derivatives of Greek "metaferein," which is the etymological root of "metaphor."[7] So now the world fit for human consumption appears as one giant metaphor! In all fairness, Nietzsche, like Kant, comes to these conclusions circuitously by actually affirming human creativity: what, essentially, is one more fabrication in art form when nothing else is totally real to begin with![8] There is certainly no means of circumventing the synthesis that lurks behind any Reality Remade.

The same may be said about the synthesis wrought by those acts of consciousness that produce speech, differ as they must from any *extralinguistic* activity yet partaking of the same *extramoral* lie no one can escape.[9] The domain of language resulting from these acts accordingly gives rise to yet another ontological *shift* Germans sometimes allude to as a "Seinsverschiebung." The human universe thus consists of several ontological layers, each attesting to their own Realities Remade—one within the other and all, in a manner of speaking, "telling lies" about some unknowable state in their own, unique fashion. How and where does language, whose bearers of meaning are words, fit into this ontological scheme of things? Certainly, attempts at pinpointing the nature of meaning itself have not exactly made great strides, not even after Michel Bréal coined the term "semantics" in the hope it would stand for a "science of meaning."[10] Unfortunately, that science quickly went awry because Bréal himself mainly focused on *diachronic* developments of *stages* instead of analyzing how language upholds its unique *synchronic states* in full self-determination.[11]

To illustrate briefly, at the synchronic level of content division English presents "sky" and "heaven" while German retains one "Himmel"; English possesses the two contents "flesh" and "meat" for the one German "Fleisch." In this manner, each linguistic inventory ends up displaying its own "world-view," or "Weltansicht" (W.v. Humboldt) once the extant contents have been validated by

---

[7] Nietzsche, "Über Wahrheit und Lüge" 1082, 1084, 1086–1087.

[8] Nietzsche, "Über Wahrheit und Lüge" 1086–1091.

[9] See Liselotte Gumpel, "Language as Bearer of Meaning; The Phenomenology of Roman Ingarden," in W. Galewicz and E. Ströker (eds.), *Ontologie und Kunst: Für Roman Ingarden zum 100. Geburtstag* (Amsterdam, Atlanta: Rodopi, 1994) 21–57.

[10] Michel Bréal, *Semantics: Studies in the Science of Meaning*, trans. Mrs. Henry Cust (New York: Dover Publications, 1964).

[11] Ferdinand de Saussure, *Course in General Linguistics*, ed. C. Bally and A. Sechehaye, trans. Wade Baskin (New York, Toronto: McGraw Hill, 1966) For the diachronic and synchronic planes in language, see chapter III: "Static and Revolutionary Linguistics" (pp. 79–102, and therein, pp. 80, 83, 87–88, 88–91). Work from now on identified as *"Course."*

a speech community.[12] Linguistic "views" of this nature, however, are hardly indices of some transparent "Weltanschauung." One dare not deduce from these differences in semantic values that Germans are more or less religious, or, in the second example, more cannibalistic by nature than their fellow Anglo-Saxons. While diachronic speculation on etymological roots may proceed and include some original contact between the given language and the extralinguistic reality, such an investigation possesses a limited purpose. It does so, because what remains paramount is the fact that extant semantic values guide native competence, enabling speakers to express *their* meaning through the meanings a language holds available for them, irrespective of any inherent idiosyncrasies.

Good evidence of how synchronic reinforcement overtakes any transparent vestiges of diachronic origin may be found in languages such as German that possess inanimate extension of gender. The great nineteenth-century philologist Jakob Grimm discovered how gender became the first attempt at translating a world through words in rudimentary personification predating some of the earliest religions.[13] At *this* point in time, gender has entered the synchronic system of set values and seems to exist for the sole purpose of irritating students of a foreign language, particularly when these are Anglo-Saxons largely unaccustomed to observing such rules for inanimate contents.

Since I have already drawn on a celestial German "Himmel," let me turn to two of its orbs. German has adopted a *feminine* sun and *masculine* moon, while French reverses the gender. In any direct perception of the extra-linguistic reality, the French version no doubt makes more sense. Surely, the sun appears the stronger of the two, the more overpowering star when compared to its planet, the gentle moon. But *logic* is not at issue here, only *language*. Indeed, for me as a German native, language has taken such a hold over logic that, from the earliest acquisition on, the sun to this day *is* a female, the moon a male, with any deviation from this interpretation seeming almost an aberration. That is what percep-

---

[12] Wilhelm von Humboldt, *Schriften zur Sprachphilosophie*, ed. Andreas Flitner and Klaus Giel (Stuttgart: J.G. Cotta'sche Buchhandlung, 1963) 434. Work will be identified hereafter as "Humboldt, *Schriften*."

[13] See Jacob Grimm, *Selbstbiographie: Ausgewählte Schriften, Reden und Abhandlungen*, ed. U. Wyss (München: Deutscher Taschenbuchverlag, 1984), where he cites gender with "sprachfindung"—literally, a language finding itself within forms of expression (p. 181 ff.). Ernst Cassirer discusses Grimm's observations on masculine/feminine gender, as this resulted from early human interpretive efforts at extracting sexual idiosyncrasies from nature. See Cassirer, *Philosophie der symbolischen Formen, Erster Teil: Die Sprache* (Darmstadt: Wissenschaftliche Buchgesellschaft, 1972) 273–274. Work will be identified hereinafter as "Cassirer, *Sprache*."

tion of the world through (these German words) has done to me in terms of "*die* Sonne" versus "*der* Mond."[14]

Meaning belies logic simply because *reference* in language never genuinely attempts to *represent* or imitate the extralinguistic reality, instead *presenting* only itself. Viewed positively, that is the miraculous power of language.[15] Whatever *is* there has considerable input, especially when revivified in a literary context. Take for example the poem "Mondnacht" by the Romantic, J. Eichendorff: it depicts a melting nocturnal horizon as a kiss between masculine "*der* Himmel" and feminine "*die* Erde."[16] An English translation could but should not rid these words of their gender, if the romantic nuance of the imagery is not to be lost, not to mention that a decision has to be reached whether "heaven" or "sky" best befits the only extant "Himmel." Before translating the poem, the speaker of English involved in the process has to grapple with the way in which each language has already "translated," and as such transfigured, a world into words within its own inventory. In view of Nietzsche's extramoral lie, there is certainly no right or wrong when having to come—quite literally!—to terms with that difference.

Language may even belie logic when contents appear *animate*, indeed *anthropomorphic*. It is hardly a secret that creatures come in male/female pairs where their sex is concerned, yet here is the "neutered" German female *"das* Mädchen" transcending masculine/feminine gender. No less ironic is the reversal between diachronic intent and synchronic outcome: the suffix "-chen," which in meaning lends a touch of the diminutive to a noun, possesses automatically a neuter gender. So, in typically sexist fashion this final syllable was supposed to keep the female nice and petite while neutering her simultaneously through a grammatical rule!

In Remaking its Reality, language in *a* language also *recycles* its contents in seemingly odd ways, in the process generating some curious homonyms that harbor several meanings under "one name" while apparently breaking the representational bounds that should separate *meaning* from *metaphor*. A case in point is

---

[14] See Liselotte Gumpel, "Die Sprache in 'panlinguistischer' Sicht," in Bernd Thum and Gonthier-Louis Fink (eds.), *Praxis interkultureller Germanistik—Forschung, Bildung, Politik*, vol. IV (München: Iudicium, 1992) 905–917). Here I briefly take up issues of acquired gender formation. Also see Liselotte Gumpel, "The Essence of 'Reality' as a Construct of Language," in *Foundations of Language*, 11 (1974): 167–185.

[15] See Richard Lederer, *The Miracle of Language* (New York: Pocket Books, 1992).

[16] Joseph von Eichendorff, "Mondnacht," in *Eichendorffs Werke*, vol. I. (Leipzig, Wien: Bibliographisches Institut, 1891) 282. Also concerning this poem's gender including its sexual symbolism: (1) Edward Stankiewicz, "Poetics and Non-Poetic Language in their Interrelation," in *Poetics, Poetyka*, vol. I. (Gravenhage: Mouton, 1961) 11–24; (2) Liselotte Gumpel, "Metaphor as Nominalized Meaning: A Phenomenological Analysis of the Lyrical Genre," Diss. Stanford Univ. 1971, 288 ff., 293–294.

an example from an article that appeared in the *Journal of Philosophy* entitled, "Conceptual Metaphor in Everyday Language."[17] Everyday indeed it is, since among the examples are listed such rudimentary function words as *prepositions* when these turn into "orientational metaphors." No longer spatial designators, the concrete dimensions of "ups" and "downs," for example, may be relayed to conveying human vicissitudes of success or failure. Indeed, these words may collaborate with extralinguistic perception in the ineluctable extramoral lie when they describe the moon as coming "up" over that hill where the sun has just gone "down." Yet, as Mr. Holmes might say to his partner Watson, all the while it remains "elementary" knowledge in physics, the sphere of science, that the earth's rotation alone causes these impressions.

To complicate matters further, there are numerous ramifications of prepositional recycling, such as their *concrete/figurative* deployment any native speaker takes for granted until a foreign language is taken up, where they may affect inflectional changes determined by changes in grammatical case. Thus "standing *at*" a door, for instance, is tangible enough, but "laughing *at*" someone says little about actual space. In translation, the latter type of usage is often unpredictable for the choice of words: Germans has "lachen über"—literally "laughing "over" or "about" rather than "at" the person. Students have to learn additionally that this kind of abstract usage mostly requires a specific (accusative) case.

But prepositional recycling does not stop there, since these elements may serve as *verbal complements* to complete the meaning of an action while outwardly looking the same. Someone may spatially "carry their luggage *on* a train," or be told to "carry *on*" by continuing to do so, or occasionally rant and rave, thus "carrying *on*" when no one is there to lend a hand. The verb "carry" by itself obviously could not convey these differing nuances in the latter two instances.

Whether orientational or plain recycling, it occurs at every level of the syntactic hierarchy. Critics have dubbed certain *adjectives*, for example, "personality metaphors," since it is possible to speak of people having "sweet" dispositions or sending out "icy glances."[18] In this instance, content bearing inanimate matter becomes superimposed on animate behavior. Then again there are the "corporal metaphors," usually rendered in *nouns*, which superimpose parts of the human body on inanimate matter, much as the "foot" may do for the base of a mountain or the "mouth" for the source of a river, with several languages often following

---

[17] George Lakoff and Mark Johnson, "Conceptual Metaphor in Everyday Language," *The Journal of Philosophy* 77.8 (August 1980): 453–486. There they list under "orientational metaphors": "up-down," "front-back," and "in-out" (pp. 461–462).

[18] The personality metaphor and its proponents are discussed by Monroe C. Beardsley, "The Metaphorical Twist," in *Philosophy and Phenomenological Research* 22 (1961/62): 293–307, specifically, p. 304. The example here was chosen at random.

suit.[19] One may include here also a "manmade quadruped" derived from the human species of bipeds, and that is the "leg," which commonly designates an extremity supporting a torso but in semantic realignment may do the same for a table top.

In the majority of (modern) languages, semantic paucity originally led to this type of swift reapplication of content. Thus, German also has its quadruped, the "Tischbein." This closely knit compound makes rather explicit, moreover, that a certain dependence on the new furniture content must be maintained. Humans can just talk about their "leg" but speak to the carpenter about a "table leg." The same applies to the "mountain" in relation to its "foot," and so on. What happened originally has been investigated by Ernst Cassirer, who discussed how the body became the first referential pivot humans relied on when expressing themselves about their immediate environment.[20] This critic of language, however, was wise enough not to tie in this evidence of primordial language acquisition with any categorical presence of meaning over metaphor. Others, who were less cautious, got entrapped instead in the *dead metaphor* phenomenon mentioned above in the introduction, making it difficult to distinguish "everyday" from idiosyncratic content, or "orientational" specialty from the most *ordinary* semantic entity.

II. Metaphor in Meaning: The Standard Assumptions

I shall now elucidate briefly how the standard assumptions on metaphor, defined as "neo-Aristotelian," came into being.[21] For Western Civilization they largely go back to Aristotle. In his *Poetics* and (to a lesser extent) his *Rhetoric*, Aristotle sought metaphor in the "strange term"—"allotrios"—and as such in a content that was incompatible with its immediate context while it still remained compre-

---

[19] Ernst Robert Curtius, *European Literature and the Latin Middle Ages*, trans. Willard R. Trusk (New York, Evanston: Harper & Row, 1963), regarding "corporal metaphors" (pp. 136–137). These examples for corporal metaphors are also in: Lakoff/Johnson, "Conceptual Metaphor in Everyday Language" 472, and Roger Brown, *Words and Things* (Glencoe, Illinois: The Free Press, 1958) 140–141.

[20] See Cassirer, *Sprache*, on the body ("Körper," "Leib") as basic source of reference (pp. 159–160, 187–188, 215–216, 227–228, passim).

[21] See L. Gumpel, *Metaphor Reexamined: A Non-Aristotelian Perspective* (Bloomington: Indiana Univ. Press, 1984), covers the "neo-Aristotelian" tradition (pp. 211–259). Future reference to work: Gumpel, *Metaphor*. Term is not to be confused with the brief contemporary period marking the "neo-Aristotelians of Chicago" who are covered in: Eliseo Vivas, *The Artistic Transaction, and Essays on Theory of Literature* (Columbus, Ohio: State Univ. Press, 1963) 243–259.

hensible when transferred through some point of analogy to another import.[22] The series of "epiphoras" that made this transference possible are so language-bound in their illustration that citing them here is of little avail. Suffice it to state that, in a highly inductive approach I have labeled "spotsighting," Aristotle focused on single contents, mostly derived from a literary text such as the Homeric epics.

Aristotle's flawed procedure in itself is puzzling, coming from a critic who (a) was the staunch promulgator of the "thetic" and as such the conventional origin of language; (b) became the father of "Categories" in his attempt at classifying the empirical world on the basis of mental synthesis; and (c) was mindful of *genre* as a holistic principle when analyzing drama.[23] Yet in this exposition Aristotle ignored the alogical foundation of language by deriving semantic deviance from such logical categories as genus-species classes while he neglected genre by going mainly after discrete contents. No wonder that some Classical scholars doubted Aristotle was the author of those parts in the *Poetics*.[24] Indeed, by basing identities and differences in *language* on the categories of *logic* he invoked tacitly the "category-mistake" that contemporaries such as G. Ryle and followers began positing in this century as a determinant of metaphor while, ironically, committing the *ontological* category-mistake in the process by confusing different states of being.[25]

---

[22] Aristotle, *The Poetics*, trans. W. H. Fyfe (London: William Heinemann/Cambridge: Harvard Univ. Press, 1960) 80–81; Aristotle, *The "Art" of Rhetoric*, trans. J.H. Freese (London: William Heinemann/Cambridge: Harvard Univ. Press, 1959) 398–399. The "epiphora[s]" I transliterated from the Greek. Gumpel, *Metaphor*, goes into all these details for both the *Poetics* and *Rhetoric* and includes my frequent reference to neo-Aristotelian "spotsighting" practices (Index there, p. 302) cited herein.

[23] Aristotle takes his stand against Plato by endorsing the conventional—transliterated, "thetic," as derived from *"synthetic"*—disposition of language. He did so in the work *On Interpretation* (pp. 116–117), which appeared together with *The Categories* treating logical classification; both are in *Aristotle in Twenty-Three Volumes*, trans. H.P. Cooke, ed. Loeb, vol. I (Cambridge: Harvard/London: William Heinemann, 1973). E.D. Hirsch, in *The Aims of Interpretation* (Chicago, London: Univ. of Chicago Press, 1976), classifies Aristotle as "the father-of-evaluation-through-the-genre" (pp. 114–115).

[24] Editors and translators have expressed doubt about chapters 19–22 on metaphor in Aristotle's *Poetics:* (1) Fyfe's edition (note 22 above) takes issue with some of their incomprehensible technical detail (pp. 74–75, 80–81); (2) G.M.A. Grube, ed. and trans., *Aristotle: On Poetry and Style* (New York: Liberal Arts Press, 1958), criticizes chapter 20 for being out of character with the rest (p. 41). (3) I. Bywater, trans., in *Aristotle's Art of Poetry: A Greek View of Poetry and Drama*, ed. H. Fyfe (Oxford: The Clarendon Press, 1966), omits Chapter 20 with similar reservations (pp. 53–54); (4) and Gerald F. Else's detailed analysis of *Aristotle's Poetics: The Argument* (Cambridge: Harvard Univ. Press, 1967), avoids the metaphor sections (20–22) for reason of too much technicality (pp. ix, 567).

[25] Gilbert Ryle, *The Concept of Mind* (London: Hutchinson, 1949/New York: Barnes & Noble, 1963). To Ryle, the category-mistake represents "the facts of mental life as if they belonged to one logical type of category (or range of types of categories), when they actually belong to another" (p. 16). See also Ryle's "Categories," *Proceedings of the Aristotelian Society* 38

Meaning and Metaphor: The World in Verbal Translation

The time span of two millennia thus made little difference in basic theory. In a less extreme historical jump, there are the followers of Roman antiquity, Cicero and Quintilian. Their principle of metaphorical "translatio" became described as a "leap," Latin "transilire," which, akin to the Aristotelian epiphoras, crossed identity in difference.[26] Of these two adherents of Latin Rhetoric, Quintilian focused on four shifts of animation that gave rise to metaphorical leaps.[27] But these language overrides, like the Aristotelian genera-species determinants, at every turn, as I tried to demonstrate briefly with the "neutered" female, the furniture "limb," feminine sun and other illustrations, many of them exemplifying Quintilian's most-admired fourth inanimate-to-animate shift.[28] The inevitable outcome of that problem is then the dead metaphor where bounds between it and (any) meaning begin to blur.

Since the approach to metaphor remained basically unaffected in the millennia that led from antiquity to the present, the dead metaphor became the real survivor, not unlike the cockroach whose longevity, one has to admit with misgivings, remains admirable.[29] If any more evidence is needed, I cite a recent *Experi-*

(1937–38): 189–206, reprinted in the Second Series of *Logic and Language*, ed. A. Flew (Oxford: Blackwell, 1961) 65–81. The First Series of this edition (curiously dated later, 1963), contains his entry, "Systematically Confusing Expressions" (pp. 11–36); it gets into the issue of linguistic "propriety" that calls to mind the "verbum proprium" espoused by Latin Rhetoric and thus demonstrates the perpetuation—and contemporary appropriation!—of the ontological category-mistake.

[26] Cicero, *De Oratore: In Two Volumes*, trans H. Rackman, vol. II (London: William Heinemann/Cambridge: Harvard Univ. Press, 1960), made the Latin leap explicit as "transilire" (p. 125). But *Quintilian in Four Volumes*, vol. III: *The Institutio Oratoria of Quintilian*, ed. H. E. Butler (London: William Heinemann/Cambridge: Harvard Univ. Press, 1959), details metaphorical *translatio* under the *trope*, literally the *"turn* of a phrase," that abides by the same basic principle of violated content selection (pp. 300–301). For details in their similarity of viewpoints, see Gumpel, *Metaphor*, 226–228.

[27] Quintilian, *The Institutio Oratoria*, regarding the four shifts of animation: (1) animate-animate, (2) inanimate-to-inanimate, (3) animate-inanimate, (4) inanimate-animate (pp. 304–305).

[28] Quintilian extols the fourth shift, animating the inanimate, for its *boldness* which transliterates into explicit "audaciousness." On that basis, it presents one point of identity with Cicero's concept, particularly where it is used to elevate a stylistic over a "natural" metaphor, which, due to semantic paucity, shares contents only out of necessity (Quintilian, *The Institutio Oratoria*, 302–307; Cicero, *De Oratore* 120–125).

[29] One indicator for this lack of change: Harald Weinrich's "Semantik der *kühnen* Metapher" [italics mine] *Deutsche Vierteljahresschrift* 37 (1963): 325–344, builds boldness on the same basic idea as that of the ancients just cited. In a historical "leap," surveys listing past definitions prove how metaphor became described with metaphor, thus relativizing the other's meaning. See (1) Warren Shibles, *Metaphor: An Annotated Bibliography and History* (Whitewater, Wisconsin: The Language Press, 1971); (2) Hans-Heinrich Lieb, "Der Umfang des historischen Metaphernbegriffs," diss. Köln, 1964; (3) Gumpel, *Metaphor*, specifically "Metaphor in a Museum of Metaphors" (pp. 235–236).

ment, duly capitalized for special effect, that a critic wrote up in an article which asked whether the term "metaphor" still designated a viable concept.[30] In typical spotsighting, a control group was asked to rate single words numerically in accordance with the degree of their metaphorical content. A seminar on *poetics* conducted this investigation yet a newspaper article whose content dealt with *politics* was selected for the purpose, which in itself hints at a curious category-mistake for the fields of study. And, of course, political rhetoric teems with colorful expressions, including such items as the political "platform" that is not the dais orators mount when holding forth but the plan they have in store for voters. As can be expected, therefore, metaphor died several times over, with raters reaching no consensus as to what constituent represented sheer meaning or deviant metaphor in a given sentence.

Not only politicians but also contemporary theoreticians revealed their penchant for describing metaphor with metaphor, as critics have pointed out.[31] There is M. Beardsley, for example, who converted description of the Latin "transilire" into a metaphorical "twist."[32] Yet in method Beardsley can also be linked to Aristotle. For much as Aristotle culled his strange term from earlier Homeric Greek, so did Beardsley seek his twist in Shakespearean, which is to say Elizabethan English, in a parallel time span of approximately 400 years between each critic and the author whose work was being examined. That temporal lapse is certainly long enough to convert any commonplace into an "alien" expression, and vice versa, if surface content alone remains the determinant. Since I have already traded on the moon, Beardsley, going by impressions of modern American English, singles it out (among other examples) to consider Shakespeare's calling the moon "inconstant" unusual, but offers no text-critical evidence for reaching his conclusion.

A more deductive approach to isolating metaphor may have been attempted by that modern contingent I term the "Fregeans" after the mathematician-

---

[30] Werner Ingendahl, "Die Metaphorik und die sprachliche Objektivität: Brauchen wir noch den Begriff 'Metapher'?" in *Wirkendes Wort* 22 (1972): 268–274, for the "Experiment" see pp. 268–269.

[31] William Kurtz Wimsatt, Jr., and Monroe C. Beardsley, *The Verbal Icon: Studies in the Meaning of Poetry* (Lexington: Univ. of Kentucky Press, 1967), where Wimsatt notes how "modern theorists" like to "shoot off ... endlessly" into a "series of metaphors" when supposedly functioning as critics (p. 128).

[32] Monroe C. Beardsley, "The Metaphorical Twist," in *Philosophy and Phenomenological Research* 22 (1961/1962): 293–307. The parallelism between Beardsley and Aristotle I go on to note concerns Beardsley's "classes" of content deviance based on Shakespearean vestiges. Among these he lists the image "inconstant moon" he extracted from *Romeo and Juliet* in typical spotsighting, minus any diachronic assessment of interim changes between Elizabethan and modern English (pp. 300–301).

Meaning and Metaphor: The World in Verbal Translation

philosopher Gottlob Frege. It was Frege's essay "On Sense and Reference" which became so popular this side of the Atlantic that at times it has been easier to locate in English translation than in the original German.[33] Frege had promulgated the idea that some meanings bore sense but no reference. The fact that he included literary texts in that group would have made "sense" had he been less subjective in his description of that kind of language, reducing its presence to little more than an effusive style. The critics of metaphor nonetheless picked up this dichotomy with alacrity. According to them, metaphor bore sense since it displayed a semantic content but no reference, which is to say it remained "non-denoting" because what was stated was not really meant.[34] So, in view of my earlier example, the "leg" of a table denoted no genuine limb people or animals walk on in voluntary movement but only some vertical support for a piece of furniture.

At first glance, the premise seems to work, but behind it lurks the representational view of reference in language that always falls short of assessing the signifying powers of language. An analogous precept in the visual arts would be to label the blue horses of the painter Franz Marc "non-chromatic" just because empirical reality possesses no equine creatures of that color. Yet color remains undeniably present, doing its job of filling out the form of these animals, and so does the denoting function that goes with *any* explicit content of word-meanings irrespective of their particular sense. As F. de Saussure has put it, in language there does not have to be any "natural connection" between the signifier and that which it signifies; he went on to state that the "arbitrariness of the sign" is precisely "what protects language from any attempt to modify it."[35] To put that arbitrariness in the straitjacket of semantic incongruity for purposes of extracting a dubious

---

[33] Gottlob Frege, "On Sense and Reference," *Translations from the Philosophical Writings of Gottlob Frege*, ed. Peter Geach, Max Black (Oxford: Basil Blackwell, 1952) 56–78. His allusion to literary texts as an instance of sheer emotional appeal to "feeling" that I cite next: pp. 62–63. Original: Gottlob Frege, *Funktion, Begriff, Bedeutung: Fünf logische Studien*, ed. G. Patzig (Göttingen 1962).

[34] On non-denoting, see (1) Samuel R. Levin, *The Semantics of Metaphor* (Baltimore: The Johns Hopkins Press, 1977) 104–106; (2) Samuel Levin, "Standard Approaches to Metaphor and a Proposal for Literary Metaphor," in *Metaphor and Thought*, ed. A. Ortony (Cambridge, London: Cambridge Univ. Press, 1979) 124–135. (3) Paul Henle, "Metaphor," *Language, Thought and Culture*, ed. Paul Henle (Ann Arbor: Univ. of Michigan Press, 1966) 173–195, covers non-denoting or "non-lexical" content projected as "icon" (pp. 176–177). (4) Paul Ricoeur, *The Rule of Metaphor; Multi-disciplinary Studies of the Creation of Meaning in Language*, trans. Robert Czerny et. al. (Toronto, Buffalo: Univ. of Toronto Press, 1977), concurs with Henle on the non-denoting, non-lexical content that "does not stand for itself" (pp. 188–189); work from now on will be identified as "Ricoeur, *Rule*." (5) Also Paul Ricoeur, "The Metaphorical Process as Cognition, Imagination, and Feeling," *Critical Inquiry* 5.1 (Autumn 1978): 143–159, where he describes non-denoting literary metaphor in such colorful—but not very illuminating—figures as the "collapse," "suspension," or "abolition of the literal meaning."

[35] Saussure, *Course*, 69, 73.

idiosyncrasy such as "metaphor" from it would—again!—only compound the presence of dead or constantly disappearing metaphors that revert to ordinary meanings.

That fact, however, did not deter the contemporary grammarians under the leadership of Noam Chomsky either from basing metaphor on violations of "selectional" rules that, in contrast to subverted "subcategorization" rules of syntax, still formed a comprehensible sentence.[36] Yet semantic selection, more specifically its violation, turns out to be just another way of describing the presence or absence of deviation in language. What may be more appropriate at this juncture is to echo the rhetorical question Paul Ricoeur posed in his *Rule of Metaphor* when he asked, "deviation from what?"[37] In other words, what is the measure for any violated selection that would stand up theoretically?

There are lastly diachronists more concerned with posing questions regarding the *provenance* and *precedence* of meaning versus metaphor. Which came first? My example of the recycled "leg" content would appear conclusive on that score. For surely, the literal meaning referring to the limbs of living organisms—bipeds or quadrupeds—precedes that of the content recycled for signifying a piece of furniture. To stress that point, I cited Cassirer on how all reference originally emanated from the corporal, indeed corporeal self associated with the human body.[38]

Even that kind of evidence, however, may be disputed in odd chronological reversals as long as no one is quite certain what linguistic meaning is in relation to metaphor. Thus it was that very corporeal closeness to vibrant nature which led some critics to assign the qualifier "poetic" to the earliest languages. The German thinker Hamann and his pupil Herder, for example, insisted that the primordial language—"Ursprache"—was truly "poetic."[39] In the past I have referred to that stance as a type of "Rousseauian Primitivism." Born out of skeptical reaction to excessive Enlightenment rationalism, critics of that era mistrusted trends toward what they considered further *rational* abstraction. In that purview, then, the early language parallels the "noble savage" Rousseau preferred to an overly civilized

---

[36] Noam Chomsky, *Aspects of the Theory of Syntax* (Cambridge, Massachusetts: The M.I.T. Press, 1965), particularly chapter 4, section 1: "The Boundaries of Syntax and Semantics" (pp. 148-163). "Sentences," he contends, "that break selectional rules can often be interpreted metaphorically ...," yielding personification, he continues (p. 149). But finally Chomsky has to concede he is about "[t]o conclude this [section with a] highly inconclusive discussion" (p. 163).

[37] Ricoeur, *Rule*, actually asks *two* questions pertaining to the identification of metaphor: "First deviation from what? ...Next, what does one mean by deviation?" (p. 137). Both questions remain essentially rhetorical in neo-Aristotelian semantics—to Ricoeur as well.

[38] Cassirer, *Sprache*, on the human body: see note 20 above.

[39] Peter von Polenz, *Geschichte der deutschen Sprache*, 9th ed. (Berlin, New York: Walter de Gruyter, 1978), confirms that conception of Hamann and Herder, where he cites "Poesie als 'Ursprache' der Menschen" (p. 126).

citizenry. Being close to vibrant nature was considered "poetic," and that quality became frequently correlated with meanings that displayed "metaphor" by harboring concrete imagery. Ergo, (poetic) metaphor preceded literal meaning since that grew out of a further (intellectual) distancing from nature.

Here it is interesting to note that Ernst Cassirer, though fully aware of the human body's referential input, saw it the other way around. Throughout his volume on language he kept emphasizing the greater "symbolic" mediacy that gradually developed when language was pried loose from its immediate environment and became accordingly more independent of it. The very distance between language and the environment it serves comes about through gradual sophistication of usage, with an increase in connotative potential. All I have presented so far about ramified (homonymic) recycling proves that point for a Reality Remade in verbal translation, causing metaphor, if anything, to follow literal meaning in development.

In any discussion on linguistic *diachronics,* moreover, it seems impossible to omit the highly touted *Deconstructionist* premise of Jacques Derrida, in this context particularly where he introduced the figure of the "palimpsest."[40] Etymologically derived from Greek/Latin "palimpsestos/ palimpsestus," the term means literally something like "rubbed again," and refers to words written over several times on parchment or a tablet while leaving behind certain traces of a previous text imperfectly erased. So, here is yet another instance of metaphor used to describe metaphor in language. And describe it Derrida did, seizing on such German verbs as "greifen," begreifen," for example, in order to prove how meanings moved from a *manual* to a *mental* "grasp" of things, an example also taken up earlier by other diachronists such as Owen Barfield.[41]

As already indicated, any advanced "mental" development in language no doubt can be traced back to more concrete, "manual" origins that have been rerouted in a series of the "retours" and "detours" Derrida invokes and whose traces come to embody the invisible ink on the palimpsest. Even Derrida's preoccupation with Hegelian dialectics, specifically the latter's precept of sublation (*Aufhebung*) fits into that picture; language destructs what it has constructed in order to build anew.[42] Critics before Derrida, such as Humboldt, Heidegger—and

---

[40] Jacques Derrida, "White Mythology: Metaphor in the Text of Philosophy," trans. F.T.C. Moore, *New Literary History* 6.1 (Autumn 1974): 5–74 (palimpsest, p. 11 ff.).

[41] Derrida, "White Mythology," on the "grasp" example, given in the German as "fassen/Fassung" and (greifen) "begreifen /Begriff" (p. 24). Cassirer, *Sprache,* also offers these examples to substantiate what was to him a move toward greater (symbolic) mediacy (p. 129). Owen Barfield, *Speaker's Meaning* (Middletown, Connecticut: Wesleyan Univ. Press, 1967), similarly cites the "grasp" example, in English (p. 53).

[42] Derrida, "White Mythology," on sublation (pp. 9, 25, 73). Ricoeur, *Rule,* discusses Derrida's sublation (pp. 284–295). But Ricoeur, who generally wants to remain descriptive

61

even the later Wittgenstein on the basis of his "language-game" (*Sprachspiel*)—have concerned themselves with such matters as to how the "spoken" remains sustained as it becomes modified within new "speaking."[43]

Derrida's palimpsest may offer some interesting speculations on past and present usage that do not, however, suffice to explicate clearly what meaning and metaphor *are* in language, at the *synchronic* plane. Rather, "deconstructive diachronics," as I have called his orientation, only lets him contend that it is because "the metaphorical ... sets out in syntax its deviations, that it carries itself away, can only be what it is by obliterating itself," as it "endlessly constructs its own deconstruction."[44] Nicely put, but still, it is simply back to deviation; when that becomes "obliterated," the "metaphorical" dies too! What actually happens to meanings in their far-reaching deconstruction is something I shall demonstrate next, albeit not without simultaneously proving that, eventually, it will take more than the standard assumptions to free meaning systematically from metaphor in language.

III. Hawk and Dove, Bull and Bear: Meaning or Metaphor, That is the Question!

Umberto Eco referred to meanings as "cultural unities," which undoubtedly they are, except that this definition does not suffice.[45] "Culture" is too broad a term.

---

rather than inflicting any kind of critical "blister" (pp. 7–8) on anyone, sheds no further light on this principle.

[43] On the dialectics between speaking and the spoken, see (1) Humboldt's *Schriften* where "Sprechen" (speaking activity) and "Gesprochenhaben" (having spoken) mutually determine one another (p. 226). (2) Martin Heidegger, *Unterwegs zur Sprache* (Pfullingen: Neske, 1959): "Im Gesprochenen (what was spoken) bleibt das Sprechen (speaking) geborgen (sealed or concealed).... Alles beruht darin, das Wohnen (dwelling) im Sprechen der Sprache (of language) zu lernen" (pp. 16, 33). (3) Ludwig Wittgenstein, *Philosopische Untersuchungen/Philosophical Investigations*, trans. G.E.M. Anscombe (New York: Macmillan, 1963), posits a "language-game" (Sprachspiel) based on "das Sprechen der Sprache" (the speaking of language, p. 11). His phrasing partially reflects *verbatim* Heidegger's statement, despite differences in their orientation—the former's Pragmatism versus the latter's (Phenomenological) Existentialism.

[44] Derrida, "White Mythology," makes the observation toward the end of this essay (p. 71). For further reference to deconstructive diachronics, see Gumpel, *Metaphor*, p. 255. Ricoeur in *Rule*, links the ideas of Ryle and Derrida where he insists that "the category-mistake is the deconstructive intermediary phase between description and redescription" (p. 22). Jürgen Nieraad's *"Bildgesegnet und Bildverflucht": Forschungen zur sprachlichen Metaphorik* (Darmstadt: Wissenschaftliche Buchgesellschaft, 1977), briefly treats the impact of Ryle's category-mistake upon Ricoeur, among others (pp. 73–74).

[45] Umberto Eco, *Einführung in die Semiotik*, ed. Jürgen Trabant (München: Wilhelm Fink Verlag, 1972), from the Italian *La struttura Assente*, 1968. The "cultural unities" (kulturelle

Meaning and Metaphor: The World in Verbal Translation

Ernst Cassirer made that clear in his *Philosophy of Symbolic Forms,* where his three volumes embody a different aspect of culture, beginning with language, then myth, and ending up with empirical science.[46] By making language the very ground of culture, Cassirer, the neo-Kantian, seems to compensate for Kant's major omission of language as constitutive domain that I cited at the outset.[47]

It is equally important for non-Aristotelian semantics to stress that all significance obtained from the cultural unities of language must be perceived through the forms of words. That is where Realities become Remade in language. How that is done I shall demonstrate from now on primarily with the aid of four meanings —"hawk" and "dove," "bull" and "bear." Since I am communicating here in written language, the orthographic dimensions of the visual sign will supersede those of the sonorous form. The point is, how do these forms come across to competent native speakers of English?

At first glance, I seem to engage in the kind of "spotsighting" so far disparaged. But singling out these contents allows me for the time being to intensify my focus in a type of Cartesian Reduction that takes nothing for granted, exactly because meaning and metaphor have been approached in this manner for so long. I may thus be playing the role of devil's advocate in part, until I offer my "non-Aristotelian" solution in a context-sensitive setting.

Upon second glance, moreover, the four nouns turn out to be not entirely context-free either. Rather, they come in *pairs,* interspersed with the conjunction "and." For beyond their plain reference to the animals any native American recognizes, they function as *antonyms* for what might loosely be described a military and commercial setting, respectively. At that point, too, each content serves as a kind of *homonym* by harboring one name that embodies (at least) two meanings. That is when "hawk" implies "war monger" and "dove" the opposite, "peace lover"; when "bull" may suggest an active and "bear" a sluggish market. In this group, "dove" no doubt most closely represents a kind of "cultural unity." As purely visual rather than verbal icon it has already assumed biblical proportions going back to the alluvial days of Noah. There it became the avian messenger that

---

Einheiten) occur throughout (pp. 73, 75, 80, 87, passim), and in one instance are used for that old transparent standby of the four Eskimo meanings for snow (p. 90).

[46] I am here recapitulating the three parts into which Cassirer's *Philosophy of Symbolic Forms* divide, with language providing the significant foundation. (Note 13 above)

[47] Cassirer, *Sprache.* He regrets that Kant's "Critique of Reason" was not extended to comprise a "Critique of Culture" (p. 11), which according to his division would begin with language, proceed to myth—standing for anything the human imagination forges—and end with the equivalent of Kant's natural sciences (note 3 above).

announced the subsiding of the flood "with a freshly plucked olive leaf in its beak."[48]

The significance of this biblical symbol most likely aided the dissemination of the word "dove" for denoting the peace lover. Similar aspects of "motivation," as linguists call such a quest for extralinguistic transparencies, are no doubt as easy to come by for the other animal imagery cited here. Is not the hawk in empirical nature as predatory a creature as a human war monger, making it the perfect antithesis of the peace loving dove? Similarly, does not the bull's movement come across as charging rather than sauntering, while no biological expert is needed to know that bears hibernate seasonally and may be deemed considerably more lethargic by comparison?

Nice as these transparencies are, they leave the nagging question behind, why just these animals? Surely, these traits exist in a large variety of species. Then it seems safer to consult the experts on diachronics by checking etymological roots. But none of these investigations lead directly to the one answer—recognizing *that* these meanings are extant at the *synchronic* level, ready to interact with the "oppositional system" of positive-privative values at the sonorous, visual, and semantic levels.[49] There, they may surface in the pun gracing the advertising poster, political slogan, or lyric poem. In that usage, the very configuration of form begins to matter, be it the vocalic assonance between "hawk" and "dove" despite their different spelling, or the alliterative combination between "*b*ull" and "*b*ear."

The same applies to grammarian preoccupation with the "selectional rules" I have previously cited; they are obviously violated here but serve little purpose if applied in order to separate plain meaning from a supposedly idiosyncratic metaphor.[50] That brings me back to the question, do these anthropomorphized homonyms that began as animal imagery represent meaning or metaphor or both? Diehard rhetoricians may also balk at the idea of homonymy, since each animal content has revealed a point of identity—the analogy in the Aristotelian anomalous term that becomes transferred—much as hawkish pugnaciousness lends credence to human war mongering. In a genuine homonym the two meanings covered by one name are supposed to be entirely disparate, as would be the English "lock" of hair from the "lock" that fastens a door.

---

[48] *Genesis* 8, 10–12; *The Holy Bible* (Cleveland, New York: The World Publishing Company, 1962) 8.

[49] Saussure, *Course,* on "opposition" and its "associate" relations (pp. 85, 117–123), where change is not *in* but operates *between* meanings.

[50] Chomsky, *Aspects of the Theory of Syntax* 149.

Meaning and Metaphor: The World in Verbal Translation

Be that as it may, who is to guarantee that despite an identity-in-difference these animal-cum-human contents are not at best *dead* metaphors and as such simply meanings whether or not the "human animals" they signify simultaneously remain very much alive? And all levity aside, it seems fair to assume that these anthropomorphized creatures have become flattened from overexposure, in this era of mass media impact. Certainly, today's Anglo-Saxons reside for the most part in an *urban* environment. Hence they are likely to encounter the human namesakes before getting to a zoo, a farm, or a bullfight and as such into situations requiring any direct naming of the animals in question.

Indeed, the Vietnam War spawned such heated hawk/dove debates that the resulting frequency of application had to flatten these word contents, killing off their essence as metaphors, as it did for those charged with rating them in the experiment I cited. As a matter of fact, only today, while writing this, I picked up a local newspaper that carried headlines about both a "hawkish commander" dealing with Russian aggression in its main section and a "bullish response" to the Dow market under its business section.[51] If these words had to be rated like those of the earlier cited experiment, the result should turn out equally inconclusive, even if these adjectival derivatives suggest already a further step in so-called literalization, away from the nouns naming the animals as such.

If, on the other hand, I were to recall the "Fregean" contingent also mentioned before, the claim could be made that the anthropomorphized versions remained "non-denoting" because the animal imagery was no longer *meant*. The "denoting" alternative would be the *explicit* reference to the animals such as the "hawk" rather than the *implicit* "war monger," for example, that this content also carries. Ultimately, it all depends on a speaker's individual state of native competence, shaped as this is to some extent by choice of wording. In this instance, it would entail preference for the literal-human "war monger" over the wording that remains outwardly avian when cast as "hawk."

The setting, too, may relativize any difference between meaning and metaphor, coupled with what I have termed elsewhere the "metalinguistic gesture," as a speaker describes how language is used while using it.[52] Take for instance the context of a masquerade ball attended by a politician in a hawk's costume to make his/her position on aggressive military intervention as tangible as possible. In the

---

[51] *Minneapolis Star Tribune*, July 7, 1995. The "hawkish" image occurs within the main section's article, "Yeltsin names general to lead Interior Ministry" (p. 2A); the "bullish" image becomes explicit in the heading of a business section's article: "Dow soars to 4,664.00 in a bullish response to Fed's cutting rates" (p. 4D, their capitalization).

[52] On the metalinguistic gesture, see Gumpel, *Metaphor*, 114, 122, 167, 220, 225, 233. In my semiotic vocabulary there, a "literal" motioning to the "Icon" points to the explicit content, and a "metaphorical" motioning to the "Index" to the implicit content (p. 114).

first *metalinguistic gesture* someone at the party may say about this individual that s/he looked "literally" like a hawk, thus skimming the meaning's *explicit* surface content. In a second gesture involving a party given in ordinary dress, someone may insist a certain guest was "metaphorically" a "hawk" in stance despite the benign appearance, and thus point at the *implicit* significance of that word.

Let me not forget to re-invoke the "orientational" metaphors here as well. In the economic setting of "bull" and "bear" markets, the prepositional "ups" and "downs" may readily return to designate fluctuations that take speculators for a ride when stock prices "rise or fall" minus any of the voluntary movement belonging to an avian hawk or dove.[53] No wonder such expressions were classed as "everyday," since on Wall Street, for instance, they may come up literally "every day"—in my own metalinguistic gesture!

These language-bound usage problems are bound to arise when the focus has to be *bilingual* in the standard meaning of "translation." In German, for example, the four nouns must assume *gender*. Less surprising is the fact that the predatory *hawk* becomes rendered in the *masculine* and its more timid counterpart, the *dove*, in the *feminine* gender. Substitution of content is another matter. Dictionaries list the "hawk," for example, on the English/German side as "hawk" = "Falke"/"falcon" = "Falke," while the German/English side offers "Falke" = "hawk, esp. falcon," as well as "Habicht" = "hawk."[54] There is thus foregrounding for both versions, the "falcon"/"Falke" or the "hawk"/"Habicht," and even that difference may be of great importance in a literary text, an issue taken up in my conclusion based on non-Aristotelian semantics.

What remains of immediate importance, however, is the evidence that even in cases of seemingly simple matters affecting translation, semantic names and logical norms never coincide enough in a language to make logical category-mistakes a criterion for anything. The versions of German *"der* Falke" ("Habicht") versus *"die* Taube" may have been based on human traits of dominance and submission in a rather sexist interpretation of gender. Yet the same examples also bear evidence of how linguistic gender may *misrepresent* the extralinguistic reality since in nature the species generally come in pairs of male and female, even if according to Simone de Beauvoir's *Le deuxième sèxe* that binary distribution may not be fully consistent in all cases.[55]

---

[53] See newspaper article of note 52 above.

[54] *Harrap's Concise German and English Dictionary* (Lincolnwood, Illinois: National Textbook Company, 1987): "falcon"/"hawk" (pp. 137, 180), "Falke"/"Habicht" (pp. 166, 236).

[55] Simone de Beauvoir, *The Second Sex* (Toronto, New York, London: Bantam Books, 1968). Of special interest here is the chapter "The data of biology" which deals with some of the uneven sexual distribution among the (lower) animal species (pp. 1–33).

Meaning and Metaphor: The World in Verbal Translation

Language, on the other hand, makes that distribution seem even more accidental by conveying largely a *unisex* foundation among the species of the animal kingdom. Neglecting that "second" or "other" sex is, after all, what caused feminist objection to the one-sided English "man," as though "he" were the sole representative of the human race. Eventually, that got to be too much for the modern *"wo*man," formerly the "man with a *womb.*" Despite such "ups" and "downs" in determination, the avian/mammalian pairs so far used will return in my non-Aristotelian response to the functional separation of meaning and metaphor.

IV. Meaning and Metaphor: Toward a Non-Aristotelian Answer

What I have tried to demonstrate so far is that a criterion such as "deviance" that supposedly separates meaning from metaphor becomes "lethal" for the latter; it repeatedly "kills" off metaphor within the *alogical* foundation that characterizes language as one domain. While critics do not fail to be cognizant of the dead metaphor, they cannot rescue it from its demise by such means. To be sure, for purely descriptive-statistical purposes geared toward identifying a taxonomy of content from flora to fauna, the deviant-dead metaphor suffices—as might apply to counting the "hawk" imagery in a text—be its import avian or anthropomorphic. Although such endeavors may fulfill these kinds of limited goals, they nonetheless cannot convert "semantics" into a "Science of Meaning," as the promulgator of that discipline, M. Bréal, had envisaged it.[56]

As I present my "non-Aristotelian Answer" to an indestructible metaphor in conjunction with the contents formerly introduced, I shall simultaneously demonstrate how drastically their application may be stretched in support of a "deviance" that is naturally inherent in language itself. To do this as systematically as possible, I name first the Polish Phenomenologist, Roman Ingarden. If it is true, as some have said, that Kant's Critical Philosophy amounted to a Copernican Revolution for turning mistaken notions around, then this accolade belongs equally to Ingarden's Phenomenology in the area of semantics.

Ingarden first of all made good Kant's omission of language as constitutive domain. He also went further in that respect than Ernst Cassirer by actually naming that domain. What Ingarden has termed "ontic heteronomy" (*Seins-Heteronomie*) specifies a mode of existence that is exclusively "dependent on" (*abhängig*) and thus "derived from" (*abgeleitet*) multiple (*hetero-*) "acts of

---

[56] Michel Bréal, *Semantics* (note 10).

meaning" (*Meinungsakte*).⁵⁷ Everything which a *Meinungsakt* produces, he added, remains freely "created," "forged," and "drafted." ⁵⁸

With a single stroke Ingarden removed language ontologically from the *representational* view of reference that assesses all identity and difference in word-content on standards derived from the extralinguistic world—to him, "ontic autonomy" where perception and cognition occur *in*dependently of linguistic activity.⁵⁹ One hardly has to be the speaker of a particular language to perceive a hawk or dove, but exactly the opposite is true when the words "hawk" or "dove" are involved. That very difference facing anyone confronting words should automatically eradicate the ontological category-mistake that foists extralinguistic categories on language. Whatever appears as "odd or even" in the world of ontic autonomy has to be detected first in the word representing ontic heteronomy.

Ingarden certainly tackles the word after having drawn those ontological dividing lines: each verbal form has embodied within it a semantic threshold—the "wordsound" (*Wortlaut*)—that allows *matter* to turn into *meaning*, whether the concrete base be sonorous or visual, since all written signs still carry mute sound.⁶⁰ Once concreted, the wordsound yields both the explicit "material" and implicit "formal" contents which together give rise to a semantic vector called "direction-factor" (*Richtungsfaktor*). This pointer literally—again, in my own metalinguistic gesture—directs consciousness to assume a content corresponding to the word in question, be it the mammalian or anthropomorphic "hawk," for example, when guiding English competence.⁶¹

---

⁵⁷ Roman Ingarden, *Das literarische Kunstwerk*, 3rd. ed. (Tübingen: Max Niemeyer, 1965), subsequently abbreviated to "Ingarden, *Kunstwerk*." On "ontic heteronomy" (*Seins-Heteronomie*, sometimes minus the hyphen), see pp. XIV–XV (where he clarifies his and Husserl's position), 104, 120–127, 131, 137, 141, 172. For ontic heteronomy's unique dependence on anything "relative" to speech activity: pp. 106, 109, 120; and dealing with its "derived" status, see § 18–21, pp. 98–133.

⁵⁸ Ingarden, *Kunstwerk*, where he uses "gestiftet" (pp. 106, 129) to mean something like "freely endowed," and "schöpferisch" to convey anything created by "spontaneous" activity on the part of acts of consciousness (Bewußtseinsakte, p. 107 ff.).

⁵⁹ Ingarden, *Kunstwerk*, on ontic autonomy, pp. XIV–XV, 99, which functions outside of language, either as "(corpo-) real" *perception* of the world (also pp. 20, 103–104, 106–107, 129, passim) or "ideal" *cognition* in conceptualizing whatever is perceived. Diagram in Gumpel, *Metaphor*, might be helpful: it illustrates where ontic heteronomy and autonomy touch and overlap (p. 45 ff).

⁶⁰ Ingarden, *Kunstwerk*, chapter 4 on the wordsound (*Wortlaut*), pp. 30–61. While I stress its concretion into a word's semantic threshold, Ingarden discusses further its rhythmic and related aesthetic input.

⁶¹ Ingarden, *Kunstwerk*, on that indigenous pointer, the pure-intentional direction-factor—"Richtungsfaktor—see pp. 65–76, 85 (including verb' direction-factor), 116, passim.

Meaning and Metaphor: The World in Verbal Translation

A former pupil of Edmund Husserl, Ingarden stresses that the direction-factor must be "pure-intentional." In plain English, this vector must be the product of language activity, in *a* language. As *pure-intentional* object, a meaning becomes the "target" (*Treffpunkt*) for an *intending* act, verbally induced.[62] Its sole purpose is to provide the requisite *content* for speaker *intent* when entering a sentence, to Ingarden, a syntactic "correlate."[63] That is another way of saying that *all* sentence formation proceeds categorically by means of an interaction between the *reference* the selected meanings bring to it and the *transference* they undergo when *shifting* to convey what a speaker aims precisely to express through them. Obviously, therefore, the idea of separating meaning from metaphor on the basis of reference and transference falls by the wayside as well, not to mention that the correlate's type of transference remains purely functional, irrespective of the content of the syntactic constituents.

Now I am ready to return to three of my meanings to demonstrate what ontic heteronomy has wrought. It is impossible to be a competent speaker of English without knowing also that "hawk," "dove," and "bear" not only function as *nouns* but also as *verbs*. This more far-reaching association, however, hardly lends itself to a neat identity-in-difference that marked "hawk" as the predatory animal and aggressive person. In ontic heteronomy it is much more important for the speaker to be aware that potentially s/he can pun about a "hawker" who, with eyes like a "hawk," watches out for the police while "hawking" illicit ware. No amount of paraphrasing in another language could reproduce the inimitable puns, at least not without losing some of that *pointe* or "sting."

Here it may be interesting to note that according to research into language acquisition, the full connotative potential of words—essentially derived from maximum input of the direction-factor—does not become firm until the age of puberty, thus keeping pace with physiological developments in young speakers.[64]

---

[62] Ingarden, *Kunstwerk*, on the reciprocity between intending act and target, the pure-intentional (mental) object; meaning then bears the full impact of what was *meant* to be said in speech activity (pp. 78, 122).

[63] Ingarden, *Kunstwerk*. He asserts: "Also kein entfalteter Sachverhalt ohne einen Satz und kein Satz ohne ein entfaltetes Satzkorrelat" (pp. 120–121). No content may "unfold" without a sentence and no sentence come into being without an unfolding correlate. Sections § 15–24 cover sentence formation, including a a somewhat dubious hierarchy of positing nouns as catalysts for syntactic constitution (pp. 61–164). The functions I term (a meaning's) "reference" and (its shift of) "transference" within a sentence Ingarden designates "Meinen" and "Vermeinen" (pp. 104–107, 122–131), together embodying the correlate's "double-intentionality."

[64] J. Nieraad, *"Bildgesegnet und Bildverflucht"* cites research (done by Ash, Nerlove, and Leondar) which proves that semantic contiguities are solidified at around puberty (pp. 115–116, 118–119, 123, 128).

My above example, furthermore, demonstrates that this input involves grasping the implementation of both syntax and semantics, since nouns and verbs may hardly turn up in the same locus within a sentence. That point is made in response to linguists such as Chomsky, who openly admitted that he could not find the boundaries governing syntax and semantics.

The same can certainly be said of "bear" either as noun or verb. Indeed, the verb "bear" no doubt offers the widest—perhaps even "wildest"?—possibilities from the standpoint of crossing logic by running the gamut from giving birth to enduring the burden of adversity. Lastly, the verb "dove" is still more language-bound from a syntactic standpoint. Compared to the other two, "dove" no longer registers an *infinitive* but rather a *finite* verb—"finitude without mortality," as I call it. For it projects *tense,* specifically the imperfect (simple) past of "dive," when cast in the *strong* rather than (its more current) *weak* form of "dived." A fully competent speaker of English also remains phonologically aware that the verb "dove" matches that of the noun as *visual* icon, while these two parts of speech are not pronounced quite the same when rendered in sound. Ingarden's wordsound carries all that information if, indeed, matter is to yield meaning.

"Bull!" someone might say in a rather derisive reaction to my observations, and thus bring me to the last content cited before. Unlike the others, this one still remains a noun of sorts. What, however, it really displays comes off as a "minisentence," replete with quotation and punctuation marks. Essentially, then, this is an exclamation, an outcry of sorts. Ingarden would also consider it a tiny syntactic correlate since it embodies a content that elicits speaker intent.[65] Granted, more situational or written context may be needed to determine the full illocutionary force: does it convey *disgust* in the suggestion of "Nonsense!" or *delight* at naming said animal when located on a farm or in a zoo?[66] Either way, *one* content has undergone the full *contextualization* required of a sentence correlate, causing the reference of this constituent to release in transference *what* this exclamation is *meant* to express.

So far I have only clarified issues revolving around meaning and metaphor which always ended up on the side of the former. As for the indestructible metaphor that my non-Aristotelian semantics promised to introduce, I first return to Ingarden, who discusses general *linguistic* aspects before dividing these into

---

[65] Ingarden, *Kunstwerk:* One of the "Einwortsätze" (one-word sentences) becomes exemplified with the exclamation "Feuer!" (Fire!), illustrating a full-fledged correlate (p. 112). Liselotte Gumpel, "The Essence of 'Reality' as a Construct of Language" (note 14 above), goes into the "holophrastic" phrases of language acquisition among the very young (pp.172–174).

[66] In Gumpel, *Metaphor,* I present some nomenclature of the speech-act theorists (J.L. Austin and J.R. Searle): basic "locution," expressive "illocution" and "perlocution" in response to or compliance with what was said, commanded or requested (p. 110).

literal and *literary* modes of application. First, the sentence correlate must come together; only then is it projected "out into" a reality-nexus forming a literal proposition, or "judgment" (*Urteil*) which embodies a truth claim (*Wahrheitsanspruch*), and accordingly becomes juxtaposed (*angepaßt*) with a corresponding objective referent. [67]

Since I have already detailed the adequating process exhaustively elsewhere, I shall bring it in more indirectly while concentrating on its opposite, the *literary* correlate Ingarden terms "quasi-judgment" (*Quasi-Urteil*).[68] The "quasi-" prefix suggests a "simulated" rather than half-hearted "semi"-state, simply because surface contents reflect a world that looks real in explicit content but remains fictitious. Speech-act theorists have similarly defined literary discourse as "pretense."[69] All that comes close, of course, to Nietzsche's extramoral "lie," except that the illusive reality here is an aesthetic product which is morally no more mendacious than objective reality itself was to this thinker.

To Ingarden, the *literary work of art* comprising a fictional realm surfaces in four "strata" (*Schichten*) that may be subdivided further into two *linguistic* and two *literary* kinds.[70] The two linguistic strata come together through comprehensible wordsounds and the amalgamated "semantic unities" (*Bedeutungseinheiten*) that are borne by coherent syntactic correlates; the two literary strata then take over the function of presenting (*darstellen*) "objects" in the shape of fictional characters and places, all of them projected in the given "aspects" (*Ansichten*) their verbal contents provide.

---

[67] Ingarden, *Kunstwerk* (pp. 170–176), on adequation and the direction-factor projection (*Hinausversetzung*) "out into" the extralinguistic reality. Its full implications are also presented, complete with diagrams, in Liselotte Gumpel, "Language as Bearer of Meaning" (note 9 above).

[68] Ingarden, *Kunstwerk*, § 20–22 (pp. 121–183). Critics have correlated the "quasi-" prefix in this context with dubious *"pseudo*-statements." See Edward Stankiewicz, "Poetics and Verbal Art," in *A Profusion of Signs*, ed. T.A. Sebeok (Bloomington, London: Indiana Univ. Press, 1977) 54–76, especially 56.

[69] Ingarden, *Kunstwerk*, asserts that the literary realm is not to be taken "in dem Modus des vollen Ernstes" since it reflects only an "Illusion der Realität" (pp. 178, 182). This type of "not earnest" or "non-serious" usage was especially proclaimed by John R. Searle, although he did not seem to know where those findings would lead him in determining the essence of language. Searle, in *Speech Acts: An Essay in the Philosophy of Language* (Cambridge: Cambridge Univ. Press, 1970), draws on Austin when he states that fictional discourse was "parasitic," operating in a "let's pretend" vein (pp. 78–79). In "The Logical Status of Fictional Discourse," *New Literary History* 6 (1974–1975): 319–332, he classes literary illocutionary acts with the "pretended" kind (p. 327).

[70] Ingarden, *Kunstwerk*: First stratum, chapter 4 (pp. 30–61); second stratum, chapters 5 and 6 (pp. 61–229); third stratum, chapter 7 (pp. 229–270); fourth stratum, chapters 8 and 9 (pp. 270–307). Page numbers indicate that the second stratum of syntactic amalgamation is by far the longest. My binary division into two linguistic and two literary strata have been elucidated in Liselotte Gumpel, "Language as Bearer of Meaning" (note 9 above).

Let me illustrate what is involved with a *hypothetical novel* whose opening word is "Bull!" With the quotation and punctuation marks intact, this is actually more then a word—an exclamation, a mini-sentence in the manner explained, thus fulfilling the requirements of the first two linguistic strata. The text has commenced with a comprehensible wordsound and a mono-verbal syntactic correlate, even if this is not sufficiently extended to require full amalgamation. Whether the word in this limited "sentence" releases a cynical response or an enthusiastic recognition of said animal may have to await a further concatenation of correlates.

Since there is no backing from a reality-nexus, all attention goes on what there *is*, with constitution starting at point zero. Meanings must give their all, putting across what they own in denotative and connotative potential. So language is essentially "on its own" when forging the fictional realm, in the process creating a type of *suspense* naturally derived from the makeup of meanings. One thing is nonetheless certain: whether "Bull!" shifts to imply "Nonsense!" or to elicit some reference to an animal, the higher strata begin to take root. For here is a fictional "object," a person, first appearing in this one aspect, "Bull!"

This "Bull!" operates as a "face" of sorts insofar as it provides the first aspect of a fictional character. Other correlates will provide further attributes, be it name, age, sex, or whatever. In that manner, the author "steers" readers through the text, which then mediates between *constitution* and *concretization*, as Ingarden calls the latter participation on the part of a reader.[71] Accordingly, the text coordinates between inception and reception, frequently far beyond the author's own life. But the text can only do so if the words, based on the idiolect of the author's time, are grasped in the way they were *meant*. That was something the anachronistic analyses of Aristotle and Beardsley failed to uncover when extracting language-bound deviance from the works of Homer and Shakespeare, respectively, texts hence constituted way before their time.

If, for example, the idiomatic and derisive usage of "Bull!" were no longer current to later readers and they interpreted it as a call for this mammal, the linguistic strata would be subverted, causing the literary strata to project a wrong "world."[72] The idea of "no longer" suggests a temporal factor I have defined else-

---

[71] On concretization, see Ingarden, *Kunstwerk*, chapter 13 (pp. 353–380). Also note Roman Ingarden, *Vom Erkennen des literarischen Kunstwerks* [from the Polish *O poznawaniu dziela literackiego* of 1939] (Tübingen: Max Niemeyer Verlag, 1968), where it is covered in the first two chapters (pp. 16–150). This treatise is less technical than *Kunstwerk*. Work will from now on be identified as "Ingarden, *Vom Erkennen*."

[72] On idiom formation, see Liselotte Gumpel, "The Structure of Idioms: A Phenomenological Approach," *Semiotica* 12 (1974): 1–40, where adequation is posited as the source of amplified semantic content through the contacts language makes with the extralinguistic reality.

where as "epochal time."⁷³ It can be illustrated more forcefully with my other example governing the past strong or weak forms of "dove" and "dived." Should future readers be no longer familiar with the strong form and take it to be the noun "dove," the rules of syntax and semantics would be sufficiently violated to block sentence correlation, to the point of "non-sense." With the linguistic strata thus distorted, a fictional aspect projecting a character could hardly take over. Epochal time thus *dates* inception; it is in that respect the "extrinsic" linguistic component which harks back to the author's era and may thus help to narrow down the period for an anonymous work.

If, furthermore, the language were functionally literal and thus of the *adequated* kind, some *paraphrasing* could be tolerated just because the focus does not remain on the pure referent of the words themselves, but on the objective one in the reality-nexus they now signify. For example, a reporter discussing an Olympic sports event could substitute "dived" for "dove" if the audience were more familiar with one of those forms, as long as the message about the diver was understood. But in a non-adequated text, where the word is all, meddling with the literary substratum and its "quasi-mirror" would be like "updating" a painting by changing its colors. The only other measure is to add a text-critical note on wording which time has modified.

Epochal time thus remains *fixed* by demanding recognition of a linguistic inventory current during the author's life, while that quasi-mirror, once formed, also contains a *fluid* temporal element at the higher levels of the literary strata. If, for example, "Bull!"—once constituted in the idiomatic expression it was *meant* to carry—ends up rendering a whistle-blower against the powers that be—in industry, politics, or whatever—s/he could attain heroic proportions during an age that celebrated these causes, much as the characters of Don Quixote or Hamlet "grew" in modern times, after psychology became such a popular field.

One aspect of time relevant to language and literature may thus be *fixed* and another *fluid*. Beyond the "vertical" succession so far discussed, there exists the "horizontal" movement of *sequence*—"Aufeinanderfolge," to Ingarden—that for Western languages goes from left to right, top to bottom of a page.⁷⁴ Yet this phenomenon becomes counteracted by the *simultaneity* embodied in the organic construct. While the *act* of concretization is always temporal, the literary work of art, constituted as a whole, remains atemporal. Whatever the impression, it is only the assimilation process that becomes temporal as the work passes (once more) through the consciousness of readers while the whole is already there. That is why

---

73 Epochal time: under "time" in the index of Gumpel, *Metaphor* (p. 303).
74 On sequence as "Aufeinanderfolge," see Ingarden's *Kunstwerk*, chapter 11 (pp. 326–336), and *Vom Erkennen*, chapter II (pp. 95–150) which delves into many temporal perspectives.

more than one reading is advocated; my hypothetical "Bull!" opener would gain as well from knowing the rest of the text.

Moreover, the "Bull!" disclaimer may also date the work in another way. Even if this "idiomatic" usage, as I have described it euphemistically, were well-known in former times, it may have been barred from inclusion in a novel for being too close to slang. In an age not long ago the *elevated* language of literature was still separated from the *everyday* lingo of ordinary discourse. Nowadays, however, the opposite may apply: on the surface, a commercial jingle might end up sounding more "poetic" than a "prosaic" looking piece of literature rich in jargon from every field, including technology. That problematic reversal should accelerate the need to get away from sheer surface content, if the labels "literal" and "literary" are not to become relativized and rule each other out as did meaning and metaphor.

On that issue, it is now time to discover how non-Aristotelian semantics keeps *meaning* and *metaphor* functionally apart. Before I can provide the definitive answer in illustration, however, I have to present the theory behind the examples, part of which is again Ingarden's. The first thing to do is to divide the non-adequated usage into *two literary genres,* one of which belongs to *fiction,* the other to *lyric poetry.* Although tradition also separates fiction from drama, thus yielding a triadic division, both these types of works comprise *plot* formation, be their words spoken (performed) or written. On those grounds, Ingarden does not systematically distinguish them either, other than attaching a few details on the "theater."[75]

Outside of the one fictional category, then, there exists the *lyric* genre. That is where a *non-Aristotelian metaphor* is to be found—categorically, irrespective of content. At first glance, to be sure, it appears easy to claim that a poem contains *ipso facto* metaphor, but the challenge lies in proving how such a constituent works. Well, to begin with its etymology, based as it is on the precept of *transference,* this now has to be of a special kind. As stated, transference always accompanies reference in non-Aristotelian semantics, specifically sentence formation, as meanings shift in content to convey speaker intent within a correlate. That is why "bull" in the exclamation "Bull!" can end up implying this or that and look outwardly—explicitly—the same. For a meaning to turn into a viable metaphor, transference must be modified: it is made to *extend* from *syntax* to *context.* "Intent" within this context pertains to the *lyric ego* which becomes pieced together *directly* by the selected contents as it suffuses the entire poem.

Stratification for this lyric construct must be changed accordingly: (1) the first stratum of wordsounds obviously remains, since without those semantic thresholds of words no meaning can be derived from meanings; (2) the explicit-

---

[75] See Ingarden, *Kunstwerk,* about "Sprache im Theaterschauspiel" (pp. 403–423).

Meaning and Metaphor: The World in Verbal Translation

material and implicit-formal contents included now *foreground* and *background* poetic context; (3) the resulting lyric ego emerges from these contents not unlike a mosaic composite. While syntactic amalgamation, which was the second stratum in fiction, may not be omitted, it becomes de-emphasized since it no longer remains primary to lyric constitution.

The difference between the two literary genres also brings me to one more temporal phenomenon I term "structural time."[76] Compared to the *mediate succession* of concatenating sentence correlates in fiction that gradually builds plot formation, lyric *expression* occurs in the *immediate present*. That difference in temporal makeup also affects the *concretization* of literary genres. Ingarden describes how a special retentive memory reinforces the simultaneity of amassing lyric immersion while fictional concatenation creates "double horizons" between what has been read and is as yet to be assimilated until all is gradually knit together.[77] A final aesthetic concretization then releases "polyphony" as all strata interact harmoniously.[78] In lyric poetry, of course, that polyphonous effect attains maximal enhancement through the sonorous/visual attributes wordsounds offer in their semantic constitution of the lyric ego.

Most of these structural idiosyncrasies remain conspicuous enough. There is basically the length itself, specifically the *brevity* of poems when compared to that of a novel or drama. Enhanced lyric immediacy also brings explicit and implicit constituents of *title* and *text* into closer alignment, with the text itself conspicuously dominated by the poetic *line*. Its length freely chosen by the poet, the line supersedes—and indeed frequently disrupts—sentence structure. While the traditional poetic line reflected the genre through rhyme, meter, alliteration, and related aesthetic accouterments, its modern counterpart achieves a similar self-identity by remaining asyntactic. But when anaphora/epiphora, rhyme, and related elements are present, they help illustrate lyric immediacy in all, even recursive dimensions when going *back* "up" from text to title in their own *vertical* linkage with former lines. At the same time, concretization continues to move *forward,* from one line to the next, until the entire (con-)text has been absorbed. Ingarden's mnemonic device aids in holding it all together.

Let me now pretend that the same contents, "hawk and dove," "bull and bear," compose a poetic line. There is of course literally no telling as yet what their full import will render. But it can be taken for granted that every one of these words is

---

[76] On details of structural time, check index in Gumpel, *Metaphor,* under "Time" (p. 303).

[77] Ingarden, *Vom Erkennen:* on retentive memory ("lebendiges Gedächtnis," pp. 101–103, 143–144); double horizon ("doppelter Horizont," pp. 105–106, 140); lyric traits in general ("immersion" and its recursive foundation, pp. 101–102, 105, 137–139, 274, 283–284, 287).

[78] For Ingarden's "Polyphonie" (adjectival "polyphone"), see *Kunstwerk* (pp. 61, 397) and *Vom Erkennen* (pp. 93, 234, 284).

functionally a metaphor, lending its signitive potential to fleshing out the lyric ego through all the assonantal and alliterative equivalence it has to offer.[79] With that kind of direct aesthetic reinforcement, it stands to reason that there could be no willful substitution of "dove" by "dived," for example, in order to accommodate a modern reader. Such interference would cause even these functional metaphors to "decay" by piecing together an unintended "pseudo-ego." Only under those conditions, however, could this type of metaphor *die*, taking the entire poetic context and its lyric ego along with it.

The other main problem would be *translation* into another language, with its own Reality Remade at every level of the word. Not without cause do Germans call that task "nachdichten"; the translator becomes an "after-poet," which is to say a "pseudo-poet" of sorts. Were it otherwise, Ingarden's sphere of ontic heteronomy, based exclusively on the productivity of speech within *a* language, would have no reason for being. To do justice to the poem, the translator has to palpate the distinctive oppositional values each system carries. My own limited attempts at translating poetry left me with the acute awareness of how difficult it is to paraphrase in one language on the basis of choices seemingly foisted upon me by the other language that I—later!—came to regret. [80]

For instance, supposing my hypothetical poetic line had to be rendered in German; how should one cope with "Falke" versus "Habicht" for "hawk" even if, at the simplest level, the animal rather than the human war monger or any of the other semantic ramifications were meant? And *all* of them could be meant, making maximum use of that inner pointer, Ingarden's direction-factor, in this asyntactic setting. Not only the backgrounding but also the foregrounding of this lyric ego requires tough decisions: one wordsound comes closer in alliteration and/or deeper sense while neither befits the cadence of the English original. Next, there is the mandatory *capitalization* of German nouns, which might prove too disruptive for what was uniformly non-capitalized in English. No doubt translators might exercise their rights as "second poets" here and follow some of their

---

[79] On lyric equivalence: (1) Roman Jakobson, "Closing Statement: Linguistics and Poetics," in *Style in Language*, ed. T.A. Sebeok (Cambridge: MIT Press, 1960) 347–358 (specifically, p. 358); (2) Heinrich F. Plett, *Textwissenschaft und Textanalyse: Semiotik, Linguistik, Rhetorik*, (Heidelberg: Quelle & Meyer, 1975), covers all types of equivalence, some of them not far removed from the lyric recursiveness I discuss here (pp. 129–130, 159, 210, 240). For the resulting intermedial impact of language on literarture, see also Liselotte Gumpel, *"Concrete" Poetry from East and West Germany: The Language of Exemplarism and Experimentalism* (New Haven, London: Yale Univ. Press, 1976) 34–66, 90–118.

[80] I am here thinking of my translation of Paul Celan's poem, "Ins Nebelhorn"/"Into the foghorn" included in K. Hamburger's *The Logic of Literature*, trans. Rose (Bloomington: Indiana University Press, 1973) 253. While analyzing this poem in Gumpel, *Metaphor* (pp. 193–209), I began to detect problems in my choices for matching resonance, length of line, and so on, that were never quite resolved.

German contemporary cohorts by abandoning this syntactic rule for the benefit of a smoothly flowing lyric.

If, on the other hand, the German poem had to be rendered in English, even something as basic as *gender* might damage the lyric ego, as discussed with the Eichendorff poem rendering a romantic kiss between masculine "*der* Himmel" and feminine "*die* Erde."[81] There would be no choice for the unisex definite article "the"; at best the pronouns could be rendered as "he" and "she" if, for example, the original's masculine falcon and feminine dove were romantically linked. Even the so-called function words structurally become metaphor, down to their very placement on the line. For instance, should "hawk and dove," "bull and bear" be split into two lines, the "middle" conjunction does its part to reinforce the paratactic style of that poem, possibly changing the nuance of the entire context.

What I have tried to prove with so limited a repertoire as I am able to present here is that the *structure* instead of the particular content determines the enhanced connotative potential of the lyric constituents. That fact should also solve the "dilemma" of the "Contextualists," as these critics were called, who could not understand how a poetic context remains so eloquently self-contained and does not desist from "denoting."[82] Such a conflict only arises with a narrowly representational view of reference in language, assuming that meanings point *at* things in the extralinguistic domain. Yet when non-adequated language is relieved of that very task, as it is in all literary works, the pointer inherent in every word meaning has the chance to expand fully.

The German poet Stefan George (1868–1933) conveyed what I have just explained in imagery when he described his text as a "garden" that, unlike its natural counterpart in empirical reality, needed neither air nor warmth to grow its "dark, big, black flower."[83] Emblematic for the print on a page, this flower's form

---

[81] For the Eichendorff poem, see note 16 above.

[82] On the Contextualists, see (1) Murray Krieger, *The New Apologists for Poetry* (Minneapolis: The Univ. of Minnesota Press, 1956). He wondered how a poem may "function referentially" when forced "to point outside itself"; how does poetic language remain "non-referential" when, to partake of "any discourse at all," it must be "referential"? (pp. 20–22). (2) Elisio Vivas, "Contextualism Reconsidered," in *The Artistic Transaction and Essays on Theory of Literature*, (Columbus: Ohio State University Press, 1963) 171–202. (3) Walter Sutton, "The Contextualist Dilemma—or Fallacy," which, together with Krieger's "Contextualism was Ambitious," appeared in the *Journal of Aesthetics and Art Criticism* 17 (1958–59): 219–229 and 21 (1962–62): 81–88, respectively.

[83] Stefan George, *Werke: Ausgabe in zwei Bänden*, vol. I. (München, Düsseldorf: Helmut Küpper, 1958) 47. The untitled poem, "Mein garten bedarf nicht luft und nicht wärme," bears the original of my translated line as: "Dunkle große schwarze blume." Examples exhibit only onset—minus noun—capitalization and missing punctuation. He rebelled early against a slavish acceptance of syntactic rules.

will never wilt nor its significance evaporate as long as the whole poem bearing it continues to cohere. Indeed, the above dates indicate that this artificial plant's imagery has already survived the death of its poet by more than half a century. Future concretizations rather than air or water are bound to endow it with renewed "life" (*Leben*), as Ingarden would put it.[84] Or, as I. A. Richards would describe it, George may well have been this flower's "father" but, ultimately, language remains its "mother," having given birth to this timeless artifact through his *mother tongue* of German.[85]

The "ups" and "downs" surrounding traditional metaphor that spurred critics on to find answers difficult to come by may thus be eliminated as long as function supervenes form as the fundamental criterion. On that basis, I claim confidently that all my own sentences here contain only *literal* word meanings instead of functional metaphors, be they plain or effusive in content. I was neither building worlds from words nor engaging in lyric self-expression. Instead, I used language to write *about* language, aiming at factual information in the form of adequated sentence correlates. It is with this kind of conviction that neo-Aristotelian semantics may be left behind while ushering in a new, non-Aristotelian era to herald the next century, indeed the third millennium.

---

[84] Ingarden, *Kunstwerk*, "Das Leben des literarischen Werkes" 353, 367.

[85] I am referring here to Richards' poem "Lighting Fires in the Snow," specifically the lines, "The wise poem knows its father/And treats him not amiss;/But language is its mother/To burn where it would rather/Choose that and by-pass this ...." Ivor A. Richards, *New and Selected Poems* (Manchester: Carcanet New Press, 1978) 12.

Part II

Translating German Philosophy and Literature
to the American Context

Kurt Mueller-Vollmer

Translating Transcendentalism in New England:
The Genesis of a Literary Discourse

> We practice our art in unsuspected ateliers.
> *Ralph Waldo Emerson*

§1. Can there be a Literary History?

My paper should be read as an argument presented through a case study against those who, for different reasons, maintain the impossibility of literary history. Of course, the rejection of the very notion of a history of literature as a viable approach to literary studies is not altogether recent, and if we look at the new criticism, Croce's idealist aesthetics, deconstructionist and some postmodernist criticism, this rejection appears to be one of the few constants among otherwise opposing schools of thought. Yet it is only after the postmodernist repudiation of an overarching meta-narrative of Western history that the very basis has been removed for constructing a history of literature, comparative or otherwise; a history that had employed as its fixed point of reference the unfolding of the various national literatures within the framework of the history of Western Culture. Yet the postmodernist claim of the end of history notwithstanding, we can observe within the evolving new world order and its prevailing globalizing and transcultural currents a peculiar resilience and reemergence of the nation state as a viable political and cultural entity. Moreover, it is an undeniable fact that the literature of modernity and postmodernity has evolved from within the boundaries of particular national literatures while these in turn have played their own part in the formation of the ideology of the modern nation state. It seems then that the announcement of the demise of literary history is at best premature, and should be seen more as the reflection of ideological blindness and epistemological deficiencies than a statement about a real state of affairs.

In current debates some of the more ardent defenders of literary history take for granted that its task is identical with the narrative construction of actual events. This assumption, however, rests on an epistemological fallacy (as though historical narratives were in a position to account for and reconstitute "what actually has happened") and on an erroneous conception of the nature of historical research and argumentation. As to the latter, already the nineteenth-century historian Gustav Droysen (1808–1884), to whom we owe what is still the most comprehensive and persuasive theory of historical scholarship, considered the narrative but one of different modes of historical presentation.[1] Being fixated on the narrative as *passe par-tout* to all the cultural sciences, the narrativists have tended to overlook essential dimensions of their subject matter and have misjudged the character of historical reconstruction altogether. The same can be said about their postmodernist opponents and of the editors and authors of the *Columbia Literary History of the United States*[2] who, alas, have replaced historical questioning and presentation with a patchwork of isolated discussions of topics from an area formerly known as the literary history of the United States. The effect of such abdication vis-à-vis the history of literature (and of culture for that matter) is similar to the one resulting from a one-sided fixation on historical narratives.

In the case of New England Transcendentalism and its relation to European literature, both attitudes amount to an effective blindfolding. For this relationship manifests itself and is accessible only through a specific set of historical sources and documents that proper investigative questioning must localize and identify, thereby enabling the questioner to observe within a determinate temporal and spatial field two different literary cultures in contact with each other. Arranging and interpreting the complexity of this relationship with an eye solely toward the construction of a one-dimensional narrative at all cost would lead to serious omissions and distortions. This is the case not merely for the simple reason that the potential protagonist of such a tale, American national literature, did not exist at the time when its narrative is supposed to begin. But rather, and this brings us back to the same epistemological fallacy, that such a narrative would create the illusion that the aim of literary history is to produce "an accurate mimesis of the past" as is claimed by one of its recent defenders,[3] instead of dealing with what still is extant of the past and reconstructing from it such interconnections that allow us to read its documents and texts as constitutive parts of a larger historical

---

[1] Johann Gustav Droysen, *Historik. Band I: Rekonstruktion der ersten vollständigen Fassung der Vorlesungen (1857) Grundriss der Historik ...*, ed. Peter Leyh (Stuttgart-Bad Cannstadt: Fromann-Holzbog, 1977).

[2] Emory Elliott (gen. ed.), *Columbia Literary History of the United States* (Columbia UP: New York, 1988).

[3] This is the opinion of David Perkins in his informative study *Is Literary History Possible?* (The Johns Hopkins UP: Baltimore and London, 1993) 73. On this and other issues see also his discussion in *The Uses of Literary History*, ed. Marshall Brown (Duke UP: Durham and London, 1995) 63–69.

context. The question then whether literary history is possible deserves an unqualified yes. Not in the sense, to be sure, that this involves a comparison of different teleological narrative constructions—the American, the British, and the German—or their possible rearrangement. Instead our concern is with a number of clearly identifiable moments of interaction between two different literary and intellectual cultures, where one of them, American literary culture, will be made transparent to reveal the genealogy of its Transcendentalist discourse. But this does not involve the construction of a cross-entry taxonomy of literary works and authors. Nor will our procedure be aimed at anything like a history of the reception of works of German literature and culture in America, or be engaged in exercises of New Historicist contextualization without end.

A discursive phenomenon shared by the German Romantic theologian Friedrich Schleiermacher and the New England Transcendentalist writer Ralph Waldo Emerson will serve as our point of departure. The question of their possible relationship confronts us with a specific set of problems that calls for an appropriate methodological response so that relevant facts and sources can be identified to help us answer the initial question. If the established methods of literary history seem to be inadequate for this task, this does not mean that literary history is impossible, but rather that it will have to be adjusted to the task at hand. Literary history after all is not a tale about something or other, but a journey of discovery, which means it deals not with things past but with their continuous presence.

§ 2. Schleiermacher: "Boldly Conceived Interconnectedness"

Transcendentalism should be taken as both the subject and the object of the title phrase of my presentation. For in one sense Transcendentalism is the translator, while in another, it is itself what is being translated into the discourse of that mid-nineteenth century movement known by the name of "New England Transcendentalism." While I was rereading Schleiermacher's discourses *Über die Religion* (*Discourses on Religion*) following heavy exposure to Emerson's essayistic prose, I was astounded at how many of Emerson's favorite and essential expressions introduced in his first published book, *Nature* (1836), have their correspondences in Schleiermacher's *Discourses* of 1799, a text that lies at the very center of early German Romanticism. Let me illustrate this rather remarkable phenomenon with some revealing textual specimens chosen from a particularly dense section in Schleiermacher's work, entitled "Das Wesen der Religion" ("The Nature of

Religion"). To the attentive reader these passages emanate an obvious, and distinct Emersonian ring:[4]

> *ursprüngliche Einfalt der Natur*
> (Original simple innocence of nature)
>
> *Wege der Bildung*
> (the paths of self-culture)
>
> *den Weltgeist zu lieben und freudig seinem Wirken zuzuschauen*
> (to love the world spirit and to joyfully contemplate its workings)
>
> *Schönheit des Erdballs*
> (the beauty of the earthly globe)
>
> *zartes Spiel der Farben*
> (tender play of colors)
>
> *lieblichte Produkte der vegetabilischen Natur*
> (the lovely products of vegetative nature)
>
> *Anschauen des Universums*
> (intuiting the Universe)
>
> *Einheit und Allgegenwart*
> (unity and omnipresence)
>
> *die Unendlichkeit zu suchen*
> (to search for the infinite)
>
> *eine erhabene Einheit*
> (a sublime unity)
>
> *einen großgedachten Zusammenhang ahnden*
> (to intuit a boldly conceived interconnectedness)
>
> *allgemeine Tendenz zur Ordnung und Harmonie*
> (the universal tendency toward order and harmony)
>
> *auch die Welt ist ein Werk höherer Einheit*
> (the world, too, is the work of a higher unity]
>
> *Individualität und Einheit*
> (individuality and unity)
>
> *im inneren Leben bildet sich das Universum ab: durch das innere wird das äußere verständlich*
> (in our inner life the universe depicts itself: through the inner the outer becomes comprehensible)

---

[4] Friedrich Schleiermacher, *Über die Religion. Reden an die Gebildeten unter ihren Verächtern*, ed. H.-J. Rothert (1799; Felix Meiner: Hamburg, 1958) 46–47; my translations.

Obviously this is more than a random assemblage of peculiar expressions; it is rather a cluster of rhetorical figures revealing a "boldly conceived inter-connnectedness" ("großgedanklicher Zusammenhang") which form part of the stock and trade of early German Romantic literary discourse, and for which the reader can find equivalent expressions—often literal ones—in the American writer Emerson. How it is that Emerson and Schleiermacher, both belonging to two different linguistic and cultural traditions, would share in a discourse and a vocabulary that we can broadly characterize as Romantic is the question that I want to address. It is, of course, a question of translation.

§ 3. New England Transcendentalism and Early American Literature

Whatever else it may have been, New England Transcendentalism principally stands for the momentous break in the cultural history of the United States when its literary community ceased to be a mere contributor to universal literature,[5] and it began instead producing a national literature of its own in overt competition with the major literatures of Europe. Attempts to explain this rise of an American national literature have been varied and for the most part not very satisfactory. The majority have failed not only because they operated from within the nationalist teleological structure whose very origin they attempted to explain, but because they did not address a strangely conspicuous fact: namely, that the new American literature, despite its overt Americanness, did make its nationalist debut precisely by emulating those European nations which were then attempting to create a literature that would be accepted as modern in accordance with prevailing international standards. This means that the question of an American national literature can be seen as a problem of the constitution of its literary discourse in relation to what was considered modern European literature at the time, and that means Romanticism. In this context, then, the old teleological models no longer hold. But the opposite attempt at explanation through the paradigm of cultural transfer, that is, the importation of literary models and ideas from Europe to America, is equally unsatisfactory, even if one might cite in its favor the impressive flow of translations, mostly from the German, that began in the eighteen thirties. For in the absence of an autochthonous modern, that is, Romantic discourse, the question is, into which idiom could these European works have been translated in the target language other than that of post-enlightenment neoclassicism, Lockean

---

[5] On the distinction between "universal" and "national" literature see A. Owen Aldridge, *Early American Literature: A Comparative Approach* (Princeton UP: Princeton, New Jersey, 1982) 11–19.

empiricism, and English Romance?[6] Yet the problem we are facing is not unique to the American situation and can be stated in general terms: When transcending their linguistic and national boundaries, literary and cultural movements have to depend on translation. If they are embedded in a novel cultural discourse, their respective idioms tend to be without semantic equivalents in the target culture. For example, the discourse of early German Romanticism and German Idealism did not have an equivalent in contemporary French culture. It was within this semantic gap between two cultures that Madame de Staël's work of 1813 *De L'Allemagne* (*On Germany*) established an intermediary idiom capable of rendering German culture intelligible to the French intellectual community.

Curiously enough, this same work, widely read in the United States at the time, was to fulfill a similar function with regard to the semantic gap that existed between the new German philosophical and literary culture and the language of the American intellectual elite. If we were to rely on the still widely accepted cliché that a "translation consists of reproducing in the receptor language the message of the source language by means of the closest and most natural equivalent,"[7] we would find ourselves in a precarious situation. Translating works from early German Romanticism into French, for example, would require, given the lack of discursive equivalents in French, the previous transfer of its discourse into the target language in order to accommodate the new translations. As strange as it may seem, this apparent paradox not only accurately describes how such translations from German into French did happen, but also how, between 1823 and 1850, translations by the New England Transcendentalists were brought about. Obviously then, transferring a discourse is not identical with the translation of individual works. To clarify the relation between discourse and translation, some methodological deliberations are therefore in order.

---

[6] The weakness of Leon Chai's highly informative work *The Romantic Foundations of the American Renaissance* (Ithaca and New York: Cornell UP, 1987) lies precisely in its disregard of the discursive side of the "process of assimilation and transformation" (xi) of European Romanticism it is trying to describe. Thus having pointed out in detail affinities between Schleiermacher on the one hand, and Emerson and Parker on the other, Chai suggests that this phenomenon was due to "their inspiration by common Romantic sources" rather than by any "individual influence"(194). He does not address the question of how these "sources" could have created equivalent discursive topoi in authors writing in two different languages.

[7] E.A. Nida and C.Taber, *The Theory and Practice of Translation* (E.J. Brill: Leiden, 1969) 12. Even though in his later writings Nida and his coworker J. de Waard have replaced the term "natural equivalence" first with "dynamic" and subsequently with "functional equivalence" (*From One Language to Another: Functional Equivalence in Bible Translating* [Nashville: Camden, 1986]), this does not change the assumption that translation involves a transfer of a language-independent "message" from one language to another by means of decoding and re-encoding.

§ 4. Polysystem Theory and Literary Discourse

According to polysystem theory[8] which looks at literature as an aggregate of different literary systems and subsystems competing with each other for readership and prestige, the function of literary translation is defined by its role and place within the target culture.[9] Translation is of primary importance in a given polysystem whenever it serves to introduce new forms and models of writing; translated works are of secondary importance where they merely conform to or reinforce existing norms. In more well-established or highly literary cultures, translation tends to be relegated to the margins of that culture, whereas in younger, smaller, weak or peripheral literatures, it plays a more vital and essential role.[10] Since American literature of the early nineteenth century can be considered both young and weak if compared to its contemporary European rivals, it should come as no surprise—and here polystemic theory seems to hold—that translations did not only increase rapidly but indeed played a central role during the period in question. But when it comes to determining the specifics of this role, polysystem theory, with its exclusive dependence on an absolutist notion of system, is of no help. This becomes evident when the question arises as to which texts are to be selected by the receiving culture for translation. It is assumed that the choice of texts would be determined always by their "compatibility with the new forms needed by a polysystem to achieve a complete, dynamic, homogeneous identity."[11] However, in the case of New England Transcendentalism, a new type of literature, a new way of writing, was called for by its advocates in opposition to the norms imposed by the prevailing polysystem. The Transcendentalists targeted foreign texts for translation not because of their potential compatibility with the prevailing literary system, but rather on account of their non-conformity with and opposition to the dominant literary and intellectual culture. Moreover, the adherents of the polysystem theory presume the ready availability in the target culture of an appropriate idiom into which texts from the source language can be translated. Their focus still rests on the individual work or individual text, making

---

[8] For a cogent account of polysystem theory within the spectrum of contemporary translation studies, see Edwin Gentzler, *Contemporary Translation Theories* (Rutledge, London and New York: 1993) 105–143.

[9] Itamar Even-Zohar, "The Position of Translated Literature within the Literary Polysystem," in: James S. Holmes, José Lambert, and Raymond Van den Broeck (eds.), *Literature and Translation: New Perspectives in Literary Studies with a Basic Bibliography of Books on Translation Studies* (Leuven, Belgium: Acco, 1978).

[10] James S. Holmes, *Translated! Papers on Literary Translation and Translation Studies* (Amsterdam: Rodopi, 1988) 107.

[11] Even-Zohar, "The Position of Translated Literature within the Literary Polysystem" 221.

it all but impossible to deal with the crucial problem of the potential and actual transfer of literary discourses.

What then is literary discourse? It is safe to say that it shares in the general characteristics of all discourse, insofar as it consists, following Foucault, of "an individualizable group of statements."[12] But in order to identify the species called literary discourse, a firm Humboldtian stance is called for to liberate what may well be the pivotal notion in Foucault's discourse theory, the *énoncé* (the *said* or the *saying*), from its disciplinary confinement, that is its attachment to a specific discipline of knowledge, and relate it to literary culture. There is, to put it in a nutshell, a class of *énoncés* that does not pertain to any specific discipline, but that is nevertheless representative of literary discourse. The term *énoncé*, misleadingly translated into English and German as *statement* or *Aussage* respectively, refers to that which is being stated, *ausgesagt* or said in its particular historical manifestation, that is, its linguistic form. To understand the linguistic nature of literary discourse and its *sayings*, we must first discard the naive belief in language as a simple tool for communicating independently existing meanings, ideas, and objective realities, that consequently forces one to look upon language as a system of neutral signifiers explicitly designed for the transfer of specific sets of signifieds.[13] Rather, language itself must be understood as the medium and organ of conceptualization. Humans live, as Humboldt put it, "with the objects primarily as they are conveyed to them by language,"[14] and it is language that makes the production of concepts possible, and that conveys them to us. Through communicative speech concepts take on form and existence, gain distinctness and may thus become *items of culture*. Literary discourse then, while occupying a definite historical space, in contradistinction, for example, to clinical, economic, or psychiatric discourses,[15] is not attached to any specific discipline, but represents a field of cultural knowledge with its own kind of *sayings* (*énoncés*).

---

[12] Michel Foucault, *The Archeology of Knowledge*, transl. from the French by A.M. Sheridan Smith (Harper & Row: New York, San Francisco, London, 1972) 80.

[13] See, for example, André Lefevere, "Translation: Its Genealogy in the West", in: Susan Bassnett and André Lefevere (eds.), *Translation, History and Culture* (London and New York: Pinter Publishers, 1990) 19.

[14] Wilhelm von Humboldt, *Gesammelte Schriften*, ed. A. Leitzmann, vol. 5. (Berlin: B. Behr, 1905) 387.

[15] Foucault, *The Archeology of Knowledge* 107–108.

§ 5. Herder and the Language of Cultural Nationalism

To what extent the transfer of such *items of culture* that are specific to one culture presupposes a distinct adaptive horizon in the target culture can be gathered from the way the language of cultural and political nationalism took hold in the United States during the decades preceding the advent of New England Transcendentalism. This seems paradoxical, because the debate on the desirability of a national literature which occupied so much space in the journals of the period involved translation and cultural transfer precisely in an area that upon first glance suggests national autonomy and self-sufficiency. For example, the editors of the *North American Review*, which was for many decades the mouthpiece of the liberal New England Unitarian intelligentsia, because they believed a literature had to "grow out of differences of country, of habits, of institutions," saw it as their task, as they put it, "to foster American genius, and by independent literary criticism, instruct and guide the public taste."[16] Not only was their journal diligently looking for signs of a nascent American literature (it carried extensive articles on James Fennimore Cooper and Washington Irving), but actively propagated an ideal of national culture that drew its principal arguments from Herder's philosophy of history and theory of culture. Among the editors, Edward Everett, professor of classics, Emerson's and Ripley's teacher at Harvard, and later President of the University, was a Göttingen graduate. So were his collaborators George Ticknor, the first professor for Romance philology and literature at Harvard, and George Bancroft, founder of modern American historiography. Along with the critical methods of philological and historical scholarship of the Göttingen philological school they had also absorbed their teachers' Herderian ideas of national culture and nationhood.

But it is not just the Herderian handwriting that can be perceived in the programmatic statements of the Göttingen alumni. In Germany they had been in close contact with that country's vital literary life and believed they had encountered a most telling example of what a young national culture and literature was able to achieve. Not surprisingly, their propagation of a specifically American national culture went hand in hand with an advocacy of the study of German authors. Thus the theoretical underpinnings for the New Englanders' idea of an American nationhood were first developed by George Bancroft in several articles for the *North American Review*, in which he introduced German literature and thought, notably the work of Goethe (1824) and Herder (1825), to the American public and developed a theory of national literature that would be expanded later by William Channing, Margaret Fuller, George Ripley, Theodore Parker and

---

[16] As quoted in Russel Blaine Nye, *The Cultural Life of the New Nation, 1776–1830* (New York: Harper, 1960) 241.

others. What were to become important *topoi* in Transcendentalist discourse made their first appearance in these articles.

The core of Bancroft's argument by which he wants to justify the study of German authors in America, and of Goethe in particular, rested on Herder's notion of the intrinsic value of different national cultures. The literature of a great nation, "must be approached with respect," Bancroft writes, because it "contains of the noble feelings, the creed, the morals, and the aspirations of a people .... Respect for human nature, therefore, allows no hasty judgment against a national literature, that is, against the wisdom of a whole nation as collected and preserved by itself in written documents."[17] Studying another literature therefore leads to an enrichment of one's own humanity, indeed it is a prerequisite, "for the perfect culture of the moral man," Bancroft argued, thereby opening the debate on the theme of "Self-culture" that was to be taken up by Channing, Marsh, Emerson and Fuller. But Bancroft went further, and embracing Herder's historicist hermeneutics, he tells his readers that because the literature of a nation is always "peculiar" and "national," "the true critic must endeavor to regard it from the same point of view with the nation, in which it was designed to produce an effect."[18] If for "point of view" we substitute the term "spirit" Bancroft's hermeneutic imperative becomes Emerson's "first law of criticism," namely that "every scripture is to be interpreted by the same spirit which gave it forth."[19]

§ 6. Romantic Historicization: Literature

The Transcendentalists's core doctrine of the immediacy and spontaneity of poetic and religious experience was[20]—their emphatic declarations notwithstanding—by no means the result of spontaneous creation but rather closely related to and associated with a specific cultural event: the historicization of literature and of Christianity. It was this event that prepared the conceptual and semantic mold into which Transcendentalist discourse would be cast. Both phases

---

[17] Bancroft, "The Life and Genius of Goethe," *The North American Review* XIX (1824): 304.

[18] Bancroft, "The Life and Genius of Goethe" 304.

[19] Ralph Waldo Emerson, "Nature," in: *Nature, the Conduct of Life and other Essays*, ed. Sherman Paul (Everyman's Library: New York and London, 1970) 17.

[20] The treatment of "Transcendentalism" as a purely theological movement separate from that of the literature of the so-called "American Renaissance" by the authors of the *Columbia Literary History of the United States* (1988) has all but obscured this essential aspect of Transcendentalism. One wonders whether these authors or their editors have read the Transcendentalists' journal *The Dial*, and taken cognizance of its subtitle: *A Magazine for Literature, Philosophy and Religion*.

of this process are linked to the name of James Marsh (1794–1842), theologian, philosopher, sometime president of Vermont University, and translator of Herder's *On the Spirit of Hebrew Poetry*. In 1822, at the instigation of George Ticknor, Marsh published a landmark article "On Ancient and Modern Poetry" in the *North American Review*, establishing the theoretical and ideological framework that American literature would have to occupy so it could perceive itself as a *modern* literature, in the sense that the Schlegels and Madame de Staël had given to this term.[21] Putting to use their distinctions between "ancient" or "classical" and "romantic" literature, Marsh offered an overview of the literary history of Europe with the aim of defining the essential features that separate modern literature from that of the Middle Ages and of antiquity.

As Marsh saw it, the state of modern literature resulted from a deeply rooted process of differentiation that permeated the European cultural system from the Middle Ages onward. The ensuing separation of poetry from history, and art from nature, the dissolution of the bond among faith, imagination and reason, and the subsequent rearrangement of their relationship under the rule of philosophical reason all had contributed to create an irresolvable conflict. The inner "powers of the soul" of the individual, awakened by Christianity but impeded from unfolding freely by the dominant system of abstract morality and religion, had directed their energy backward upon themselves. Therefore for Marsh the preeminent characteristic of modern literature was its turn toward inwardness, from "the world without" to "the world within."[22]

On the surface Marsh's characterization of modern literature might seem remote and abstract, pointing, as far as America is concerned, to an as yet empty cultural and mental space. Nevertheless the article's significance for the genesis of Transcendentalist discourse can hardly be overestimated. Although starting out as a review of a work by the Italian critic Lodovico di Breme (1780–1820)[23] in which he defended the Romantic literary theory of the Schlegel brothers and Madame de Staël against its Italian detractors, Marsh's essay soon leaves the reviewed text behind and puts forth its own point of view and historical perspective, self-consciously placing American literature into the same lineage with the literatures of modern Europe. Judging by the utterances of Emerson, Fuller, Ripley and Hedge, it appears that the acceptance of this European line of descent would become an essential part of American literature's understanding of itself.

---

[21] James Marsh, "On Ancient and Modern Poetry," *The North American Review* VI (1822): 94–131.

[22] The title of one of Thoreau's poems for the *Dial*.

[23] Lodovico di Breme, *Intorno all'ingiustizia di alcuni giudizii letterarii Italiani: Discorso di Lodovico Arborio Gattinari di Breme, figlio* (Milano, 1816).

But Marsh's text also conveys an important topos from the center of Romantic aesthetics in a revealing manner that may serve as an index for the supersession of the prescriptive mimetic aesthetic of neoclassicism by a new conception of the creative power of the poetic imagination. At a prominent place in his text Marsh inserted a translation of a lengthy quote from di Breme's work in which the new theory of creativity is explained in terms similar to those introduced first by the philosopher Schelling in his influential work *System des transcendentalen Idealismus* (*System of Transcendental Idealism*) of 1800. The quote betokens the radical transformation in Romantic discourse of the traditional concept of the imitation of nature into its opposite, replacing imitation with competition. Marsh's English rendering of di Breme reads in part: "You are yourself also nature and more than her imitator, her rival.... Instead then of humbly imitating, let us venture to emulate nature in the work of creation."[24] On another occasion Marsh would reformulate this same idea in his own words, thus putting a final seal on this multilingual instance of transatlantic transference of key elements of Romantic literary discourse.[25]

§ 7. Literature as Cultural Knowledge: The *Encyclopaedia Americana*

Literary discourse, since it is not just comprised of words and metaphors, but consists of something that is said through them, necessarily implies a concept of literature that involves cultural knowledge. If the rise of American literature and the constitution of its discourse are closely linked through the offices of translation to the literary discourse of another language and culture, the student of this process has to account for the availability of the specific knowledge that makes what is said in that other language and culture accessible to the translator. When confronted with a foreign text, we usually take recourse to a dictionary to look up the words that are unknown to us. In the case of a discourse, we instead need an encyclopedia. To fulfill this need, the New England Transcendentalists who were engaged in the business of translation (and that was a good number of them)[26]

---

[24] Marsh, "On Ancient and Modern Poetry" 102.

[25] "That spirit of nature which is at work in the interior of things and speaks forth in form and shape, only as symbols, is the true object of the artist's emulation and so far only as he seizes this, in living imitation, does he produce anything of genuine excellence." *The Remains of the Reverend James Marsh, D.D. Late President and Professor of Moral and intellectual Philosophy in the University of Vermont, with a Memoir of his Life.* Compiled by Joseph Torrey, reprint of the 1843 edition (Kennikat Press: Port Washington, N.Y. and London, 1971) 174.

[26] Among the major figures of New England Transcendentalism, James Freeman Clarke, Margaret Fuller, Frederic Hedge, Theodore Parker, and George Ripley were active as translators.

had at their disposal the *Encyclopaedia Americana*, the first general encyclopedia produced in the country that embodied the contemporary state of the art in all relevant departments of knowledge. Sponsored and actively supported by the Göttingen alumni group in Boston, the work appeared in thirteen volumes from 1829 to 1833.[27] Its general editor Francis Lieber, a German emigré who was a former student of the historian Niebuhr and a friend of Wilhelm von Humboldt, used Brockhaus's *Allgemeine Deutsche Real-Enzyklopaedie für gebildete Stände* (7th ed. 1827–29) as a basis for his enterprise.[28] What resulted was not a simple translation or adaptation of the German work, but a complete reworking and augmentation of the transatlantic model to make it conform with the requirements of contemporary American society and the ideal of a national culture propagated by the New England intellectuals. Entire sections and numerous articles were added to cover the sciences, the Anglo-Saxon legal system, American history, economy, culture, linguistics and geography. All were written by American experts in their respective fields. Extensive articles on European, in particular, German literature, philosophy, science and education were supplied by Lieber himself, who at times employed eleven translators to complete the task. Not surprisingly, the density of information regarding German culture is extraordinary. The article on Germany covering her history, geography and general culture is not only equal in length to the one devoted to England, but also supplemented by numerous lengthy articles on the German language, German literature and science, German prose, the German lyric, German criticism, German art, German music, German law, etc. Under "German philosophy" are included Hegel, Schelling, Schleiermacher, and Schopenhauer, who were at that time still among the living. Articles were devoted to all important German writers, from Gryphius to contemporary authors. There are lengthy entries on the Nibelungen epic (five columns), Goethe (four columns), Schiller (five columns), the Schlegel brothers (four columns). The entries on general and comparative topics such as the definition and history of the different literary genres make use of the critical distinctions developed by A.W. and F. Schlegel. What we find then in the literary sections of this first edition of the *Encyclopaedia Americana* is what I would like to call the encyclopedization of the categories and semantics of literary culture as it had been defined previously in

---

[27] *Encyclopaedia Americana. A Popular Dictionary of Arts, Sciences, Literature, History, Politics and Biography, Brought Down to the Present Time;... On the Basis of the Seventh Edition of the German Conversations-Lexicon*, ed. Francis Lieber, assisted by E. Wigglesworth and T.G. Bradford, 13 vols. (Philadelphia: Carey and Lea, 1829–33).

[28] On Lieber's work as organizer and editor of the *Encyclopdaedia Americana* see Thomas J. Kennedy, "Francis Lieber (1798–1872): German-American Poet and Transmitter of German Culture to America," in: Don Heinrich Tolzmann (ed.), *German-American Literature* (The Scarecrow Press: Metuchen, N.J and London, 1977) 151–163.

historical terms in Romantic discourse.[29] It contained all the information pertaining to a modern literature that the advocates of an American national literature would need for their work.[30]

§ 8. Romantic Historicization: Christianity

New England culture was—at least until the middle of the nineteenth century—predominantly theological, and most of the important social and intellectual issues were treated under the guise of theology. This was also the way by which Transcendentalist discourse officially entered New England culture, making its debut in the prestigious journal of the Unitarian elite, *The Christian Examiner*. The Unitarians had challenged central portions of the orthodox Calvinist dogma, notably the doctrine of the trinity and the belief in the necessity of Christ's sacrifice as a prerequisite for God's forgiveness of mankind's fallen state.[31] But shortly they became themselves the target of attacks by the new generation of intellectual theologians who were to comprise the core of the New England Transcendentalist movement. As students they had been exposed to the new historical Bible criticism introduced into New England by the recent Göttingen graduates. Soon they were reading and studying on their own works by Herder, Eichhorn, Schleiermacher, de Wette, and those by the German Romantic poets. Much of the ensuing theological debate was carried out on the pages of the *Christian Examiner*, until the widening ideological rift between the old and the new school led to the exclusion of the young radicals who, in 1840, under the editorship of Margaret Fuller, and later Emerson himself, began publishing their own journal, *The Dial*. Meanwhile, the genesis of Transcendentalist discourse was taking place within the established theological culture with its protagonists usurping the rhetorical forms and the outlets that this culture had provided. What we are witnessing here is a process of translation in the double sense that the transference (*translatio*) of Romantic discourse was at the same time a Transcendental rendering of the central beliefs of traditional Protestant Christianity.

---

[29] Among the contributors were William Ellory Channing, Cornelius Felton, the translator (in Ripley's series specimen of foreign standard literature) of Menzel's *German Literature* (1840), Charles Follen, Henry W. Longfellow, Eduard Everett, George Bancroft, Nathaniel Hawthorn and William Bryant.

[30] A copy of the first edition of the *Encyclopaedia Americana* was found in Emerson's library. There are entries from this work in his notebooks, see *The Journals and Miscellaneous Notebooks of Ralph Waldo Emerson*, ed. E. William H. Gilman et al., vol. VI (1824–1838), ed. Ralph H. Orth (Harvard UP: Cambridge, Mass., 1986) 370.

[31] Perry Miller (ed.), *The American Transcendentalists. Their Prose and Poetry* (1957; The Johns Hopkins UP: Baltimore, 1981) 104–105.

Translating Transcendentalism in New England

At its beginning we find James Marsh's American version of Herder's *The Spirit of Hebrew Poetry* which appeared in book form in 1833[32], and which signaled the coming of historicism to American theology. In his preface the translator embraces Herder's historicist creed, echoing and expanding on Bancroft's language. Marsh argues that to understand a foreign literature, like that of the ancient Hebrew nation, one must first "divest" one's mind of all that is peculiar to one's own society and "acquired forms of thought." The Biblical scholar must then "place himself entirely in *the point of view*" of the other culture. Only then will he be in a position to understand why its poets "thought, and felt, and wrote as they did." Only under such conditions will "the living spirit of their poetry ... be kindled up in his own imagination."[33] Responsible for such divinely inspired "kindling" was, according to Herder in the voice of his American translator, the same creative power which originally had moved the Hebrew poets of the Old Testament. Their verses were "Naturpoesie", natural poetry, expressing the same feelings that can be found in religious experience. The natural poetry of the Hebrews then was religious principally for the reason that as "Naturpoesie" it sprang directly from mankind's God-given creative powers, and only secondarily because of its religious subject matter.[34]

It is apparent, though never fully stated in the open, that the connection between poetry and religion that Herder established rested on a notion of an inner worldly omnipresence of the Divinity in nature and in human affairs. This underlying pantheistic view is intimated in expressions like "that great being, who pervades and surrounds us" or "the spirit of God" which fills heaven and earth and "gives to man his elevation" and "kindles up the nature poetry of the heart and understanding"[35]—expressions that we shall find again in many of the Transcendentalists' writings.

An important outlet for the advocacy of religious ideas that the theological culture of New England provided was the public sermon. How it was used by the Transcendentalists in their favor is best exemplified by Theodore Parker, a major contributor to the *Christian Examiner* and the *Dial*, with his "Discourse of the

---

[32] J.G. Herder, *The Spirit of Hebrew Poetry*, transl. from the German by James Marsh, 2 vols. (Burlington: E.Smith, 1933). The text had appeared previously in installments in the *Biblical Repertory*, vols. 2–3 (1826–27).

[33] Herder, *The Spirit of Hebrew Poetry* 5. Although Marsh cites Herder, he pretends to be quoting from a British publication; see note 1 on page 171.

[34] The role the Bible has played in the formative process of Romantic poetics was examined by Murray Roston, in his *Prophet and Poet: The Bible and the Growth of Romanticism* (Northwestern Univ. Press, Evanston, Ill., 1964). Although Herder's *Spirit of Hebrew Poetry* is interpreted by him as the culmination of this process, no attention is paid to the American development.

[35] Herder, *The Spirit of Hebrew Poetry* 9, 50.

Transient and Permanent in Christianity," a sermon which he delivered at the South Boston Church on May 19, 1841. Not coincidentally, this "discourse" is one of the frequently quoted and anthologized classical statements of the Transcendentalists' theological position. Parker commences appropriately with a quote from the Scriptures, "Heaven and earth shall pass away, but my words shall not pass away" (Luke XXI: 33), but then proceeds to interpret this quote in unexpected ways.[36] Jesus's words will remain, not because but in spite of their having been recorded in the *Scriptures*. For Jesus, distrustful of the culture of writing and textuality, "did not even write his words in a book" in order to save them from becoming subjected to the process of history and the arbitrariness of interpretation.

By his refusal to commit his words to writing, Jesus has, in the eyes of Parker, set an example for the necessary separation of what is merely historical and transitory in human affairs from what is permanent: that is, the realm of true religion. The Bible, an amalgamate of vastly different texts written at different times and under different circumstances, was part of the realm of the transitory. In order to effect the separation of religion from its institutional and dogmatic forms, Parker argued for a radical historicization not only of the *Scriptures*, but of Christianity itself. For the latter could not be anything but a human, that is, a social and political, institution whose rituals and beliefs change with the tides of history. The upshot of Parker's radical historicization was that the doctrine of the literal truth of the *Scriptures* had become untenable, and therefore the Christian religion could no longer derive from them its legitimacy and authority.

Parker's "Discourse of the Transient and Permanent in Christianity" thus effectively rehearses the major arguments of the German school of Biblical criticism and even derives its conclusions from that source. But its ultimate message is that the acceptance of the historical nature of Christianity and its doctrines should make room for the true religion which can be experienced by individuals at all times and places in their "innermost feelings." No wonder then that the sentiment for the infinite, the omnipresence of the divine in the world that we first encountered in Schleiermacher's *Discourses on Religion*, would resurface. God being but another name for the infinite, the historical Jesus then becomes "the organ through which the infinite spoke." The one and only creed admissible in this religion is "the truth which springs spontaneous in the holy heart: there is a God"; and its only sanction "is the voice of God in your heart, the perpetual presence of him who made us and the stars over our head; Christ and the father abiding

---

[36] Theodore Parker, "A Discourse of the Transient and Permanent in Christianity," in *The American Transcendentalists: Their Prose and Poetry*, ed. Perry Miller (1957, Baltimore and London: The Johns Hopkins UP, 1981) 106–136.

within us."37 In expressions like these with their typical rearrangement of traditional concepts into new metaphoric contexts, the fusion of Christian theology and Transcendentalism, or better, the translation of orthodox and Unitarian Christianity into Transcendentalism is accomplished.

Certainly, Parker's sermon of 1841 is not an isolated instance of Transcendentalist theological discourse, nor is this discourse limited to texts such as sermons, public addresses or journal articles on theological issues. If earlier I distinguished the translation of discourse from that of individual works, I did so to single out the specific problems of the former. It is now time to assess the role that the translation of individual works has played in the process of discourse formation. When Parker delivered his discourse "On the Transient and the Permanent in Christianity" he was about to complete his translation of *Beiträge zur Einleitung in das alte Testament* (Halle, 1806–07), the *magnum opus* of the German theologian Wilhelm Martin Leberecht de Wette (1780-1849).38 De Wette had been a student of Herder's before becoming a colleague and friend of Schleiermacher's at the newly founded University of Berlin in 1810. His *Beiträge* is one of the key works of historical Bible criticism of the nineteenth century, whose first American edition, under the title *A Critical and Historical Introduction to the Canonical Scriptures of the Old Testament*, appeared in Parker's translation in Boston in two volumes in 1843.39 Parker's qualifications as a translator of this important text derived from his considerable expertise in German studies. He was a personal student of Karl Follen, the first German professor at Harvard University, and a close friend of Ripley's, whose extensive German library he used.40 Besides being acquainted with the major and minor authors of German literature, he was one of the few Transcendentalists able to read and understand the philosophers Kant, Fichte, Schelling, and Hegel in the original and familiar with the works of the important religious thinkers and theologians—the Herder,

---

37 Parker, "A Discourse of the Transient and Permanent in Christianity"128.

38 According to a journal entry from August 11, 1836, Parker began work on the translation on that day. See Henry Steele Commager, *Theodore Parker: Yankee Crusader* (Beacon Press: Boston, 1960) 38.

39 Wilhelm Martin Leberecht de Wette, *A Critical and Historical Introduction to the Canonical Scriptures of the Old Testament*, from the German ... transl. and enlarged by Theodore Parker, minister of the second Church in Roxbury, 2 vols. (Boston: Rufus Leighton, Jr., 1843).

40 Ripley was well acquainted with Schleiermacher's work. In 1836 he had published in the March issue of the *Christian Examiner* (pp. 1–46) an article entitled "Schleiermacher as a theologian." In the same year Ripley came forth with his *Discourses on the Philosophy of Religion, addressed to Doubters who wish to believe* (Boston), which echoes the title of Schleiermacher's discourses *Über die Religion* of 1799 that had been addressed to the "Gebildeten unter ihren Verächtern" (educated among its despisers).

Eichhorn, Schleiermacher, Jacobi, and de Wette.[41] But the reader who expects Parker's translation to be an accurate and faithful rendering of the original will be greatly surprised at the liberties the translator has taken with the original. His work seems to be a typical case of a state of affairs described by polysystemic theorists, namely that when a translation assumes a primary position in the literature and culture of the target language, "the borders between translated texts and original texts diffuse," so that the notion of translation is expanded to include such items as "versions, imitations, and adaptations."[42] However, translation as an act of rewriting is not peculiar to works of *belles lettres*, as Parker's translation clearly demonstrates. In his "translator's preface" he states that a simple translation of the work would have been "intelligible to but a few," so he had found "it necessary to supply much that the author took for granted." In explaining his procedure and its underlying principles Parker evokes the ancient topos of the *fides interpretes* and the Ciceronian distinction between *verbo a verbo* and *sensu a sensu* translation, but only in order to expand its meaning beyond recognition to include changes in the composition of the text itself. "In translating," Parker writes, "I have aimed more to give the sense of the author than to render his language word for word. I have not hesitated, therefore, to condense or to expand the original, as the case seemed to require. I have removed notes into the text, or placed text into the notes, as I found it convenient for my purpose."[43] With this procedure of partial rewriting of the original, the translator was convinced to have "faithfully given the author's opinions, but in a form very different from his own." The success of Parker's translation in the target culture was to justify his procedure: three editions of the work appeared within a short time.

§ 9. A Transcendentalist Program of Translation

When in 1840 Emerson, Ripley, Hedge and Fuller began with the publication of the *Dial*, this was not the group's first and only concentrated publication effort. It had been preceded by and ran parallel with an ambitious translation project through which important works in philosophy, cultural history, theology and *belles lettres* of modern Europe were to be brought to the attention of the American public. George Ripley, organizer and editor-in-chief of the series, called

---

[41] Stanley Vogel, *German Literary Influences on the American Transcendentalists* (New Haven: Yale UP, 1955) 119.

[42] Edwin Gentzler, *Contemporary Translation Theories* (London and New York: Routledge, 1993) 119.

[43] De Wette, *A Critical and Historical Introduction to the Canonical Scriptures of the Old Testament* vol. 1: X.

Specimens of Foreign Standard Literature, explained in his preface to the first volume that its main purpose was to promote and cultivate the cause of an American national literature. Following up on the suggestions made by William Ellory Channing in 1830 in his widely discussed article on the future American national literature,[44] Ripley argued that translations from other languages, notably German and French, were necessary to break the dominance that English literature had enjoyed from colonial times, and to impart "fresh impulses of thought" and "enrich" the fledgling American literature. Ripley's prospectus of authors to be translated is extensive. It includes, besides the French Germanophiles Cousin, Jouffroy, Guizot and Benjamin Constant, the names of Herder, Schiller, Goethe, Wieland, Lessing, Jacobi, Fichte, Schelling, Jean Paul, Novalis, Uhland, Körner, Hölty, Menzel, Schleiermacher, and de Wette. From these authors fourteen volumes of translations were published in the following years—including a translation of Eckermann's *Conversations with Goethe* (1838) by Margaret Fuller,[45] a three volume collection of German poetry, Menzel's three volume *History of German Literature,* and two works by de Wette, his *Practical Ethics* (1842)[46] and *Theodore, or the Skeptics Conversion* (1841).[47]

There is a conspicuous absence of core philosophical titles among these translations. For obvious reasons since the series was aimed at the widest possible audience, and difficult texts would have kept away readers unfamiliar with the new philosophy rather than attracting them. Placed in the forefront were works whose principal function was to help the new ideas of Romantic literature and philosophy gain acceptance. It was these works that became important vehicles for the translation and transmission of Transcendentalist discourse to the larger literary public.[48]

---

[44] William Ellory Channing, "On National Literature," *Christian Examiner* 36 (Jan. 1830): 269–95. Without mentioning the name, Ripley uses a quote from Channing's article in his preface to *Philosophical Miscellanies,* transl. from the French of Cousin, Jouffroy, and B. Constant, with introductory and critical notes by George Ripley, 2 vols. (Boston: Hilliard, Gray, and Co., 1838) vol.1: x, xi.

[45] Johann Peter Eckermann, *Conversations with Goethe,* transl. Margaret Fuller, Specimens of Foreign Standard Literature, ed. George Ripley, vol. 6 (Boston: Hilliard, Gray, and Co., 1839).

[46] Wilhelm Martin Leberecht de Wette, *Human Life; or, Practical Ethics,* transl. from the German ... by Samuel Osgood, 2 vols. (Boston: James Munroe and Co., London: John Green, 1842).

[47] Wilhelm Martin Leberecht de Wette, *Theodore; or the Skeptic's Conversion: History of the Culture of a Protestant Clergyman,* transl. from the German by James Freeman Clarke, 2 vols., vols. XII and XIII of the *Specimens of Foreign Standard Literature,* ed. George Ripley (Boston: Hilliard, Gray and Co., 1841).

[48] Octavius Brooks Frothingham reports that the translation series had been quite successful and that it "brought many readers into close acquaintance with the teaching and the spirit of the

A telling example is provided by de Wette's novel *Theodore*,[49] a theological *Bildungsroman* of sorts that was of negligible significance in the source language and its culture—it is not listed in any of the better known histories of German literature—but of some importance in the target language nevertheless. The book portrays the character development and education of a young clergyman-to-be who lives amidst the major social and political upheavals of the period while conveniently being exposed to the major trends of contemporary German philosophical, religious, and aesthetic thought. The work thus offered a unique opportunity for Transcendentalist discourse to assert itself through the medium of translation. In his preface to the American edition the translator, James Freeman Clarke—known amongst his contemporaries for his editorship of the *Western Messenger*, the first Transcendentalist journal with numerous articles on German literature and thought[50]—explained why he thought the translation of German theological works was important. His first reason is that German literature differed from that of other European nations by being "an original and living one, when everywhere else we can only find ingenious variations of what has been thought and said before. German theology partakes of that spirit." More importantly, he thought German theology had articulated tendencies found "more or less active among ourselves" for which American writers had not yet discovered the appropriate concepts or words.[51] In Clarke's rendering of de Wette's novel *Theodor oder der Zweifler* they were now about to discover what they had been missing; for the tale is as much about the protagonist, Theodore, as it is a genealogy of Transcendentalist discourse. Let me point out briefly two highlights in this genealogy that are marked by the names of Schelling and Schleiermacher. While searching for the meaning of religion "above the sphere of Kantian morality," the protagonist discovers the writings of Schelling, and finds himself irresistibly attracted by the "style" and "the mysterious depth" of that thinker.[52] The narrator sums up this encounter in a passage that is replete with Emersonian phrases and gestures such as these: "The view of life spread over all nature,—of all personal life

---

writers of the new school." Frothingham, *Transcendentalism in New England* (1875, New York: Harper Torchbook, 1959) 117.

[49] Wilhelm Martin de Wette, *Theodor oder der Zweifler: Bildungsgeschichte eines evangelischen Geistlichen*, 2 Theile, 2. wohlfeile Ausgabe (Reimer: Berlin, 1828).

[50] See John Wesley Thomas, James Freeman Clarke. *Apostle of German Culture in America* (Boston: John W. Luce & Co., 1949) 54–81, and his listing of Clarke's publication in the bibliography.

[51] De Wette, *Theodore; or the Skeptic's Conversion* XI.

[52] De Wette, *Theodore; or the Skeptic's Conversion* 56.

swallowed up in the universal life—the resolution of all finite things in the infinite."[53]

More revealing still than the Schelling episode is Theodore's encounter with Schleiermacher's *Discourses on Religion*—the turning point of his character development. Not surprisingly therefore did the author enrich his narrative with lengthy quotes from Schleiermacher. Moreover, the conclusion of the chapter in which the theologian's importance for Theodore's spiritual education is discussed, reads in the English rendering by Clarke like a Transcendentalist definition of religion—in harmony with Parker's similar utterances in his "Discourse on the Transient and the Permanent in Christianity."[54]

The extensive notes that were added by Clarke to the translated text[55] offer weighty philological evidence on the translation of Transcendentalist discourse. There is, for example, a three and one-half page entry on "Schelling's Philosophy of Nature" in which the translator introduces a whole series of neologisms, such as "realizing the ideal and idealizing the real," and "to spiritualize the natural world, and bind in one coherent whole all forms of mind and matter." Finally, when Clarke speaks about Schelling's *Treatise on Human Freedom*, which is often viewed as the culmination of German Idealist thought,[56] he is close to transforming the Protestant theological idiom into speculative discourse, by distinguishing in the vein of Schelling's philosophy "God simply considered" (*Gott schlechthin*) from "the existing or self-revealing God who proceeds from the other, which is the dark ground of his existence, and unfolds himself out of it into perfect Deity."[57]

---

[53] De Wette, *Theodore; or the Skeptic's Conversion* 57.

[54] De Wette, *Theodore; or the Skeptic's Conversion* 161–162. At the time he was undertaking his translation Clarke had been quite familiar with the works of Schleiermacher. When he met Francis Lieber for the first time in 1832, the topic of conversation was Schleiermacher. Lieber told Clarke "about his life in Berlin and his admiration for Schleiermacher, of whom I was glad to hear something more, as I had been so much interested in his published writings"; see James Freeman Clarke, *Autobiography, Diary and Correspondence*, ed. Edward Everett (Hale, Boston and New York: Houghton, Mifflin & Co., 1891) 63. Readings of Schleiermacher also took place at the Transcendentalist (Hedge) Club. In December 1834 Emerson notes in his Diary: "And Hedge read me good things out of Schleiermacher..."; see Emerson, *The Journals and Miscellaneous Notebooks of Ralph Waldo Emerson*, vol. IV, ed. Alfred R. Ferguson (Cambridge, Mass.: Harvard UP, 1964) 360.

[55] They contain several references to articles in the *Encyclopedia Americana*.

[56] For example, by Heidegger and some of his students.

[57] Other relevant entries concern the philosophy of J.F. Fries, the distinction between "reason and understanding," and the concept of "originality." Where the hero Theodore discusses a well-known passage from Goethe's play *Tasso*, Clarke added an English translation of the passage done "by a friend, [i.e., Margaret Fuller] in a MS version, which we hope will one day be given to the public." See De Wette, *Theodore; or the Skeptic's Conversion* 293–311.

§ 10. Transcendentalist Discourse: Contending against a Cloud?

There was among the Transcendentalists' most vocal critics at least one who noticed that the movement was not confined to the advocacy of a novel set of philosophical ideas, but that its message was tied to a new idiom that appeared dangerously incomprehensible to him and to all those who were accustomed to different discursive norms. The critic, Harvard philosopher Francis Bowen, advanced a scathing critique of Transcendentalism in a series of articles that appeared in 1837 in the *Christian Examiner*.[58] The major flaw of Transcendentalism he identified was in its adaptation of the German philosophical, and hence inherently vague, terminology. In fact the entire movement appeared to him but "one of the first fruits of a diseased admiration of everything from that [German] source." In the entire "literary history of the last half century," Bowen states, "there is nothing more striking to be recorded, than the various exhibitions of this German mania."[59]

Certain usages and terms of the Transcendentalists' idiom appeared exceptionally injurious to Bowen, namely their creation of abstract nouns such as "the infinite," "the beautiful," "the unconscious," "the good," and "the true." He felt particularly offended by verbs like "to individualize" or "to materialize" and castigated neologisms like "adolescent," "unconditioned," and "symbolism," Because of the use of such terms, Bowen thought it impossible to argue effectively against the Transcendentalist position: "There is nothing tangible for a common person to strike; even Don Quixote never thought of contending against a cloud."[60]

Disregarding the subsequently successful career of these offensive words, there is more than a simple grain of truth in this condemnation. Obviously, the Transcendentalist terminology does not make sense if placed into the context of Lockean empiricism—as Bowen did—and in vain will the Lockean reader look for appropriate referents behind the "mixed mode" Transcendentalist terms. If they are to be understood, they must be taken not as signs, but as something said, *sayings* to be understood from within the context of Transcendentalist discourse, and that in turn requires a mental attitude attuned to this objective. In 1833 Henry Hedge had already said as much about Transcendentalist discourse, namely that the works of the German idealist philosophers like Kant or Fichte "may be

---

[58] Francis Bowen, "Transcendentalism," *Christian Examiner* XXI (1837): 371–85; Bowen, "Locke and the Transcendentalists," *Christian Examiner* XXIII (1837): 170–94. Bowen is discussed by Ronald Vale Wells in the introduction to his study *Three Christian Transcendentalists: James Marsh, Caleb Sprague Henry, Frederic Henry Hedge* (New York: Columbia UP, 1943) 4–10.

[59] Francis Bowen, "Locke and the Transcendentalists" 175.

[60] Francis Bowen, "Transcendentalism" 382.

translated word for word, but still it will be impossible to get a clear idea of their philosophy, unless we raise ourselves at once to a Transcendental point of view." And this means, as Hedge put it, we must "take our station with the philosopher and proceed from his ground as our starting point. If we fail to do so, the whole system will appear to us as an inextricable puzzle."[61]

§ 11. The Genesis of a Literary Discourse: Emerson

> Le sentiment de l'infini est le véritable attitude de l'âme.
> (Madame de Staël, *De L'Allemagne*, vol. V: 13)

In our investigation into the formation of the Transcendentalist discourse we have up to now only dwelled (however incompletely) upon instances that pertain to the public arena, such as sermons, published articles, translated works and the like. We now have to change direction and turn our attention to the sphere of the individual writer. When Emerson's *Nature* appeared in 1836, a prototypal text for the discourse of New England Transcendentalism, it was not altogether obvious that this work represented a point of crystallization and the culmination of a long and complex process—one that had been documented meticulously by the author himself in his *Journals and Notebooks*. Its beginnings can be located, as the entries show, in the traditional New England Protestant education Emerson received, which not only allowed exposure to the classical works of European literature, but also admitted works of the eighteenth century English and French Enlightenment.

The first stirrings of the new literary discourse can be detected in Emerson's reaction in 1820 to a sermon delivered by his Harvard teacher Edward Everett, about which he commented awkwardly: "The immediate presence of God is a fine topic of sublimity."[62] As we read further into the Journals and Notebooks, we find how the "immediate presence of God" changed from being merely a topic of sublimity to an article of faith that spawned numerous topological metaphors. During long periods of that process there is no discernible presence of any modern German author. The first two volumes of his journals, covering the years from 1820 to 1826, do not mention the names of Goethe, Herder, or Schlegel, and that of Kant occurs but once in 1822.[63] Only in 1830 do we find two references to Goethe as against one hundred twenty-three to God. However, beginning in that

---

[61] Henry F. Hedge, "Coleridge's Literary Character," *Christian Examiner* XIV (1833): 7–8.

[62] Emerson, *The Journals and Miscellaneous Notebooks*, ed. William H. Gilman and Alfred R. Ferguson, vol.1 (Cambridge, Mass,, Harvard UP, 1960) 9.

[63] Emerson, *The Journals and Miscellaneous Notebooks*, vol. 2: 357.

year, a radical change occurs in this Goethe-to-God ratio. Volume Four of the *Journals* registers fifty-nine entries for Goethe and eighty-six for God. Finally, in the sixth volume the tables seem to have turned in favor of Goethe: fifty-eight entries for the German poet against God's merely fourteen. This Goethe-to-God ratio can serve as a useful index for the transformation of Emerson's thought from its traditional theological orientation to its grounding in Transcendental philosophy and theory. The question therefore arises as to how this transformation manifests itself on the discursive plane and to what extent it can be seen also as a process of translation.

In 1829 Emerson defined the office of the Christian minister and demanded that he "show the beauty of the moral laws of the Universe" and "watch the divinity in this World."[64] Although one of his earliest bonafide Transcendentalist statements, the expressions used are not metaphors created by Emerson; rather they embody some typical *topoi* of Romantic discourse. Yet they did not come to Emerson via the German, but through Madame de Staël's work *De L'Allemagne*. In his "Thoughts on Modern Literature" (1840, *The Dial*), Emerson saw as the main characteristic of modern poetry its "subjective tendency" and the "feeling of the Infinite" it expressed. This "new love of the vast" he claims had always been native to Germany; moreover, it was imported into France by Madame de Staël before it appeared in England in Coleridge, Wordsworth, Byron, Shelley, "and now finds a most genial climate in the American mind."[65] However, credit ought to be given to de Staël, because it was through her—and the evidence is overwhelming—that Emerson discovered this "German feeling of the infinite" for himself.[66] What matters here is not the (surely significant) fact that practically all the Transcendentalists received their initiation into German literature and thought through de Staël's book—and this includes besides Emerson himself Margaret Fuller, James Freeman Clarke, Charles T. Brooks, George Ripley, Theodore Parker and Henry W. Longfellow.[67] It is rather that de Staël's book, besides being about Germany, its culture and its literature, offered an entryway to Romantic discourse by embodying a particular variant of that discourse itself.

---

[64] Emerson, *The Journals and Miscellaneos Notebooks*, vol. 3: 152.

[65] Ralph Waldo Emerson, *Essays and Lectures*, ed. Joel Pork (The Library of America: New York, 1983) 158–159.

[66] Emerson's early notebooks contain a number of significant references to de Staël's book on Germany. Records show that he checked out the book from the Boston Public Library from March 21–May 23, 1822. See Emerson, *The Journals and Miscellaneous Notebooks*, vol.1: 348 (note).

[67] On this issue see my essay on "Staël's Germany and the Beginnings of an American National Literature," in *Germaine de Staël: Crossing the Borders*, ed. M. Gutwirth, A. Goldberger, K. Szmurlo (New Brunswig: N.J. Rutgers UP, 1991) 141–158; 217–222.

There are numerous instances of specific *topoi* that came to Emerson via de Staël. In his *Journals and Notebooks* we find not only quotes in French or English from her book, but frequently variations and mutations of these quotes cast in Emerson's own language. Finally, in Emerson's *Nature*, the transformed Staëlian *topoi* assume an existence of their own. Foremost among them are different variations of the Romantic notion of correspondence. For example, in *De L'Allemagne* de Staël had written: "Almost all axioms of physics correspond with the maxims of morals."[68] For this Staëlian *Urtext*, quoted in its English translation, there are several mutational offsprings in his Journals, where the name de Staël is mentioned, whereas in the *Nature* book such passages occur without a reference.[69]

In the reworkings and emendations of the Staëlian *Urtext* we can witness the formative process that is characteristic of Emerson's discourse. It is a process of accrual, that is, elements of one literary text from a different language are decomposed and reconstituted to form part of a new text, thereby assuming an added meaning in the new environment. This process involves not only *topoi* from De Staël's book on Germany but also those from other texts, notably those by Goethe and Novalis. It is precisely this aspect of Romantic discourse formation that Emerson's text shares with Madame de Staël's *De L'Allemagne* where, in its concluding part, her own philosophy emerges that had guided the author in her assessment of Germany in the first place. It appears then that she was able to articulate her own views only after she had acquired through her exploration and translation of German literary texts the discourse that was appropriate for her message. This transition from description to exposition occurs in a chapter fittingly called "De la contemplation de la nature" where the author in concluding her discussion of Novalis' *Lehrlinge zu Saïs (Disciples at Saïs)* pretends to be quoting from this work. But what starts out as a genuine translation evolves into a text entirely of de Staël's own making, with no linguistic equivalent any longer to the original. It is a rewriting of Novalis in her own language, ultimate proof of the translatability of Romantic discourse, demonstrating that "in order to know nature," one "must become one with her."[70]

It was in formulations like these that the Transcendentalists would not only recognize their own creed, to which Emerson's *Journals and Notebooks* attest, but would at the same time discover the model for rewriting poetic discourse from another language and expanding it, and through such creative exercise make that

---

[68] The original reads: "Presque tous les axioms de physique correspondent à des maximes de morale." Madame de Staël, *De L'Allemagne,* Nouvelle Edition, d'après les manuscrits ... par La Comtesse Jean de Pange, avec le Concours de Simone Balayé, vol. IV (Paris: Hachette, 1959) 204–205; translation mine.

[69] Emerson, *Nature, the Conduct of Life and other Essays* 18.

[70] Madame de Staël, *De L'Allemagne,* vol.V: 166; translation mine.

discourse part of their own. Continuing the Novalis / de Staël permutation, therefore, Emerson would write about nature in his *Nature* book: "A Life in harmony with nature, the love of truth and of virtue, will purge the eyes to understand her text."[71]

To sum all this up, we can quote one more time Emerson, who is quoting Goethe about the German poet's discovery of Immanuel Kant's Transcendental philosophy. The quote reads in Emerson's translation: "Yet for all this I had no word, still less phrases. But now, a Theory seemed for the first time to smile before me."[72] American Transcendentalism likewise had reason to smile before itself and the world—now that it had acquired the proper words and phrases for its thinking and its theory.

---

[71] Emerson's formulation reads like a condensation of de Staël's reworked Novalis passage. She writes: "One must, in order to know nature, become one with her. A poetic and inner directed existence, a saintly and religious soul, all the strength and all the vital forces of our existence are necessary to understand her, and the true observer is he who knows how to uncover the analogy of that nature with man, and that of man with the heavens" (*De L'Allemagne*, vol.V: 166; translation mine).

[72] Emerson, *The Journals and Miscellaneous Notebooks*, vol. 6: 290; Emerson translates here from Goethe's essay "Einwirkung der neuern Philosophie."

Cyrus Hamlin

Transplanting German Idealism to American Culture: F. H. Hedge, W. T. Harris, C. T. Brooks

My concern in this paper will be to trace some aspects of the complex process whereby the intellectual culture of German Idealism was transmitted to America and became accessible to the thought and work of American writers in the course of the nineteenth century. This process was complicated by more than differences in language and differences in the traditions of thought and letters separating the two cultures at the time when German Idealism first emerged during the last years of the eighteenth and the early years of the nineteenth century. Despite a number of similarities in cultural background, particularly in the area of religion and theology, the conditions of life in the early decades of the United States made the transplantation of Idealist thinking difficult and precarious indeed.

I

One anecdote which makes the challenge of that process of translation clear concerns the visit in 1804 by the German scientist and world traveller Alexander von Humboldt to Thomas Jefferson in Washington, DC. Humboldt, though still relatively young, had already established an international reputation, having recently completed his journey of exploration into the jungles and mountains of South America. Jefferson, serving at that time as the third President of the United States, was perhaps the American citizen best qualified to appreciate the essential intellectual and cultural concept which motivated Humboldt's journey of scientific exploration. Having himself spent a number of years in Europe, Jefferson had absorbed the culture of the European Enlightenment to a degree unequalled by any other American with the possible exception of his older colleague in government, Benjamin Franklin. Humboldt, a native of Berlin, which had formed the center of the Enlightenment in the German speaking lands, and uniquely privileged by his aristocratic background and personal wealth, had also during the mid 1790s, along with his older brother Wilhelm, been associated with the spirit of German Classicism in Weimar and Jena through close personal association with

Goethe and Schiller. The young Humboldt had absorbed in particular the theories of natural science from the former and theories of human and artistic culture from the latter.

No human being living at that time knew more about the natural history of the planet than Alexander von Humboldt, not to mention his firsthand experience of the diversity of cultures in the Americas; and few citizens of the United States, or indeed anywhere else, would have been in a position to appreciate and understand what Humboldt had to offer so well as President Jefferson. So far as I am aware, however, this remarkable meeting in Washington in 1804 between these leading representatives of their respective cultures produced little more than a sense of mutual respect. Humboldt may have indirectly conveyed some awareness of the culture of German Idealism to Jefferson at a personal level, but I do not believe that his visit achieved any direct influence of German thought upon American life. Yet such a failure of influence, if it may be so described, could not be blamed on either of them. Neither Humboldt nor Jefferson could have been expected to serve as the mediator or translator of German culture to American soil. It was simply not the right time or the right place for such a transplantation of ideas between German Idealism and American thought to begin.

A far more telling, if not equally more oblique anecdote, based upon a seemingly occasional conjunction of published texts four decades later, provides further evidence for the problem I wish to address in this paper. So far as I know, this specific intercultural connection has never before been noted by scholars.

In the leading periodical of New England Transcendentalism, *The Dial*, there appeared in the issue for October 1843 (during the fourth year of its publication) a text of approximately eight pages entitled simply "A Letter." As with many items in the journal, no author was identified, though scholarly studies of *The Dial* have since indicated that it was written by none other than Ralph Waldo Emerson. The letter is presented as an editorial response to a series of unnamed "correspondents" on a variety of issues. These range from the prospect of the railroad and the impact it will have on American life—"Let it come," says Emerson, "in Heaven's name, I am not afraid on't"—to the prospects for American literature, "that great absentee," a question which apparently had attracted some discussion at the time in Cambridge (by which Emerson presumably means Harvard College). We might argue from our own perspective today, not without a sense of irony, that *The Dial* itself, above all through the writings of Emerson, was contributing to the rise of an authentic American literature to a degree that no one at Harvard or even among the readership of *The Dial* would have yet been fully aware.

My concern here is with another question addressed in the "Letter." From rather oblique comments it becomes apparent that Emerson has been asked to remark on a tendency among the best educated American youth to despair of finding careers in America, so that many of them were packing up and leaving for Europe in order to immerse themselves in its life and culture. Emerson regards this practice with some scorn as a form of escape from reality: "a postponement of their proper work, with the additional disadvantage of a two years' vacation." Such a problem, he remarks, is not new or unique to America, evidence for which he finds in a recent book published in Berlin—Theodore Mundt's *Geschichte der Literatur der Gegenwart* (1842)—where "the despair of Germany" is described in a literary passage dating, to Emerson's admitted surprise, as far back as 1799. This "Jeremiad" is taken from the novel *Hyperion, oder der Eremit in Griechenland* by the poet Friedrich Hölderlin. It is the famous "Scheltrede gegen die Deutschen" (as the passage has come to be called), which occurs at the end of the second volume, when the main character, an eighteenth century Greek, visits Germany. Emerson proceeds to offer a translation into English of the entire passage, filling an entire page of his "Letter" to *The Dial*.

I have no idea how Emerson found this passage in a history of contemporary German literature published only a year earlier. Mundt was one of the leading critics of the post-Hegelian era, a member of the group usually referred to as *Junges Deutschland*, and his history was intended to be a continuation of Friedrich Schlegel's important work published a generation earlier, *Geschichte der alten und neuen Literatur* (1815). Nor is it apparent to me whether Emerson made this translation on his own or whether he might have needed assistance from someone with a stronger command of German. Mundt includes his discussion of Hölderlin alongside the novelist Jean Paul in a chapter which deals with peripheral aspects of what he labels (following Heine?) "die romantische Schule." His brief remarks on the poet are concentrated on the novel *Hyperion* and, curiously, on the extremely complex notes on tragedy which Hölderlin appended to his translations from Sophocles (1804). Mundt also refers in passing to the first collection of Hölderlin's poems, edited in 1826 by Gustav Schwab and Ludwig Uhland (though he mentions only the former editor), yet he hardly discusses the poems at all, nor does he quote from any of them. Nonetheless, within his brief presentation of Hölderlin's novel, Mundt quotes the entire "Scheltrede," which thus served as the basis for the text translated by Emerson for *The Dial*.

We need to remind ourselves that Hölderlin was still alive at the time Mundt wrote about him, though he had been living in a state of mental derangement in the now famous tower over the Neckar River in Tübingen for more than thirty-five years, as Mundt also acknowledges. To all but a devoted few Hölderlin had been long forgotten by 1842, and indeed he died only a year later, five months before Emerson's "Letter" appeared in *The Dial*. It is remarkable enough that Mundt should have included even five pages on the poet in his history, which was probably the first discussion of Hölderlin's work ever to appear in the context of

German Romanticism. But for Emerson to have picked up on this so quickly from Mundt, to have translated a full page from Hölderlin's *Hyperion*, and to have used this passage to illustrate his polemical point about young educated Americans despairing of their own country and leaving to study in Europe is nothing short of astonishing.

So far as I am aware Hölderlin's name was unknown in America for a full century following this long forgotten instance in 1843. The rediscovery of Hölderlin in Germany, as is well known, only began during the early years of this century, though isolated discussions of his work did occur later in the nineteenth century, as in Rudolf Haym's *Die Romantische Schule* (1870), more briefly in Nietzsche's *Unzeitgemäße Betrachtungen* (1876) and in the essay by Wilhelm Dilthey subsequently included in his book *Das Erlebnis und die Dichtung* (1905). Virtually no consideration of Hölderlin's work beyond the borders of Germany occurred in any significant way before the 1930s. So what should be said about Emerson's citation from *Hyperion*? Does it suggest some implicit affinity between the two writers? I would doubt that Emerson could have intended as much. Is there even any likelihood that Emerson knew more about Hölderlin than he read in Mundt's history? Probably not. Where in the entire United States would it have been possible in 1843 even to find a copy of Hölderlin's novel? And did Emerson's translation in *The Dial* have any impact on the readership of the journal, which was itself a rather limited and privileged sampling of American culture? So far as I am aware, this "Letter" of 1843 has not figured centrally in any subsequent scholarly or biographical study of Emerson. I do not believe that this text has ever been included in collected editions of Emerson's work, and certainly no acknowledgment has ever been made that Emerson was the first American by almost a century to take any notice of Hölderlin.

This anecdote indicates just how unpredictable and how complex the process of intercultural translation can be, especially with regard to German Idealism and its influence in America. Emerson's translation of Hyperion's "Scheltrede" against the Germans from Hölderlin's novel, as indicated, cannot be regarded as evidence of any significant influence by the leading poet of German Idealism on the leading author of American Transcendentalism. At the very least it would be necessary to point out that Mundt takes the passage from the novel completely out of context and Emerson's quotation of it essentially distorts and misrepresents what Hölderlin was trying to convey. Mundt's reading of *Hyperion* in his history, more than four decades after Hölderlin's novel first appeared, may be of interest for an evaluation of *Junges Deutschland* in its relation to German Romanticism. Emerson, however, could not possibly have known enough about the original context of the novel to have formed an opinion about Hölderlin's motives for writing the "Scheltrede," and he was probably indifferent to the cultural and political concerns of *Junges Deutschland* as represented by Mundt's History. Emerson's "Letter" in *The Dial* was exclusively concerned with making a point to an unnamed correspondent about an attitude among the educated American youth at that time toward their own culture. Even if Emerson's use of the "Scheltrede" in his own translation is appropriate to the point he was trying to make, it says nothing whatsoever about how Hölderlin's Idealism might be related to American Transcendentalism. That was not Emerson's concern anyway.

I thus find myself, after the initial excitement of discovering this passage from Hölderlin in Emerson's translation in *The Dial*, unable to offer any argument at all about its significance. Such a negative outcome provides an object lesson, I submit, concerning the complexity of cross-cultural transmission in general. Even today from a distance of nearly two centuries it is difficult to mediate between the culture of German Idealism and the alien scene of higher education in America, as any teacher who has attempted to do so can bear witness. Most of the texts are available to us in modern editions, often with excellent translations into English. We also enjoy the elaborate apparatus of the Humanities curriculum in our universities, within which German Idealism finds its proper place, both in literature and in philosophy. We have access furthermore to the vast scholarly and critical resources about Idealism which have accumulated over the decades in our research libraries. None of this was available to Emerson and his contemporaries. Indeed, most of the relevant names—Hölderlin being a good example—would not even have been known at that time. Hegel would be another example of a central figure in German Idealism whose name was probably unknown to Emerson and the other authors of *The Dial*, though it should be acknowledged that certain of the major writers in Germany from the era of Idealism—Kant and Goethe in particular, Fichte and Schelling to a lesser degree—were already known within the still limited confines of American letters and learning prior to the middle of the nineteenth century. More on all this shortly.

II

In order to achieve successful translation of new and unfamiliar ideas from one language to another and from one culture to another, at least three factors need to be considered. First, there must be access in some form or medium to the appropriate source material. This could involve published work, such as a book, or written material in manuscript, or there might be some individual or group of persons to mediate such material in a reliable way. Second, there must be a competent translator, usually an individual, though possibly also a group of individuals working together, who are in a position to represent the target culture but who also have valid access to the original material, if only because of sufficient familiarity with the original language. In other words, most essentially, there must be a competent translator. Third, perhaps most problematic for the challenge with which I am concerned here, there must be some valid form of community within the target culture which is in a position to respond adequately to the new material. There must be, in other words, an audience for the work which is to be translated.

These three factors in abstraction will be self-evident. In actual practice, however, each individual instance of cross-cultural translation looks very different, depending on specific historical contingencies. In order for the ideas of German Idealism to be successfully transplanted into American thought there had to be (1) access to these ideas through the pertinent source texts; (2) competent translators within the target culture—i.e., native Americans who were in a position to mediate between the original German and the idiom of American culture; and (3) a community of readers, however small, within the relatively naive and untutored cultural scene of the United States, which was prepared to respond sympathetically and productively to these new ideas from Germany.

For my purpose in this brief overview of specific instances from the reception of German ideas in America during the first half of the nineteenth century, the careers of three translators may be considered. Their work is now largely forgotten, their books for the most part are gathering dust on the shelves of our libraries, and the representative works which they translated are generally available in more reliable and up-to-date versions. Yet their pioneering efforts deserve our attention and praise, especially considering the adverse conditions under which they lived and wrote. The first is Frederic Henry Hedge, the second William Torrey Harris, and the third Charles Timothy Brooks. All three were native New Englanders, born and raised in the traditions of American congregationalism, all three educated at the leading colleges of early nineteenth century New England—the first and third at Harvard, the second at Yale—and all three provided by accidental circumstance with access to the materials of German Idealist literature and thought in the original language. Two of them, Hedge and Brooks, were trained for the ministry and conducted successful careers within the Unitarian church. The third one, Harris, initially dropped out of the academic community, which he found to be too rigid and sterile for his inquiring spirit, and headed west to the frontier, where from his base in St. Louis, Missouri, he became the leading figure in American education during the latter decades of the century. The life story of each man is quite distinct, though representative also of the challenge and complexity, ultimately perhaps of the limitation, for translating the ideas of German Idealism into the native vein of American thought.

III
Frederic Henry Hedge (1805–1890)

Hedge was the son of a progressive academic philosopher, Levi Hedge, trained at both Harvard and Yale in the early years of the century, who was ultimately appointed the Alford Professor of Natural Religion, Moral Philosophy and Civil Polity at Harvard, where he taught from 1810 to 1827. He received the affectionate nickname of "old brains" from his students and published a widely used college textbook *Elements of Logick, or a Summary of the General Principles and Different Modes of Reason*, a work largely indebted to the rationalist tradition of John Locke and the Scottish Enlightenment. In 1818 Professor Hedge decided to send his twelve-year old son Frederic to Germany in the company of George Bancroft, later to become the leading American historian at Harvard, who intended to study at the universities of Berlin and Heidelberg, following the advice of Edward Everett, then a colleague of Levi Hedge's and the first American to earn a doctorate at a German university.

The young Hedge, who had until that time been tutored at home by his father, subsequently spent four years (from 1818 to 1822) at school in the area of Germany near Göttingen, first at Gotha, then at Ilfeld, finally at the famous Schulpforta, which the philosopher Fichte had attended and where later the young Nietzsche also studied. Hedge then returned home and enrolled in Harvard College, receiving his degree after two years in 1825, where he earned the reputation of being "a fountain of knowledge in the ways of German." He was offered a position as Instructor in German upon graduation—the same year in which Charles Follen was appointed at Harvard for the same purpose—but Hedge turned down the offer in order to enroll in the Divinity School. At that time he also became a close friend of both Ralph Waldo Emerson and Margaret Fuller, both of whom were encouraged by Hedge to learn German.

After graduating from the Divinity School in 1829, Hedge was ordained minister of the Unitarian Church in West Cambridge, where he remained until 1833, at which time he was called to the church in Bangor, Maine, where he remained until 1847. In 1833 Hedge published a lengthy review of Coleridge's later writings in *The Christian Examiner*, the leading progressive religious journal at that time, "Coleridge's Literary Character," in which he also included a remarkably astute and well informed survey of recent German philosophy. Arguing that the Germans had achieved a sophisticated and systematic tradition of transcendentalist thought, Hedge surveyed the works of Kant, Fichte and Schelling, comparing and contrasting their work within the space of about six pages. This was the earliest occasion in print when serious attention was given in America to German Idealist philosophy.

At about the same time Hedge also persuaded Emerson, Fuller and several others in Boston to form with him what came to be called the Transcendental Club, or also the "Hedge Club." Hedge himself had come to be called "Germanicus Hedge," and meetings continued, after he had removed to Bangor, whenever he could manage a trip to Boston. Hedge also first proposed that a journal be founded to address aspects of Transcendentalism. This proposal was finally realized in 1840, when Margaret Fuller agreed to edit *The Dial*—an assignment which Hedge turned down. During the four years in which it appeared Hedge contributed surprisingly little, even though the journal had been largely his idea. In 1847, however, Hedge published the first of his two major contributions to the study of German Idealism in America, a large anthology entitled *Prose Writers of Germany*. This collection contains representative excerpts from twenty-eight authors, including most of the major writers and thinkers of the age of Goethe. The translations were done by Hedge along with eight others, including Thomas Carlyle, whose work had appeared in England a quarter of a century earlier. A brief selection from Hegel was also included, presumably the first excerpt from this philosopher to appear in America, though the translator chose to remain anonymous. This may reflect a sense of the difficulty involved in translating this philosopher.

Hedge continued to write about things German and to translate from German authors throughout his long career. As a Unitarian minister he relocated twice to other churches, to Providence, Rhode Island, in 1847 and to Brookline, Massachusetts, in 1857. In 1872 he abandoned the ministry to become Professor of German at Harvard, a position which he held for more than a decade until his retirement in 1884. He was apparently not a successful teacher. One student is quoted as calling him "the worst teacher of German that ever lived," while others described him as "a testy and fussy old gentleman." But his publications in later years were prolific, including several volumes of literary essays and addresses on a wide variety of topics, most of them relating to German literature and thought. In 1886 Hedge also published a remarkably thorough and learned history of German literature, including extensive excerpts in his own translations, entitled *Hours with the German Classics: Masterpieces of German Literature Translated into English*. In that same year, as part of the 250th anniversary of Harvard's founding, Hedge received an honorary degree as Doctor of Laws. Hedge also published an edition of Goethe's collected works in English, consisting of twelve volumes with translations by various hands, including Hedge's own work, with notes and commentary prepared by him.

Hedge died in 1888, having been ill for the last two years of his life, though he had appeared in May of that year to address the American Unitarian Association in Boston, an organization which he had served as President for several years earlier in his career. In that same year he also published a slim volume entitled *Metrical Translations and Poems*. A large portrait of Hedge hangs in the central hallway of the Harvard Faculty Club to this day. By the time of his death, furthermore, the study of German literature and philosophy had become established in the curriculum of most major universities in the United States. Hedge had witnessed this development and contributed directly to it during a career spanning more than half a century. His achievement as mediator and translator deserves recognition above all for the influence he exerted on American Transcendentalism.

Among the verse translations contained in his final slim volume of poetry, a number are taken from Goethe, including songs from *Faust*. Allow me to single out two of them, one of which is known to anyone familiar with the tradition of Protestant church hymns in this country, entitled simply "Luther's Hymn," and beginning "A mighty fortress is our God /A bulwark never failing." The second is a translation of Goethe's great and extremely difficult hymn "Harzreise im Winter," where Hedge's version may still be compared favorably with any subsequent attempts to render this poem in English. I quote only the first stanza:

> On heavy morning clouds
> With downy pinions resting,
> Intent on prey,
> Soar thou my song!
> For a God hath to each
> His path prescribed,
> Where the happy rush swift
> To the joyful goal.
> But he whose heart is
> Shrunk with misfortune,
> He vainly struggles
> Against the strong bond
> Of the iron thread
> Which only the too-bitter shears
> Shall one day sever.

IV
William Torrey Harris (1835–1909)

Born and raised on a farm in northeastern Connecticut in the town of Putnam, Harris was descended on both sides of his family from English Puritans who settled in Massachusetts in the 1630s. After attending several private schools, including Phillips Academy in Andover, from which he graduated, Harris entered Yale College in 1854 at a time when the curriculum still consisted of required courses in Latin, Greek, Mathematics and Rhetoric (i.e., declamation). Modern languages were not taught—he studied German on his own—and philosophy as a subject did not yet exist. After two years Harris had become fed up with a course of study he regarded as antiquated and useless. He dropped out of Yale and headed west to St. Louis, then still a frontier town on the Mississippi River, where he took a job teaching in the grammar school.

In St. Louis Harris helped found the Literary and Philosophical Society, where at a meeting in 1858 he met Henry Brokmeyer, who had emigrated to the United States from Germany in the mid-1840s and was an avid, though self-taught Hegelian. Harris had been struggling with Kant's "Transcendental Aesthetic" in the *Critique of Pure Reason*—so he later reported—when Brokmeyer urged him to read Hegel's *Science of Logic*, which Harris ordered from Germany and proceeded to study from cover to cover through all three volumes. Little of this, if anything—so he also later stated—was comprehensible to him. Brokmeyer, who was supporting himself as an iron monger and living in a cabin on the edge of the wilderness, proceeded to translate the entire work into English for his friend Harris, whose translation subsequently circulated in manuscript from reader to reader for decades, became the sacred text of the St. Louis school of Hegel, and apparently still survives, though never published even to this day.

This is a well-known story in the history of Hegel's influence in America, an American frontier story which would be of interest at best as a curiosity along the strange byways of Hegel's international reception, were it not for Harris's subsequent remarkable career as a pioneer in American education. He was never an independent thinker and probably does not even merit the title of philosopher, but he became a brilliant and astonishingly effective mediator, organizer and administrator. In 1867 he founded in St. Louis the *Journal of Speculative Philosophy*, which he edited for thirty years and which became the leading vehicle for disseminating German thought in America through numerous translations, critical commentaries and philosophical essays by virtually all the emerging American philosophers—from Frederic Henry Hedge and Bronson Alcott to Josiah Royce, Charles Sanders Peirce, William James and the young John Dewey. Much more than author and editor, however, Harris also became superintendent of schools for St. Louis, in which capacity he completely reformed the curriculum, introducing science, the arts, music and philosophy, championing also the modern languages—German was used in some of the schools for the large immigrant community. He supported co-education and led the movement to introduce the *Kindergarten* based on the German model. He developed a public library for the city and invented a system for cataloguing books using philosophical categories, which was subsequently adapted by Melvil Dewey as the Dewey Decimal System." He fostered the Philosophical Society in St. Louis, of which he was a founding member, and he invited such speakers on the newly opened railway as Alcott and Ralph Waldo Emerson. In return, when Alcott, who had become a good friend of Harris', founded the School of Philosophy in Concord in 1879, Harris was appointed the resident philosopher. For almost a decade he lectured every summer on Kant and Hegel to the assembled New England elite from Boston and Cambridge.

The crowning achievement of Harris's career followed in 1890, when he was appointed by President Harrison to be the fourth United States Commissioner of Education, a position he held for the next sixteen years. In that same year Harris also published his most important book, the product of thirty years' work, entitled *Hegel's Logic. A Book on the Genesis of the Categories of the Mind: A Critical Exposition*, dedicated to his friend Brokmeyer. I am not in a position to judge the authority of Harris's reading of the *Logic*, but what most impresses a reader of the book is the lucidity and freshness of the writing. Harris presents Hegel's argument in a language which is neither strictly translation nor paraphrase, but with a commentary free of jargon and obscurity. The fact that the author of this book had just been appointed Commissioner of Education, the first to hold this office—established only in 1867—with any serious philosophical commitment to education as institution, qualifies Harris in my view to be called the only truly American Hegelian. It was Harris who established policies for public education, which were put into effect nationwide around the turn of the century, a time of crucial importance for the development of conceptually coherent standards and procedures as perhaps never before or since.

Two other achievements by Harris deserve mention. He believed that the key to education is reading. On that conviction he introduced a series of graded readers for schools, which included passages and selections from the great works of literature and philosophy extending across the entire history of human thought. These textbooks, called *Appleton's School Readers* (Appleton was the name of the publisher), were initially attacked and scorned when they first appeared in 1877. Within one year, however, over a million copies had been sold. Income from such sales quickly made Harris a wealthy man. These readers continued to be used in schools for many years and established the earliest model for graded texts as the basis for a coherent approach to the history of culture and thought through the exercise of reading at all stages of education. Harris's last Project, carried out during the final years before his death in 1909, was to revise and completely rewrite and expand the famous dictionary of American English by Noah Webster. The edition edited by Harris was called the *New International*, and it held the market for more than a quarter of a century. Harris himself wrote the entries for every philosophical term, numbering several thousand items in all. His influence was thus felt, even if anonymously, at the level of lexical definitions in America's most authoritative dictionary, as also in the graded readers used throughout the nation's schools.

Harris is now largely forgotten except in the history of American education. Nor does he deserve to be called a translator in the strict sense of the word, even though his service as a mediator of Hegel is perhaps unique. Harris's work as an educator and editor, as a policy maker and an administrator, as mediator for European, especially German ideas and as spokesman for a coherent, conceptual model of education contributed more than anything else to assure that—as has been claimed—we are all Hegelians whether we know it or not. This may no longer hold true in a strict sense, since the system of education established by Harris has suffered a great deal in recent memory and has come under attack from all sides. But Harris's essential achievement remains significant in more than just historical terms. His emphasis on language and the importance of reading as the instrument and medium of an education toward philosophical thought, as well as the development of a curriculum based on the study of appropriate texts which represent the tradition and heritage of our culture and thought, involving a critical and conceptual encounter with such texts through reading—all this remains fundamentally true and important for education today. The debt which American education owes to this mid-nineteenth century dropout from Yale may finally be just as great as the debt he claimed to owe to Hegel, filtered through the study of an unpublished frontier translation of the *Wissenschaft der Logik*, achieved in St. Louis, Missouri, during the late 1850s.

V
Charles Timothy Brooks (1813–1883)

The career and work of Charles Timothy Brooks is perhaps least well known today among the three translators discussed in this paper, but his achievement as a literary translator in the strict sense of the term is by far the most distinguished of the three. By report Brooks was a quiet and sensitive, almost saintly human being, whose entire career subsequent to his studies at Harvard College and the Harvard Divinity School was devoted to the Unitarian Church in Newport, Rhode Island, where he served as the inaugural minister. He made only one trip to Europe near the end of his life, at which time he was quite well known as a translator and was in direct correspondence with several of the authors he had translated. His work as a translator seems in the best sense of the word to have been his avocation, as much for the pleasure it afforded him as for the challenge to his modest poetic talent. Yet the amount of work he completed and the general quality, especially of poetic texts, places him among the very best in this poorly celebrated company.

Transplanting German Idealism to American Culture

Brooks may indeed deserve to be called the finest translator of German literature during the entire nineteenth century in America.

Brooks was born in Salem, Massachusetts, to a family which had been settled there for eight generations. Unusually bookish and intellectual from his early years, he entered Harvard in 1828 and became associated with a sophisticated group of friends, including George Ticknor Curtis, John S. Dwight, Samuel Osgood, John Parkman, Charles Sumner, Oliver Wendell Holmes and, somewhat later, Theodore Parker. Brooks was appointed class poet and head of the Hasty Pudding Club (at that time primarily a literary society) and worked closely with the leading teacher of German in North America at that time, Charles Follen. He began serious study of German literature as an undergraduate and was already at work on Goethe's *Faust* during the spring of his senior year in 1832, when news of the poet's death was received. He also translated a number of poems and ballads from a variety of poets and came under the spell of German music at that time. Brooks began his theological studies when American Unitarianism was entering its strongest ecclesiastical phase, the year in which Emerson abandoned the ministry and the Transcendentalist movement in Boston was in its ascendancy. All these strains of influence converged for Brooks at the time when he completed his studies and entered the ministry in 1836 with the call to found the church in Newport.

Brooks began his public career as a translator with a version of Schiller's *Wilhelm Tell*, published in 1837. This was followed the next year with a volume of German lyric poems, published in the *Specimens of Foreign Standard Literature*, edited by George Ripley, a member of the Transcendentalist group in Boston. Along with a number of poems by Goethe, Schiller and others, Brooks included lyrics by Uhland, Theodor Körner (including Follen's memorial to the poet after his death in battle in 1814), and Friedrich Rückert, along with a group of anonymous folk songs and ballads. He went on to devote much of his adult efforts as a translator to the novels of Jean Paul, publishing *Der Titan* in two volumes in 1862, *Hesperus* in two volumes in 1864, and *Die unsichtbare Loge* just before his death in 1883. Several other works by Jean Paul which Brooks translated are reported to survive in unpublished manuscripts. His verse translation of *Faust. Part One* appeared in 1856, the first English translation of this work to be published in America, the first to be complete and accurate in all aspects of the poetic form of the original. This version was reprinted many times in subsequent decades and was only displaced by the more successful complete version of *Faust* (both parts) by Bayard Taylor toward the end of the century. Brooks's translation bears comparison with Taylor's version on all counts and deserves to be considered one of the best ever done in English in a field that now counts nearly one hundred versions of Part One.

More interesting as indication of the changing directions of taste and literary sensibility during the later decades of Brooks's career, which also reflects a marked decline of interest in Transcendentalism and Idealism, are the translations he published of novels by Berthold Auerbach, the satirical poems of Wilhelm Busch, and the long verse epic by Rückert, *The Wisdom of the Brahmin*, which Brooks appears to have regarded as his most ambitious effort (six books were published in 1882, the remaining twelve books were completed but remained in manuscript). He also translated a number of poems by his contemporary, the radical political poet Ferdinand Freiligrath, whom Brooks met in London during his only visit to Europe. According to report, Brooks also left a number of other translations complete but unpublished at the time of his death: Schiller's *Maria Stuart* and *Die Jungfrau von Orleans*, a play by Hans Sachs, Grillparzer's first play *Die Ahnfrau*, and many individual poems, including also works from French, Italian, Latin, Greek and other languages. This all adds up to a respectable corpus of work, which, given the generally high quality of linguistic accuracy and literary style, justifies the claim that Brooks was the leading translator of German literature in America during the nineteenth century. His reputation as translator would be considerably greater if he had been less retiring in his manner and reticent in his career. Particularly important still are the translations from Jean Paul, which remain, apart from the few early samplings by Carlyle, among the only English versions ever done of these novels. They deserve to be reread, at least insofar as the novels of Jean Paul themselves deserve to be reread. Above all I would single out Brooks's translation of *Faust* as a truly exceptional achievement in the long and complex history of reception for this supreme masterpiece of German literature.

I offer as a sample from Brooks's version of *Faust* the speech in which Mephistopheles presents himself to Faust in the first Study-scene:

> Part of the part am I, which once was all, the Gloom
> That brought forth Light itself from out her mighty womb,
> The upstart proud, that now with mother Night
> Disputes her ancient rank and space and right,
> Yet never shall prevail, since, do whate'er he will,
> He cleaves, a slave, to bodies still;
> From bodies flows, makes bodies fair to sight;
> A body in his course can check him,
> His doom, I therefore hope, will soon o'ertake him,
> With bodies merged in nothingness and night.

Transplanting German Idealism to American Culture

VI

What can be said in conclusion concerning the achievement of these three nineteenth century American translators of the German cultural tradition? Does their work constitute a success story? And if so—or even if not—what general implications may be drawn from their work for a conference on translation?

The first point I would offer is that the translation of the thought or ideas of one culture to another through the mediation or transference of languages cannot be limited to questions of verbal competence or linguistic equivalence alone. This is particularly true in the instance (as here indicated) of such supremely complex and great works as Goethe's *Faust* or Hegel's *Logic*. The success or failure of translation—"die Aufgabe des Übersetzers" (to cite the familiar title of Walter Benjamin's essay)—is far more complex and ultimately less pure, less privileged, less positive than the exclusive domain of language as vehicle of thought might imply.

I believe that the example of all three translators—Hedge, Harris, and Brooks—offers evidence which is both reassuring and cautionary. The act of translation is indeed always possible, insofar as one language may be considered to be an adequate vehicle for what has been expressed and written in another. But the criteria for successful reception depend on so many factors, most of them unpredictable and even indeterminate within the target culture, that go beyond the limits of language as such and beyond the control of individual translators. All three of these translators learned the lesson of limitation from their work; yet all three also achieved a success which deserves recognition and praise as instances which are representative (in Emerson's sense) and exemplary (in Goethe's and Hegel's sense).

As the true pioneer of German Idealist culture on New England Transcendentalist soil, Hedge was perhaps the only native American in the year 1833 (when he was still in his twenties!) who could have compared the work of Kant, Fichte and Schelling in so brief a format and with such confidence and legitimacy as occurred in his review of Coleridge. Yet Hedge's writings in general were a disappointment, both to his friends associated with *The Dial* (both Emerson and Fuller are clear on this) and to his readers a century and a half later. But Hedge persevered and even outlasted the movement of Transcendentalism which he helped to found, as he also outlived most of his friends from the movement. His ultimate achievement may reside more in the institution of the academy, the modern university (rather than the Unitarian church), which Hedge served far more capably than his students at Harvard seem to have understood. The edition of Goethe which he edited in English during his later years and his history of German literature provide a model and even a norm for the institutional and collective labor of the culture, which remains valid even to this day.

Harris is for me a true hero of American education. His work as translator must be viewed within the larger framework of his career as teacher and policy maker. Not so much his book *Hegel's Logic*, however remarkable an achievement that may have been more than thirty years after the still unpublished translation prepared with his friend Brokmeyer, but his entire life and career bear witness to his work as mediator between German and American culture. His disparate publications offer traces of the task which Harris undertook of making Hegel accessible to American readers. Yet how oblique and even remote were the forms in which this work was attempted: the *Journal of Speculative Philosophy*, which helped to found the field of philosophy in America; the teaching offered by Harris for a full decade at Bronson Alcott's School of Philosophy in Concord; the policies established for the public schools in America, beginning in St. Louis during the era of the Civil War and ending in Washington at the turn of the century; the graded readers for schools; the revised dictionary entries for *Webster's New International*. All these together provide the media for the process of intercultural translation which made the legacy of Hegelian philosophical thought accessible to the intellectual life of the United States.

Finally, Charles Brooks as a modest and almost saintly laborer in the vineyards of translation pursued his work as avocation throughout a long career in the ministry with a success far greater than the culture in which he lived was prepared to acknowledge and remember. I have called Brooks's version of Goethe's *Faust. Part One* perhaps the finest English translation of the century, one which still deserves to be reread. I suspect, however, that Brooks's devotion to the labor of translating the novels of Jean Paul may be an even more significant achievement. The fact that a number of his translations still remain unpublished suggests that the full measure of Brooks's legacy as a translator may not yet be known.

One final word of caution may be in order. The claim has often been made with conviction and persuasion that deep affinities and parallels pertain between German Idealist and American Transcendentalist thought. One might thus argue that the work of Emerson and Thoreau should be regarded for American culture as comparable to what the work of Goethe and Hegel signify for German culture. That claim may or may not be true, but its truth does not—and cannot!—reside upon the basis of translation. Emerson's essay on Goethe in *Representative Men* should be judged a miraculous achievement in the history of cross-cultural understanding, more so perhaps than the case of Hedge's discussion of Kant, Fichte and Schelling in his review of Coleridge or Harris's lifelong preoccupation with Hegel's *Logic*. Yet the validity of Emerson's understanding of Goethe ultimately derives from Emerson's native intellect and not from the work of Goethe itself,

Transplanting German Idealism to American Culture

which Emerson may or may not have read in the original German. The hermeneutics of equivalency as a norm or ideal for the act of translation may finally be an illusion. What Emerson—and Thoreau, for that matter—brought to their own writing—as Goethe and Hegel brought to theirs—goes far beyond the limits of translation, as such genuine and successful translators as Hedge, Harris, and Brooks would probably have been the first to acknowledge.

Bibliography

BROOKS, Charles Timothy (transl.)

—. Johann Wolfgang von Goethe. *Faust: A Tragedy*. Boston: Ticknor and Fields, 1856.

—. Jean Paul Friedrich Richter. *Titan: A Romance*. Boston: Ticknor and Fields, 1862.

—. Jean Paul Friedrich Richter. *Hesperus; or Forty-Five Dog-Post-Days: A Biography*. 2 vols. Boston: Ticknor and Fields, 1864.

—. Jean Paul Friedrich Richter. *The Invisible Lodge*. New York: U.S. Book Co., 1883.

The Dial: A Magazine for Literature, Philosophy and Religion. Vol. 1–4. Boston, July 1840–April 1844.

HARRIS, William Torrey. *Hegel's Doctrine of Reflection*. New York: D. Appleton, 1881.

—. *Hegel's Logic. A Book on the Genesis of the Categories of the Mind: A Critical Exposition*. Chicago: S.C. Griggs & Co., 1890.

HEDGE, Frederic Henry. "Coleridge's Literary Character." *The Christian Examiner*. 14 (1833): 108–29.

—. *The Prose Writers of Germany*. Philadelphia: Carey and Hart, 1847.

—. *Hours with German Classics*. Boston: Roberts Brothers, 1886.

—. and Annis Lee Wister. *Metrical Translations and Poems*. Boston: Houghton, Mifflin, 1888.

KLENZE, Camillo von. *Charles Timothy Brooks: Translator from the German and the Genteel Tradition*. Boston and London, 1937.

LEBEAU, Bryan F. *Frederic Henry Hedge: Nineteenth Century Transcendentalist: Intellectually Radical, Ecclesiastically Conservative*. Allison Park, PA, 1985.

LEIDECKER, Kurt Friedrich. *Yankee Teacher: The Life of William Torrey Harris*. New York: Philosophical Library, 1946.

LONG, Orie William. *Frederic Henry Hedge: A Cosmopolitan Scholar*. Portland, Maine: The Southworth-Anthoensen Press, 1940.

LYONS, Richard Gerald. *The Influence of Hegel on the Philosophy of Education of William Torrey Harris*. Diss. Boston University, 1964.

MUNDT, Theodor. *Geschichte der Literatur der Gegenwart*. Berlin: M. Simion, 1842.

NEUFELDT, Leonhard. "Frederic Henry Hedge." In: Joel Myerson, ed. *The Transcendentalists: A Review of Research and Criticism*. New York: MLA, 1984.

POCHMANN, Henry A. *New England Transcendentalism and St. Louis Hegelianism*. New York: Haskell House, 1970.

SCHAUB, Edward L, ed. *William Torrey Harris (1835–1935): A Collection of Essays Including Papers and Addresses Presented in Commemoration of Dr. Harris' Centennial at the St. Louis Meeting of the Western Division of the American Philosophical Society*. Chicago and London: The Open Court Publishing Company, 1936.

Ernst Behler

Translating Nietzsche in the United States: Critical Observations on *The Complete Works of Friedrich Nietzsche*

The project entitled *The Complete Works of Friedrich Nietzsche* is dedicated to the translation of all of Nietzsche's writings, including his unpublished fragments, with annotation, postscripts on the individual texts, and indexes in twenty volumes. Volume 2, *Unfashionable Observations I–IV* has already appeared, Volume 3, *Human, All Too Human I* is in the process of technical production at Stanford University Press, and the manuscripts for several other volumes are about to be sent to press. Within a reasonable period of time (10–12 years), the project will result in the first complete and coherent English translation of Nietzsche's works. The aim of this collaborative effort is to produce a critical edition for scholarly use and to establish a readable and accurate text in contemporary English. All texts will be translated anew by a group of scholars, and particular attention will be given to maintaining consistent terminology throughout the volumes. Besides listing textual variants, the annotation to this English edition provides succinct information on the text and identifies events, names, titles, quotes, and biographical facts of Nietzsche's life. The Afterword to the individual volumes presents the salient facts about the origin of the text, the stages of its composition, and the main events of its reception. The Index of Names at the end of each volume identifies all persons named in the text, including mythological figures.

The significance of this undertaking owes to Nietzsche's own influence in the modern world, which has been decisive in shaping contemporary thought not only in philosophy, but also in the literary disciplines and theology. This influence extends beyond particular academic disciplines to artists in the fields of poetry and fiction, music, and architecture, as well as to the public at large. Nietzsche has also become an essential part of today's humanities and social sciences curricula. His stature in our intellectual world can easily be ascertained by the attention paid to him by contemporary authors of the most diverse backgrounds and orientations. The new English edition of Friedrich Nietzsche's complete works therefore constitutes a major endeavor in the realm of international cultural exchange.

Ernst Behler

In relation to the Stanford conference "Translating Cultures—Translating Literatures," this project offers at least three major themes for discussion. The first concerns the more practical and technical problems of this enterprise, its organization as a collaborative effort, and the demands of translating the complete works of Friedrich Nietzsche in contrast to the translation of individual writings. This section includes matters of a textual nature, such as which edition to choose as the basis for the translation, the importance of the unpublished writings, the *Nachlaß*, for a Nietzsche translation, and the relationship of the new to previous English translations. A second set of questions relates to the particular demands of a Nietzsche translation as far as stylistic, linguistic, and "cultural" expectations are concerned. Every modern philosopher exhibits idiosyncrasies in terms of his discourse and his manner of argumentation, and to render these features is an essential task of the translation. There seems to be agreement that the greatest challenge Nietzsche offers to the translator in this regard is his style, which generally has the reputation of being one of the most refined and versatile modern prose styles. In addition to writing an excellent prose style, however, Nietzsche has said much about style, including his own, and this topic shows a basic relationship to the theme of translation. A similar affinity to translation can be discovered in yet a third group of topics centering around Nietzsche's theory of language and the particular character of his literary expression. The present essay traces these themes and is divided into three sections: (1) the project of *The Complete Works of Friedrich Nietzsche*; (2) Nietzsche on the translatability of style; and (3) Nietzsche's theory of language and the expressive character of his writings.

I

1. *Textual Basis of the Translation*

Nietzsche's prominence in the intellectual world has led to a critical questioning of the reliability of his texts in the German tradition as well as in countries where most readers encounter him in translation. Although in German-speaking countries there have never been serious textual problems with the texts published by Nietzsche himself, the editions of his unpublished writings and fragments have always been of dubious authority. The main critical Nietzsche editions in German are:

- Großoktav-Ausgabe: Werke in 19 Vols. and 1 Vol. of Indexes (Leipzig: Naumann, 1894)
- Musarion-Ausgabe: Gesammelte *Werke* in 23 Vols. (Munich: Musarion, 1920-1929)
- Kröner-Ausgabe: *Sämtliche Werke* in 12 Vols. (Leipzig: Kröner, 1930)

- Historisch-Kritische Gesamtausgabe: *Werke und Briefe* (Munich: Beck, 1933–1940, incomplete)
- Schlechta-Ausgabe: *Werke* in 3 Vols. (Munich: Hanser, 1954)

While each of these editions presents the texts published by Nietzsche himself in a generally reliable form, the editing of his unpublished manuscripts is unsatisfactory, even defective, in all of them. The *Historisch-Kritische Gesamtausgabe* was instituted to remedy this failure, but came to a halt in 1940 and has remained unfinished. Karl Schlechta, the editor of the "Schlechta-Ausgabe," was aware of all previous deficiencies, but did not have access to the materials necessary to remedy them because these materials were preserved in the *Nietzsche Archiv* in Weimar, then in East Germany. To put this point in sharpest relief: The most significant *Nachlaß* materials—what we are calling Nietzsche's "literary fragments" (i.e., the unpublished notes, plans and lectures from which the published texts were derived in modified form)— from 1869 to 1889, prior to the publication of *The Birth of Tragedy* in 1872 up to his mental collapse in 1889, total approximately 3,500 pages in the most comprehensive previous German edition, the *Großoktav-Ausgabe*. The Colli-Montinari edition, by contrast, contains approximately 6,000 *Nachlaß* pages, approximately 42 percent more of Nietzsche's unpublished manuscript material.

One portion of these manuscripts has become particularly notorious for editorial mishandling: the unpublished fragments from about April 1885 to January 1889, the time of Nietzsche's mental breakdown. At the request of Nietzsche's sister, Elisabeth Förster-Nietzsche, some editors compiled a central and systematic work from these fragments, which allegedly expressed the philosophical doctrine of the late Nietzsche. Although this compilation was partly based on previous plans by Nietzsche, those plans were constantly shifting and had finally been dropped by the author in favor of a continuation of his former aphoristic style. This editorial intervention resulted in *The Will to Power*, which in its first edition contained 483 fragments and in its second 1,067. The title alone made the book appear to be one of the paramount philosophical works of modern times. Critics have repeatedly exposed the editorial irresponsibilities of this manipulation, which fabricated a false principal work and paved the way for misleading systematic and ideological interpretations of a thought process that essentially escapes systematic closure.

The new Nietzsche edition initiated by Giorgio Colli and Mazzino Montinari after the Second World War corrects these and other deficiencies in previous Nietzsche editions and presents the best and most reliable textual basis for a study of Nietzsche to date. The edition began to appear in 1963 and was continued by Montinari alone after Colli's death. When Montinari later died on November 24,

1986, all of the texts published by Nietzsche, the unpublished fragments, and the correspondence had been edited. Yet Nietzsche's early autobiographical texts and most of the philological writings on classical antiquity from the Basel period of Nietzsche's professorship had not appeared, and most of the annotation remained unfinished. Montinari's main accomplishment was the complete edition of all of Nietzsche's unpublished fragments from Fall of 1869 to late January, 1889. Among these fragments, the sections from which the *Will to Power* was compiled best illustrate the contribution of the new edition. They now appear in their entirety and in chronological order from April, 1885 to January, 1889 in the last three volumes of the new edition. In 1980, Montinari published a condensed paperback version of his new Nietzsche edition in 15 volumes. This edition contains all of Nietzsche's texts from the hardcover edition, whether published texts (Vols. 1–6) or unpublished manuscripts (Vols. 7–15), but with less annotation and textual criticism. The new editions by Colli and Montinari are known as:

KGW: *Kritische Gesamtausgabe der Werke* in 25 Volumes (to date). Edited by Giorgio Colli and Mazzino Montinari. Berlin: de Gruyter, 1963–. [complete works]

KGB: *Kritische Gesamtausgabe der Briefe* in 16 Volumes (to date). Edited by Giorgio Colli and Mazzino Montinari. Berlin: de Gruyter, 1975–. [complete letters]

KSA: *Kritische Studienausgabe* in 15 Volumes. Edited by Giorgio Colli and Mazzino Montinari. Berlin: de Gruyter, 1980. [paperback edition, hereafter *KSA*]

These editions have decisively changed the conditions for Nietzsche research not only in Germany but far outside it. Italian, French, and Japanese editions appeared simultaneously with the German one. Lacking a translation of the unpublished fragments, the English-speaking world is at an obvious disadvantage in comparison with other countries. The present edition will remedy this discrepancy. For reasons of convenience, *KSA* forms the textual basis of the translation, but *KGW* will be consulted whenever needed.

2. Relationship of 'The Complete Works of Friedrich Nietzsche' to the Colli-Montinari Edition

The project, *The Complete Works of Friedrich Nietzsche*, will produce a complete English edition of Nietzsche's works in accurate translation with consistent terminology, annotations, critical afterwords, and indexes. Here is a breakdown of the planned edition, listing its director and translators as they have been determined thus far:

Translating Nietzsche in the United States

The Complete Works of Friedrich Nietzsche
Based on the Giorgio Colli and Mazzino Montinari Edition; edited by Ernst Behler

Vol. 1:	*The Birth of Tragedy/Early Writings* (trans., with an afterword, by Diana I. Behler)
Vol. 2:	*Unfashionable Observations I–IV* (trans., with an afterword, by Richard T. Gray)
Vol. 3:	*Human, All Too Human I* (trans., with an afterword, by Gary Handwerk)
Vol. 4:	*Human, All Too Human II* (trans., with an afterword, by Gary Handwerk)
Vol. 5:	*Dawn* (trans., with an afterword, by Brittain Smith)
Vol. 6:	*The Gay Science* (trans., with an afterword, by Steven A. Taubeneck)
Vol. 7:	*Thus Spoke Zarathustra* (trans., with an afterword, by Bernd Magnus)
Vol. 8:	*Beyond Good and Evil/On the Genealogy of Morals* (trans., with an afterword, by Ernst Behler and Bernd Magnus)
Vol. 9:	*The Case of Wagner /Twilight of the Idols/The Antichrist/Ecce Homo/Dionysus Dithyrambs/Nietzsche Contra Wagner* (trans., with an afterword, by Ernst Behler and Bernd Magnus)
Vol. 10:	*Unpublished Fragments: From the Period of 'The Birth of Tragedy'* (trans., with an afterword, by Diana I. Behler)
Vol. 11:	*Unpublished Fragments: From the Period of 'Unfashionable Observations'* (trans., with an afterword, by Richard T. Gray)
Vol. 12:	*Unpublished Fragments: From the Period of 'Human, All Too Human'* (trans., with an afterword, by Gary Handwerk)
Vol. 13:	*Unpublished Fragments: From the Period of 'Dawn'* (trans., with an afterword, by Brittain Smith)
Vol. 14:	*Unpublished Fragments: From the Period of 'The Gay Science'* (trans., with an afterword, by Steven A. Taubeneck)
Vol. 15:	*Unpublished Fragments: From the Period of 'Thus Spoke Zarathustra'* (trans., with an afterword, by Bernd Magnus)
Vol. 16:	*Unpublished Fragments: From the Period of 'Thus Spoke Zarathustra'* (trans., with an afterword, by Bernd Magnus)
Vol. 17:	*Unpublished Fragments: From the Period of 'Beyond Good and Evil'* (trans., with an afterword, by Ernst Behler and Bernd Magnus)
Vol. 18:	*Unpublished Fragments: From the Period of 'On the Genealogy of Morals'* (trans., with an afterword, by Ernst Behler and Bernd Magnus)

Vol. 19:   *Unpublished Fragments: From the Period of the Late Writings*
(trans., with an afterword, by Ernst Behler and Bernd Magnus)

Vol. 20:   *Unpublished Fragments: From the Period of the Late Writings*
(trans., with an afterword, by Ernst Behler and Bernd Magnus)

Although this edition is based on the Colli-Montinari edition, it is not simply a copy, but rather a revised and improved version of *KSA*. In particular, the volumes of texts published by Nietzsche will correspond more precisely to their counterparts in the volumes of unpublished fragments. Such correspondences are of great importance for any translation, because Nietzsche often experiments in the unpublished fragments with ideas later expressed in his published writings. Each volume containing a particular work (e.g., Vol. 6: *The Gay Science*) has been assigned to a translator together with its counterpart among the unpublished fragments (e.g., Vol. 14: *Unpublished Fragments: From the Period of 'The Gay Science'*). Volume 1 will differ from the first volume in *KSA* in that it will include writings on classical antiquity from the Basel period that are presently lacking in the Montinari edition and are planned for future sections of it. Another important difference between the projected *Complete Works* and the *KSA* concerns the apparatus. The notes in *KSA* relate mainly to problems of a philological nature. The notes in the *Complete Works*, however, will comment in succinct fashion on events, quotes, biographical facts of Nietzsche's life, and problems related to the translation. The annotation will make a considerable contribution to Nietzsche research. The afterwords in *KSA* by Giorgio Colli are of an uncritical, personal nature and will be replaced by factual essays on the history of the text and its reception. Each volume will have an index of names.

3. *Need for a Translation of Nietzsche's Writings in Their Entirety (including the previously translated ones)*

Although various translations of individual works by Nietzsche are available in English, the new edition is only conceivable as a translation that includes retranslation of texts which have been translated into English before. This demand is in part contractual. The European publishers who control rights to the edition, Adelphi and Gallimard, would grant rights to the edition only as an edition—that is, to the texts, arrangement, and apparatus overall. Although the texts published during Nietzsche's lifetime are long out of copyright, the crucial unpublished writings entered copyright only with the Colli-Montinari editions and are therefore the property of the European houses that financed the original work. The need for a new translation of these writings follows even more cogently from the particular nature of Nietzsche's oeuvre. Instead of hewing to sustained, systematic, and linear argumentation, Nietzsche tries out a multiplicity of "perspectives" and develops his ideas by constantly shifting from position to counter-position. The unpublished fragments are an integral part of this process and often indicate how the thoughts expressed in the published works developed. Often, in fact, the fragments go considerably beyond the published formulations. The interconnection of published and unpublished writings and the enhanced awareness of this interconnection in contemporary Nietzsche scholarship make a new, coordinated translation of all Nietzsche texts imperative.

Moreover, conformity in terminology, critical apparatus, and afterwords among the twenty volumes of the edition require a new translation of all of Nietzsche's texts. One of the main scholarly contributions of this edition is its critical apparatus, which consists in annotations and textual variants. None of the previous Nietzsche translations has a consistent notational system; indeed, many of them have been published without any annotation. The textual variants derive mainly from the manuscripts Nietzsche delivered to the publisher and the proof sheets he returned after his proofreading. They list textual differences between earlier stages of his text and the final printed version. These variants were not known to previous Nietzsche translators. It would be inconceivable to add these variants, never translated before, to texts translated by others a long time ago. The notes include comments relating to instances in the text that were difficult to translate. The afterwords, together with translation and annotation, form an integral part of each volume.

The full range of Nietzsche's thought process has never been accessible in English. There is no complete, reliable, and coherent English translation of all of Nietzsche's works. *The Complete Works of Friedrich Nietzsche* edited by Oscar Levy (17 vols., 1909–1919) does not satisfy the demands of today's Nietzsche criticism; in particular, it fails to include Nietzsche's unpublished writings and fragments. On the whole, these translations, undertaken by a group of about 10 translators, lack accuracy and consistency. They frequently distort the original and have contributed to serious misunderstandings in the British and American Nietzsche receptions.

After the Second World War, Oscar Levy's English translation of Nietzsche's complete works (1909–13) was progressively replaced by more reliable translations. As recognition of Nietzsche has grown, some of his writings, such as *The Birth of Tragedy, Thus Spoke Zarathustra, The Gay Science, Beyond Good and Evil, and On the Genealogy of Morals*, have been translated several times by different translators with varying degrees of success. Of special value for their accuracy and their critical annotation are the translations by the late Walter Kaufmann. R. J. Hollingdale has produced the most reliable translations published in England. Between the two of them, Kaufmann and Hollingdale have translated all of the works published by Nietzsche. Although contemporaries and occasionally even collaborators, they have produced Nietzsche translations that differ considerably in terms of style, idiom, philosophical terminology, and general vocabulary. Only fractions of the unpublished texts are available: in W. Kaufmann and R. J. Hollingdale's translation *The Will to Power* (New York, 1967), based on the arbitrary German compilation of that text; and in Daniel Breazeale's reliable translation of excerpts from Nietzsche's early notebooks in *Philosophy and Truth* (New Jersey, 1974). In intellectual terms, the distinctly individual characteristics of the existing translations would clash intolerably, and a great freight of annotation would be needed to signal differences in their terminology.

In practical terms, it is neither desirable nor possible to make up a *Complete Works* as a pastiche of existing Nietzsche translations. All the translations are still in copyright, and their owners would part with rights only at a prohibitive expense, if at all. This practical necessity of retranslation is also an intellectual opportunity. No translation can avoid a certain degree of personal idiosyncrasy, but in the proposed edition such idiosyncrasy will be minimized since one primary objective will be to work toward a common and consistent terminology.

II

Considering an author as language conscious as Nietzsche, one should be surprised that among his manifold writings there is only one instance in which he deals directly with the topic of translation. This is Aphorism 28 from *Beyond Good and Evil* devoted to the *tempo* of style which according to Nietzsche, "is most difficult to render from one language into another" (*KSA* 5: 46).[1] Nietzsche is of the opinion that there are "honestly meant translations that, as involuntary vulgarizations, are almost falsifications of the original, merely because its bold and merry *tempo* (which leaps over and obviates all dangers in things and words) could not be translated." In his view, a German is "almost incapable of *presto* in his language" and therefore also "of many of the most delightful and daring *nuances* of free, free-spirited thought." For the German, "the buffoon and satyr are foreign," and "so Aristophanes and Petronius are untranslatable for him."

In this manner, Nietzsche's thoughts on translation soon turn into a critique of the German language that is typical for him, but here he even includes Goethe, who usually enjoys a favored position in his general defamation of the Germans by being projected as their counter-image:

---

[1] Nietzsche is quoted from *Kritische Studienausgabe* (in the following *KSA*), ed. Giorgio Colli and Mazzino Montinari, 15 volumes (Berlin: de Gruyter, 1980) according to volume and page number. The English translation is taken from Friedrich Nietzsche, *Beyond Good and Evil*, trans. Walter Kaufmann (New York, 1989); hereafter *BGE*, followed by number of aphorism.

> Everything ponderous, viscous, and solemnly clumsy, all long-winded and boring types of style are developed in profuse variety among Germans—forgive me the fact that even Goethe's prose, in its mixture of stiffness and elegance, is no exception, being a reflection of the 'good old time' to which it belongs, and a reflection of German taste at a time when there still was a 'German taste'—a rococo taste *in moribus et artibus* (*KSA* 5: 46; *BGE*, 28).

Only Lessing is an exception for Nietzsche in this regard because of "his histrionic nature which understood much and understood how to do many things." Lessing was also a great expert in style. He had translated Bayle and liked the "neighbourhood of Diderot and Voltaire, and better yet that of the Roman comedy writers."

From that point on, Nietzsche talks only about style in the image of an adverse relationship of the German language to style. The initial topic of translation serves more and more to illustrate the excellence of particular qualities of style such as *tempo* and *presto* through their untranslatability, at least into German. We might then expect Nietzsche to turn to himself, to his own style, and to his ability to capture such features even in German. But he stays with foreign authors and describes his ideas through the various styles of Machiavelli, Petronius, and Aristophanes. He first relates to "Machiavelli's tempo," especially in his *Il Principe*, that ostensibly could not be imitated in German, not "even in the prose of Lessing." Furthermore, Machiavelli's *Il Principe* "lets us breathe the dry, refined air of Florence." The most spectacular trait in Machiavelli's style, however, is a contrast of content and form, insofar as this author

> cannot help presenting the most serious matters in a boisterous *allegrissimo*, perhaps not without a malicious artistic sense of the contrasts he risks—long, difficult, hard, dangerous thoughts and the *tempo* of the gallop and the very best, most capricious humor (*KSA* 5: 47; *BGE*, 28).

The main obstacle to a German translation of Petronius is this author's musical inclination because "more than any great musician so far," he was a "master of *presto* in invention, ideas, and words." "He had the feet of a wind"—"the rush, the breath, the liberating scorn of a wind that makes everything healthy by making everything *run*." As to Aristophanes, his stylistic excellence consists in a "transfiguring, complimentary spirit for whose sake one *forgives* everything Hellenic for having existed, provided one has understood in its full profundity *all* that needs to be forgiven and transfigured here." Nietzsche exemplifies this enigmatic thought with Plato, whose "secrecy and sphinx nature" is nowhere better revealed than by the "happily preserved *petit fait:*"

> that under the pillow of his deathbed there was found no 'Bible,' nor anything Egyptian, Pythagorean, or Platonic—but a volume of Aristophanes. How could

even Plato have endured life—a Greek life he repudiated—without an Aristophanes? (*KSA* 5: 47; *BGE*, 28)

On the whole, Aphorism 28 from *Beyond Good and Evil*, Nietzsche's only aphorism on translation, exemplifies the highest stylistic accomplishment through untranslatability, at least into German, but by implication and in various degrees of success, into all other languages, too. One is certainly not mistaken in assuming that in addition to all the great masters of style, Nietzsche is also referring to himself, to his style, and thereby to his own untranslatability. To read this message from his text, however, requires some effort because Nietzsche wrote in that language which in his opinion is so terribly adverse to style. One would have to proceed in two steps and first say that Nietzsche excelled beyond all the other great stylists named in this aphorism—Aristophanes, Plato, the Roman comedy writers, Machiavelli, Diderot, Voltaire, Lessing, and Goethe—because he surpassed in German what they had done in a more supple language medium. Proof of real mastership is shown by competing in a more difficult medium, by working against obstacles that the other stylists do not encounter or encounter only to a lesser degree. A second consideration reveals that the task of translating Nietzsche's style presents an enhanced difficulty in translation. If stylistic virtuosity is to be measured according to the degree of untranslatability, then Nietzsche's style, because of its manifestation in an unfavorable language, has to be both the most excellent and the most untranslatable. That this is not an extravagant reading follows from the aphorism itself. In terms of both brevity and scope, Nietzsche describes the entire European history of style, at least a great deal of it in the space of about 50 lines. He furthermore points out the relationship of style to freethinking, to transfiguring, and to forgiving. By way of imitating, of translating Machiavelli, he lets us breathe "the dry, refined air "of Florence, maybe also of Sils Maria in the Upper Engadin, where this aphorism was written. Above all, this aphorism illustrates the perhaps most distinguished quality of style for Nietzsche, that risky antagonism of "long, difficult, hard, dangerous thoughts and the *tempo* of the gallop and the very best, most capricious humour." All in all, however, this is a text on style accomplished through style and thereby an exponentiated form of style. If it is difficult, perhaps even impossible, to translate Machiavelli's prose into German, how much more difficult must it be to translate Nietzsche into Italian, French, or English.

This antagonistic relationship between style and translation is indeed a major theme in Nietzsche, whereby the issue of translation gains much greater importance for him than is obvious at first glance. To visualize the full scope of this topic in Nietzsche's writings, one has to relinquish the narrow meaning of translation and understand the designation metaphorically. There is one text among Nietzsche's writings which is of special significance in this regard, i.e., Nietzsche's own translation of the third book of Aristotle's *Rhetoric* devoted to style.[2] Nietzsche selected this text out of his high esteem for Aristotle in the field of rhetoric and his own keen interest in the phenomenon of style.[3] Among the ancient rhetoricians, Aristotle provided Nietzsche with the most impressive conception of rhetoric. Rhetoric for Aristotle is "δύναμις," power, strength, namely, the "power to employ all possible means for the purpose of persuasion." In this quality, rhetoric is neither knowledge (ἐπιστήμη) nor skill (τέχνη), but something in itself, a power, a "δύναμις." Rhetoric is not a mere persuasion ("πείθειν"), but a persuasion that exhausts all possible means of persuasion ("κατὰ τὸ ἐνδεχόμενον πείθειν"). What Aristotle lacks for Nietzsche, however, is a sense for the performative in rhetoric. He probably considered the delivery of the speech as not "essential" and thought about rhetoric only in books, similar to his conception of the art of poetry. In his *Poetics* he saw the "function of drama independent from its performance and did not include the sensual appearance on stage in its definition" (*RH*, 419–20; *RL*, 9–11). As far as the performance of rhetoric is concerned, Demosthenes is deemed the greatest rhetorician among the ancients. But Aristotle is the greatest theoretician of rhetoric for Nietzsche because he grasped the idea of the power of speech like nobody else.

This power of speech is style and obviously the most exquisite quality of language for Nietzsche. One aspect of the relationship between style and translation has been discussed already, namely, the experience that the more refined style is, the more difficult its translation turns out to be. There is yet another kind of relationship between style and translation in that style is nothing originary, nothing in itself, but entirely derived, made up—a translation, so to speak. Style has to be adopted, learned, and the greatest models of style for Nietzsche were the ancient authors, but also some of the moderns, as Aphorism 28 from *Beyond Good and Evil* has shown. This relates to the notion of translation in the broader, metaphorical sense, and style is perhaps the most prominent example for it, at least in Nietzsche's text. He considered "only quite a small number of books of antiquity," the most famous not even among them, as essential from his study of style. Sallust is included because Nietzsche's "sense of style, of the epigram as style," responded at once to this author:

---

[2] Friedrich Nietzsche, *Aristoteles Rhetorik. Drittes Buch: Kritische Gesamtausgabe* (in the following *KGW*) II, 4 (Berlin: de Gruyter 1995) 529–612.

[3] See Friedrich Nietzsche, *Darstellung der alten Rhetorik* (in the following *RH*), in *KGW* II, 4: 413–520. The English translation is taken from *Friedrich Nietzsche on Rhetoric and Language* (in the following *RL*), trans. Sander L. Gilman, Carole Blaire, and David J. Parent (Oxford University Press, 1989).

Compact, severe, with as much substance as possible, a cold malice toward 'fine words,' also toward 'fine feelings'—in that I knew myself (*KSA* 6: 254).[4]

Just as important was Horace, whose ode conveyed an "artistic delight" to Nietzsche aroused by no other poet. He was convinced that "what is achieved here" can not even be "willed" in other languages:

> This mosaic of words in which every word, as sound, as locus, as concept pours forth its power to left and right and over the whole, this minimum in the range and number of signs which achieves a maximum of energy of these signs—all this is Roman and, if one will believe me, *noble par excellence*. All other poetry becomes by comparison somewhat too popular—a mere emotional garrulousness...(*KSA* 6: 254).

Nietzsche's most direct statement on style, on the "art of style," and its relationship to translation occurs in Aphorism 4 of the section "Why I write such good books" from *Ecce Homo* (*KSA* 6: 304–05).[5] According to this aphorism, the "meaning of every style" is to translate, to "communicate a state, an inward tension of pathos, by means of signs, including the tempo of these signs." Style thereby is one of the most individual expressions of the human being. And yet with Nietzsche, style is not bound to one and the same expression of his individual nature but arises from the "multiplicity of inward states" which Nietzsche believed to be "exceptionally large" in his case. In hybrid manner he claims, "I have many stylistic possibilities—the most multifarious art of style that has ever been at the disposal of one man." A style is good for him when it accomplishes translating or communicating an inward state, when it "makes no mistake about the signs, the tempo of signs, the gestures—all the laws about long periods are concerned with the art of gestures." Here Walter Kaufmann adds this note to his translation: "This sentence suggests some of the difficulties faced by a translator of Nietzsche." In view of these manifold possibilities of style, the assumption of a "good style in itself" appears to be for Nietzsche "a pure folly, mere 'idealism,' on a level with the beautiful in itself,' the 'good in itself,' the 'thing in itself.'" He believed that nobody would understand "the art that has been squandered" by him, that "nobody ever was in a position to squander new, unheard-of artistic devices" and continues

> That this was possible in German, of all languages, remained to be shown: I myself would have rejected any such notion most unhesitatingly before. Before me, it was not known what could be done with the German language in general.

---

[4] The English translation is taken from Friedrich Nietzsche, *Twilight of the Idols/The Anti-Christ*, trans. R.J. Hollingdale (Penguin, 1968) 116.

[5] The English translation is taken from Friedrich Nietzsche, *On the Genealogy of Morals/Ecce Homo*, trans. Walter Kaufmann (New York, 1967) 265–66.

> The art of the *great* rhythm, the *great* style of long periods to express a tremendous up and down of sublime, of superhuman passion, was discovered only by me...(*KSA* 6: 304–05).

All of these qualities culminate in what Nietzsche called "the grand style," a form of expression he liked to illustrate through architecture. In terms that can easily be related to translation in the broader as well as in the narrower sense, he describes the accomplishment of great style in the image of the architect:

> The *architect* represents neither a Dionysian nor an Apollonian condition: here it is the mighty act of will, the will which moves mountains, the intoxication of the strong will, which demands artistic expression. The most powerful men have always inspired the architects; the architect has always been influenced by power. Pride, victory over weight and gravity, the will to power, seek to render themselves visible in a building; architecture is a kind of rhetoric of power, now persuasive, even cajoling in form, now bluntly imperious (*KSA* 6: 118).[6]

At this point, Nietzsche connects style, grand style, architecture, and translation to the will to power, which for him is the apotheosis of style and, in an implied manner, also of translation. This impression clearly emanates from the concluding section of this aphorism:

> The highest feeling of power and security finds expression in that which possesses *grand style*. Power which no longer requires proving; which disdains to please, which is slow to answer; which is conscious of no witness around it; which lives oblivious of the existence of any opposition; which reposes in *itself*, fatalistic, a law among laws: *that* is what speaks of itself in the form of grand style (*KSA* 6: 118)).

To round off this image of Nietzsche's style, one would have to add that its character is not only appealing and persuasive through the pleasant features of style, but often rebuffs and deliberately offends the reader in order to exert a calculated effect upon him. Nietzsche said: "Our highest insights must—and should—sound like follies and sometimes like crimes when they are heard without permission by those who are not predisposed and predestined for them" (*KSA* 5: 48; *BGE*, 30). He thought that "all the more subtle laws of any style have their origin at this point," namely, at this wish "not to be understood." These laws of style "at the same time keep away, create a distance, forbid 'entrance,' understanding as said above—while they open the ears of those whose ears are related to ours" (*KSA* 3: 633–34).[7] These nuances of style refer to the statement "whatever is profound

---

[6] The English translation is taken from Friedrich Nietzsche, *Twilight of the Idols/The Anti-Christ* 84.

[7] The English translation is taken from Friedrich Nietzsche, *The Gay Science*, trans. Walter Kaufmann (New York: Vintage, 1974) 381; in the following *GS* followed by number of aphorism.

loves masks" (*KSA* 5: 57; *BGE*, 40), to the "masquerade of styles," the great "storage room for costumes," the "carnival in the great style" (*KSA* 5: 157; *BGE*, 223), to irony, and the entire complex of indirect communication which will not be pursued here, although it is, of course, also intimately related to Nietzsche's conception of style. It appears, however, that this brief investigation into Nietzsche's views of style has already sufficiently evidenced the greatest obstacle for any translation of Nietzsche. This is his style, its superior quality, but also its enormous versatility, and last but not least, Nietzsche's own consciousness of it. These characteristics of style are the first impressions in any encounter with Nietzsche and raise the demands for a translation to an unusually high degree. For these artistic qualities of style in the sense of a velocity like the wind, a physical power of persuasion, an absolute individuality of expression, and a refusing gesture of masking require artistic qualities from the translation. If among all German philosophers, one had to distinguish Nietzsche's particular requirements for a translation, the choice would be his style in the sense of not *what* he said, but *how* he said it.

III

This brief investigation also brings to light the artistic, artificial, derived, in short "translated" character of style which Nietzsche liked to expose in images such as the art of "showcasing," of "display," of window-dressing (*KSA* 5: 138–39; *BGE*, 208). Analyzing this character of style more closely, one soon discovers that it is an artistic continuation and enhancement of what Nietzsche has to say about language and communication in general. His theory of language ("language as art"), in other words, has an immediate relationship to translation, and it is here that Nietzsche's profound affinity to translation has yet to be discovered. It appears to be of the greatest significance in this regard that Nietzsche, from the beginning of his academic and literary career, has been engaged in theoretical and critical reflections on language. The first sketch for his Basel lectures *On Latin Grammar* of 1869 is a long fragment "On the Origin of Language" describing language on the basis of Kant and Herder as an instinctual endowment of the human race without which we could not exist.[8] *The Birth of Tragedy* of 1872 ascribes to music the greatest power of expression. Music is capable of something no other means of expression can accomplish, namely, an unmediated representation of the absolute, the "thing in itself," the ground of being (*KSA* 1: 103–04).

---

[8] Friedrich Nietzsche, *Vorlesungen über lateinische Grammatik*, *KGW* II, 2 (Berlin: de Gruyter, 1993) 183–85.

This view of musical expression articulates itself as a metaphysical theory of absolute expression in this early text by Nietzsche, an assumption from which he soon departed in favor of a more critical and restricted theory as far as representation is concerned. Yet it is obvious that Nietzsche in these early texts conceived of language and representation in terms of translation, of rendering a previous or original state as closely as possible. Shortly after the appearance of *The Birth of Tragedy*, Nietzsche began to prepare himself for another lecture course, his *Lectures on Ancient Rhetoric* of winter semester 1872-73, a topic that led him much more deeply into the theory of language and verbal communication.

In these lectures, delivered in the winter semester of 1872/73,[9] Nietzsche claims that what one calls "'rhetorical' as a means of conscious art" is really only a "development guided by the clear light of the understanding of the *artistic means which are already found in language*" (*RH* 425; *RL*, 21). There is no use in appealing to an "unrhetorical 'naturalness' of language" because "language itself is the result of nothing but rhetorical arts." Aristotle had called rhetoric that power which discovers and exhibits what is effective and impressive in a thing. That, however, is already "the essence of language." Language, like rhetoric, is not related "to the true, the *essence* of things." Language does not intend to instruct, "but to convey to others a subjective impulse and its acceptance." The one who forms language "does not perceive things or events, but impulses." He does not render "sensations, but merely copies of sensations." A sensation, caused by a nerve stimulus, "does not take in the thing in itself," but presents it only "externally through an image." Nietzsche says, "It is not things that pass over into consciousness, but the manner in which we relate to them, the πιθανον [persuasive]. The full essence of things will never be grasped" (*RH*, 426; *RL*, 23). Instead of a thing, we receive only a sign. This is the first aspect for Nietzsche: "*language is rhetoric* because it desires to convey only a δόξα [opinion], not a ἐπιστήμη [knowledge]."

The second aspect concern the tropes, the "nonliteral significations," as Nietzsche designates them. All words are "in themselves and from the beginning" nothing but tropes. Words do not represent "that which truly takes place," but only a "sound image": "language never expresses something completely but displays only a characteristic that appears to be prominent." In this way we say "sail" instead of ship, "waves" instead of sea, "δράκων" (that which looks shiny) or *serpens* (that which creeps) for snake. This is the rhetorical figure of *synecdoche*, the understanding of one thing by another. The next tropical form is that of

---

[9] See on the following text listed in note No. 3, especially the third section of these lectures "The Relation of the Rhetorical to Language" (*RH*, 425–28; *RL*, 21–27). See also Ernst Behler, "Nietzsche's Study of Greek Rhetoric," *Research in Phenomenology* 25 (1995): 3–26.

metaphor, which does not create new words, but gives a new meaning to existing ones. This is how we speak of the summit of mountains, of "γλῶσσα" (tongue) as the mouthpiece of the flute, and of "μαστός" (breast) as a hill. Metaphorical practice is also operative in the designation of gender, since gender, in "the grammatical sense, is a luxury of language and a pure metaphor." The third tropical form is *metonymy*, a "substitution of cause for effect" (*RH*, 427; *RL*, 25). This form appears when we say "perspiration" for work, "tongue" for language, or call the drink "bitter," the stone "hard," and the leaf "green." Bitter, hard, and green are not objective qualities, but only subjective sensations, reactions on the part of the subject. At this point, Nietzsche comes to a conclusion and states:

> In sum: the tropes are not just occasionally added to words but constitute their most proper nature. It makes no sense to speak of a 'proper meaning' that is transformed [made tropical, translated into a trope] only in special cases (*RH*, 427; *RL*, 25).

In another instance, he says even more directly:

> All *rhetorical figures* (that is, the essence of language) are *logical fallacies*; with that, reason begins (*KSA* 7: 486).

Finally, there is just as little difference between "straightforward *speech* and *rhetorical figures*" as there is between words and tropes. In the last analysis, all that is called language is actually figuration for Nietzsche. Language is created by "individual speech artists," but then determined "by the fact that the taste of the many makes choices." If individual language artists do not succeed with their creations, everyone appeals to a common usage and calls their figures of speech "barbarism and solecism": "A figure that finds no buyer becomes an error." The "delight in the similarity of sound" is also an important factor in the rhetorical formation of language (*RH*, 427–28; *RL*, 25). Although Nietzsche used different sources and handbooks for his lectures *On Ancient Rhetoric*, we can discover a typically Nietzschean argumentation in these early texts—an argumentation that will soon become an essential feature of his own discourse. The notion of anthropocentrism is the key term in this regard. The lectures an *Ancient Rhetoric* convey an anthropocentric view of language that encloses us within an entirely human world of communication that cannot be transcended and verified by "objective" knowledge. The key sentence for this impression is the one that limits language to the function of conveying subjective reactions to others. Yet one also notices a certain hesitation on the part of Nietzsche to transform and expand discoveries made on the restricted level of ancient rhetoric to the entire realm of language. A sentence like: "What is usually called language is actually all figuration" ("Eigentlich ist alles Figuration, was man gewöhnlich Rede nennt") does not sound terribly convincing, since it conveys too many reservations ("eigentlich," "gewöhnlich"). There is a tension in these lectures between the limited sphere of ancient rhetoric and the wide field of language in general, a tension not overcome until the writing of *On Truth and Lie in an Extramoral Sense* (1873). There is no doubt, however, that Nietzsche's reflection on language, a theme of major importance for his thoughts on translation, had its starting point in these lectures *On Ancient Rhetoric*.

The first recognition of Nietzsche's theory of language and its importance for his own writings occurred relatively early, in 1890 already, long before his star as an author began rising and the great wave of Nietzsche reception started at the beginning of our century. At that time, the Austrian writer Fritz Mauthner, himself a prominent theorist of language, noticed an immediate link between the critique of language and the critique of knowledge in Nietzsche's theory, in that his critique of morality, for instance, proceeded primarily via a critical analysis and dissolution of the traditional designations for "good" and "evil." Mauthner seems to have taken Nietzsche's project of a "revaluation of all values" quite literally, but saw the result of his attempts only in a "new superstition of words." He characterized Nietzsche's attitude as that of a "trumpeter of immorality," a "moralist" who only wanted to set up "new tablets" and thereby manifested a new belief in language.[10] After this brief flash, interest in Nietzsche's theory of language almost completely vanished. Later interpretations, when they turned to Nietzsche's theory of language at all, tended to interpret his conception of language as relating to prior, more fundamental principles such as grammar, reason, or instinctive moves in the primordial drive for self-preservation on the part of the human being. As far as the expressive, communicative, rhetorical, and stylistic character of his own writings was concerned, especially in regard to their constant self-contradiction, one did not use linguistic but epistemological models to explain this particular character of his text. The most commonly recognized theory of this sort is that of "perspectivism," that of a continuous switch of "perspectives," emphasized by Nietzsche himself in prominent parts of his writings.[11] Karl Jaspers, who studied Nietzsche's cognitive perspectivism perhaps more thoroughly than anyone else, speaks of an "infinite and total dialectic" ("unendliche Totaldialektik") that animates Nietzsche's writings, that draws every finite form of rationality into the process of infinite reflection, and brings all apodictic statements into question

---

[10] Fritz Mauthner, *Beiträge zu einer Kritik der Sprache*, 3 vols. (Stuttgart: Cotta, 1901–02) vol. 1: 366–69.

[11] See Robert C. Salomon, "Nietzsche ad hominem: Perspectivism, Personality, and *ressentiment* revisited," *The Nietzsche Companion*, ed. Bernd Magnus and Kathleen M. Higgins (Cambridge University Press, 1996) 180–222.

through the consideration of new possibilities.[12] In contrast to this approach to Nietzsche during the first half of our century, interest in our time has decisively shifted back again to his theory of language. Investigations into his language theory and the linguistic aspects of his writings have complemented the concern with his theory of knowledge and epistemology. His thoughts on language serve to explain the ambiguity of his statements and to confirm the impossibility of ascribing a definite meaning to them. Of decisive influence on this trend was the discovery of the importance rhetoric had on the formation of Nietzsche's philosophical discourse.[13]

This discovery is of course also of great relevance for any translation of Nietzsche. One notion frequently used in this regard is quite misleading as far as Nietzsche's theory of language is concerned. This is the notion of a "prisonhouse of language," which we find, for instance, in the title and as an epigraph in Fredric Jameson's book *The Prison House of Language* of 1972.[14] Jameson ascribes this concept to Nietzsche, but upon closer scrutiny it turns out that he must have borrowed the phrase from a very loose translation of a Nietzsche quotation in Erich Heller's essay "Wittgenstein and Nietzsche" of 1963.[15] Nietzsche's corresponding text is Aphorism 522 of *The Will to Power* which is now part of the unpublished fragments in the Colli-Montinari edition (*KSA* 12: 193–94). The text reads in Walter Kaufmann's more accurate translation:

> We cease to think when we refuse to do so under the constraint of language [sprachlichen Zwange]; we barely reach the doubt that sees this limitation as a limitation. Rational thought is interpretation according to a scheme that we cannot throw off.[16]

The difference between "prisonhouse of language" and "constraint of language" may appear small, but is really not when Nietzsche is read as a language theorist. Then the notion of a prison house of language conveys a sinister finality which

---

[12] Karl Jaspers, *Nietzsche. An Introduction to the Understanding of His Philosophical Activity*, trans. Charles F. Wallraff and Frederick J. Schmitz (Chicago: Gateway, 1966).

[13] This is the merit of Philippe Lacoue–Labarthe, "Le détour (Nietzsche et la rhétorique)," *Poétique* 5 (1971): 53–76. See also Paul de Man, "Nietzsche's theory of Rhetoric," *Symposium: A Quarterly Journal in Modern Foreign Literature* (1974): 33–51.

[14] Fredric Jameson, *The Prison House of Language: A Critical Account of Structuralism and Russian Formalism* (Princeton University Press, 1972).

[15] Erich Heller, "Wittgenstein and Nietzsche," in Erich Heller, *The Importance of Nietzsche: Ten Essays* (The University of Chicago Press, 1988) 152. The essay "Wittgenstein and Nietzsche" first appeared in 1963: Erich Heller, *The Artist's Journey and Other Essays* (New York, 1963).

[16] Friedrich Nietzsche, *The Will to Power*, trans. Walter Kaufmann and R.J. Hollingdale (New York: Vintage, 1968) 283; insertion mine.

Nietzsche's text actually does not express. For we are always capable of outdoing and outwitting the "constraint of language" through style, metaphorical language, irony, and other rhetorical means. There is even a certain enjoyment in these games with language. This ironic mood comes forth in another fragment of Nietzsche's later period which concludes: "'Reason' in language: oh what a deceitful old woman! I fear we are not getting rid of God because we still believe in grammar..." (*KSA* 6: 78).[17]

The most articulate formulation of Nietzsche's early language theory and his most resolute linkage of the basic character of language with translation occurs in the essay *On Truth and Lie in an Extramoral Sense* of 1873 (*KSA* 1: 873-90).[18] That our language essentially is translation, i.e., transformation, transfiguration of inner states of experience, comes to light, Nietzsche argues, when we look at the genesis of language in the broadest way. For the signs of language are hardly products of knowledge, a congruent designation of things, an adequate expression of reality, but rather "illusions" and "empty husks" (*KSA* 1: 878; *RL*, 248). Only convention, not truth, had been decisive in the genesis of language. Properly speaking, we are not at all entitled to say "the stone is hard" because "hard" is only known to us as a "subjective stimulation." Only a little are we entitled to "separate things according to gender" and to designate the tree as masculine and the plant as feminine. If we placed the various languages side by side, we would realize "that with words it is never a question of truth, never a question of adequate expression; otherwise there would not be so many languages." The "thing in itself" is something toward which the "creator of language" is indifferent, something that for him is "not in the least worth striving for." He only "designates the relation of things to men, and for expressing these relations he lays hold of the boldest metaphors" (*KSA* 1: 878–79; *RL*, 249).

In describing this creation of language, Nietzsche uses a transformation theory which states that during the formation of language "each time there is a complete overleaping of one sphere, right into the middle of an entirely new and different one." He writes, "To begin with, a nerve stimulus is transferred into an image: first metaphor. The image, in turn, is imitated in a sound: second metaphor." At any rate, our language does not relate to things too well. We believe that we know something about the things themselves, when we speak of trees, colors, snow and flowers, although "we possess nothing but metaphors for things—metaphors which correspond in no way to the original entities" (*KSA* 1: 879; *RL*, 249). On the whole, the origin or genesis of language is not a logical procedure, "and all the

---

[17] The English translation is taken from Friedrich Nietzsche, *Twilight of the Idols/The Anti–Christ* 48.

[18] The English translation is taken from *Friedrich Nietzsche on Rhetoric and Language* (*RL*).

material within and with which the man of truth, the scientist and the philosopher later work and build, if not derived from never-never land is at least not derived from the essence of things." The inadequate relationship of the human being to objects is further elucidated by Nietzsche's analysis of the transformation from metaphor to concept. This occurs when "the unique and entirely original experience" which leads to the origin of a word is relinquished in favor of the concept and "now has to fit countless more or less similar cases—which means, purely and simply, cases which are never equal and thus altogether unequal." Nietzsche writes, "Every concept arises from the equation of unequal things." As if there is something in nature that would correspond to our concepts of "leaf" or "honesty!" Only by overlooking "what is individual and actual" do we arrive at concepts, "whereas nature is acquainted with no forms and no concepts, and likewise with no species" (*KSA* 1: 880; *RL*, 249–50).

As is obvious in these arguments, Nietzsche's critique of language is a critique of the language of philosophy and the claim to truth traditionally connected with this language. "What then is truth?" he asks and responds

> A moveable army of metaphors, metonymies, and anthropomorphisms: in short, a sum of human relations which have been poetically and rhetorically intensified, transferred, and embellished, and which, after long usage, seem to a people to be fixed, canonical, and binding. Truths are illusions which we have forgotten are illusions; they are metaphors that have become worn out and have been drained of sensuous force, coins which have lost their embossing and are now considered simply as metal and no longer as coins (*KSA* 1: 880; *RL*, 250).

The importance of this language theory for the topic of translation, including the Nietzsche translation, is obvious and can be exemplified with a brief glance at the language theory of early Romanticism, especially that of August Wilhelm Schlegel. Similar to Nietzsche, Schlegel assumed an original poetic and creative principle in the human mind ("ποίησις") as the formative faculty of language. Language thereby had an originally poetic character for Schlegel; language was for him "the most marvelous manifestation of the human poetic power."[19] The consequence of this poetic understanding of language was of course that poetry in the stricter sense, having its medium in language, was right from the very start a "poetry of poetry," an enhanced or exponentiated artistic expression.[20] This gave the

---

[19] August Wilhelm Schlegel, *Briefe über Poesie, Silbenmaß und Sprache* (1795), in: August Wilhelm von Schlegel, *Sämtliche Werke*, ed. Eduard Böcking, 16 vols. (Leipzig: Weidmann, 1846) vol. 7: 98–154.

[20] August Wilhelm Schlegel, *Vorlesungen über schöne Literatur und Kunst. Erster Teil: Die Kunstlehre*. 1801–1802, in: August Wilhelm Schlegel, *Kritische Ausgabe der Vorlesungen*, ed. Ernst Behler with the collaboration of Frank Jolles, 6 vols. (Paderborn: Schöningh, 1989–) vol. 1: 387–88.

romantic theory of poetry its innovative, unmimetic character. Nietzsche, by viewing language as an artistic translation or transformation of states of the mind, assigns a similarly derived and "unreal" character to language. In Nietzsche's case, this is of the greatest importance for his conception of style which indeed is, in many regards, at the center of reflections concerning a translation of his writings.

As far as the expressive character and communicative value of his writings is concerned, Nietzsche remained faithful to his conviction, first formulated in *On Truth and Lie*, according to which we cannot achieve objective knowledge, but only register our impressions, reactions, and interpretations. This is what he has done in his writing. In the most extreme manner, as no other author has ever dared it, he has involved in his text his own person, his sickness and states of euphoria, the places where he produced his writings, his own New Year's wishes, and even his culinary predilections. Every aphorism reflects his own experience. What Nietzsche presents in his writings are events which announce their arrival or which still cast a shadow, although they have passed; processes which continue and will perhaps always endure; thoughts which evaporate at the moment one articulates them; acts of self-recognition which do not succeed because we are too far from ourselves. These are by no means ascertainable facts but conjectures for which the language of science and traditional philosophy is unsuited. For these phenomena can only be communicated in a language that suggests through images and attempts to persuade through its tone—the language of rhetoric. The language of rhetoric, however, by its nature depends on a listener whose consent this language not only attempts to gain with all the arts of speech, but whom this language also confronts with all rhetorical figures of challenge, condemnation, shock, offense, denunciation, and curse. This appears to be the communicative character of Nietzsche's writings—a character that immediately follows from this theory of language and is of the greatest importance for a translation of his text.

I should like to illustrate this particular character of reality in the sense of the imagined, the poetic, the mythical by one of Nietzsche's many aphorisms on dreams, not only because dreams are a favored medium for his explorations but especially because this offers the opportunity to quote Nietzsche according to the new English edition. I am referring to Aphorism 13 ("Logic of Dreams") of *Human, All Too Human I*, translated by Gary Handwerk, which is part of a longer series on dreams in preceding and succeeding aphorisms of this section. The particular problem of this aphorism is the question why "the first available hypothesis for explaining a feeling suffices" for the mind of the dreamer "to immediately believe in its truth," while "the same mind when awake tends to be so sober, so careful, and so skeptical in regard to hypotheses?" Nietzsche's answer to this question is:

145

> Just as even today people draw conclusions while dreaming, so for many millennia, humanity drew conclusions *while awake*: the first *causa* that occurred to the mind explaining anything that needed explanation was sufficient for it and counted as truth. (According to the tales of travelers, primitive people still behave the same today.) While we are dreaming, this primeval piece of humanity continues to exercise itself in us, for it is the foundation upon which a higher reason was developed and is still developing in every human being: dreams take us back to the distant circumstances of human culture and give us the means for understanding them better. Dream thinking is now so easy for us because during enormous stretches of human development, we have been so thoroughly drilled in precisely this form of fantastic and cut-rate explanation by whatever idea happens to occur to us first. Dreams are therefore recuperation for a brain that during the day has to satisfy the strict demands of thinking, as they have been established by higher culture.

Nietzsche concentrates his analysis mainly on the confusion of cause and effect in dreams insofar our dream imagination deduces the ostensible cause from the effect and puts it after the effect:

> all this occurs with extraordinary rapidity, so that judgment gets confused, just as it might in watching a magician, and something successive can appear to be simultaneous, or even to occur in a reverse order.

Nietzsche concludes from that:

> We can infer from these processes *how late* a stricter logical thought, a more rigorous perception of cause and effect, came to be developed when *even now* our functions of reason and understanding involuntarily reach back to those primitive forms of deduction and we live roughly half our lives in that state.—The poet and the artist also *foist* causes upon their moods and mental states that are simply not the true ones; to that extent, they remind us of an older humanity and can help us to understand it.

Part III

Translating Prose, Poetry, and Drama

HELGA ESSMANN

Weltliteratur Between Two Covers:
Forms and Functions of German Translation Anthologies

I

For about two hundred years anthologies have been an outstanding phenomenon of the German book market. A recently published and—as we found—incomplete bibliography of German poetical anthologies lists about 2,000 collections published between 1840 and World War I.[1] Statements that the German book market has virtually been flooded by anthologies are legion.[2] Although the German production of lyrical anthologies has been considered extremely intense during the second half of the nineteenth century,[3] the situation in the twentieth

---

[1] Günter Häntzschel (ed.), *Bibliographie der deutschsprachigen Lyrikanthologien 1840–1914*, 2 vols. (München, etc.: Saur, 1991).

[2] Cf. Friedrich Hebbel, "Zur Anthologien-Literatur" (1854), *Sämtliche Werke*. Historisch-kritische Ausgabe, Ed. Richard Maria Werner, vol. 12 (Berlin: Behr, 1903) 76–77. Robert Prutz, "Ueber poetische Blumenlesen und Mustersammlungen," *Deutsches Museum: Zeitschrift für Literatur, Kunst und öffentliches Leben* 9.52 (1859): 929. Theodor Storm, "Vorrede" zum *Hausbuch aus deutschen Dichtern* (1870), *Sämtliche Werke in acht Bänden*, Ed. Albert Köster, vol. 8 (Leipzig: Insel, 1920) 113. Carl Meißner, "Anthologienblüte," *Der Türmer* 32 (1930): 552. Gottfried Benn, "Anthologien," *Verlags-Praxis* 3 (1956): 341.

[3] Cf. Joachim Bark, *Der Wuppertaler Dichterkreis: Untersuchungen zum poeta minor im 19. Jahrhundert*, Abhandlungen zur Kunst-, Musik- und Literaturwissenschaft 86 (Bonn: Bouvier, 1969) 139. Joachim Bark, "Rezeption als Verbreitung von Texten: Am Beispiel von Anthologien und Lesebüchern," Walter Raitz and Erhard Schütz (eds.), *Der alte Kanon neu: Zur Revision des literarischen Kanons in Wissenschaft und Unterricht* (Opladen: Westdeutscher Verlag, 1976) esp. 212. Günter Häntzschel, "'In zarte Frauenhand: Aus den Schätzen der Dichtkunst.' Zur Trivialisierung der Lyrik in der zweiten Hälfte des 19. Jahrhunderts," *Zeitschrift für deutsche Philologie* 99.2 (1980): 199-226. Dietger Pforte, "Die deutschsprachige Anthologie: Ein Beitrag zu ihrer Theorie," Joachim Bark and Dietger Pforte (eds.), *Die deutschsprachige Anthologie*. Vol. 1: *Ein Beitrag zu ihrer Theorie und eine Auswahlbibliographie des Zeitraums 1800-1950*, Studien zu Philosophie und Literatur des neunzehnten Jahrhunderts 2.2 (Frankfurt a.M.: Klostermann, 1970) XIV. Jörg Schönert, "Die populären Lyrik-Anthologien in der zweiten Hälfte des 19. Jahrhunderts: Zum Zusammenhang von Anthologiewesen und Trivialliteraturforschung," *Sprachkunst: Beiträge zur Literaturwissenschaft* 9 (1978): 272-99.

century has hardly changed, and in the 1990s dozens of new—meanwhile mainly prose—anthologies are published each year.

The focus of my paper is on German-language literary translation anthologies, that is, anthologies containing literary texts translated into German. Since the early nineteenth century more than 3,000 literary translation anthologies have been published in the German-speaking countries, and their number, too, is increasing yearly. Thus the role of translation anthologies in the transfer of literature between other nations and Germany must not be underestimated. German translation anthologies are, in fact, the most important medium for making foreign literature known to German readers. Between 1920 and 1960, for instance, 140 American poets of the twentieth century were anthologized in German translation; about 50 of these poets were represented with translations in magazines and newspapers, and only 18 could boast of book-length translations.[4] The total number of American poets anthologized in German-language collections amounts to about 650 with more than 2,800 poems. We know today that anthologies and especially translation anthologies are a typically German phenomenon, since in many other countries this kind of publication quite obviously has not occupied such an outstanding position for so long a time.[5]

This prominent role of literary translation anthologies in Germany can be explained historically. During the nineteenth century the Germans wanted to find their own national identity by trying to get rid of foreign influences. In literature, especially, this was achieved by what might be called literary imperialism: foreign literature was translated extensively, thus giving the Germans a feeling of universality which in turn was considered the distinguishing feature of German literature and culture.[6] Translation anthologies were, of course, a very suitable and effective medium of this literary imperialism. Thus, Johannes Scherr, the editor of *Bildersaal der Weltliteratur*, the first voluminous international anthology in Germany (more than 1,200 pages in its first edition of 1848, close to 1,600 pages in its third and last edition of 1885) could boast of his collection:

---

[4] Cf. Helga Eßmann, *Übersetzungsanthologien: Eine Typologie und eine Untersuchung am Beispiel der amerikanischen Versdichtung in deutschsprachigen Anthologien, 1920–1960*, Neue Studien zur Anglistik und Amerikanistik 57 (Frankfurt a.M. etc.: Lang, 1992) 24. The total number of anthologized American poets during these years was 215, with about 940 poems.

[5] Cf. the papers in Harald Kittel (ed.), *International Anthologies of Literature in Translation*, Göttinger Beiträge zur Internationalen Übersetzungsforschung 9 (Berlin: Schmidt, 1995).

[6] For a more detailed discussion of this phenomenon and the role of anthologies in the process of cultural self-definition in Germany, see Ulrich J. Beil, "Zwischen Fremdbestimmung und Universalitätsanspruch: Deutsche Weltliteraturanthologien als Ausdruck kultureller Selbstinterpretation," Helga Eßmann and Udo Schöning (eds.), *Weltliteratur in deutschen Versanthologien des 19. Jahrhunderts*, Göttinger Beiträge zur Internationalen Übersetzungsforschung 11 (Berlin: Schmidt, 1996) 261–310.

Forms and Functions of German Translation Anthologies

Ein Buch wie das vorliegende ist nur in Deutschland möglich. Erstlich hat die Universalität des deutschen Geistes, die Unermüdlichkeit der deutschen Wissenschaft sich des Verständnisses der geistigen Producte aller Völker und Zeiten zu bemächtigen gewußt in einem Grade, wie es kein anderes Volk vermochte, und zweitens sind durch eine Fülle meisterlicher Uebersetzungen, wie sie sonst ebenfalls keine andere Nation aufzuweisen hat, die Literaturschätze der Fremde zu deutschem Gemeingute geworden. Wir Deutsche dürfen uns in der That die Besitzer der Weltliteratur nennen, auf welche Göthe hingewiesen, ...

(The present book is only possible in Germany. For one, the universality of the German spirit and the tireless pursuit of German science have been able to appropriate the understanding of the intellectual products of all people and times to an extent no other people were able. Secondly, the literary treasures of foreign cultures have become German common property through a wealth of masterly translations which no other nation can, likewise, claim to possess. We Germans can rightfully call ourselves the owners of *Weltliteratur* [world literature] to which Goethe referred, ...)[7]

The reference to Johann Wolfgang von Goethe and his concept of "Weltliteratur" in this quotation is misleading, for Goethe was neither the first nor only one to use the term "Weltliteratur." It was first coined —as "Weltlitteratur"—toward the end of the eighteenth century by Christoph Martin Wieland, a representative of the German literary rococo.[8] A first *concept* of "Weltliteratur" was developed by Johann Gottfried Herder, who in 1778-79 published his collection of *Volkslieder*, better known under its later title *Stimmen der Völker in Liedern* (1807). Herder considered the literature of the world as one big entity and hoped that the publication of this first German "Weltliteraturanthologie," that is, this first German anthology with texts translated from many languages from all over the world (from Greenland to Peru and Madagascar), would stimulate German literature. Herder and others thought that translating foreign poetry would be a good exercise for German poets and might help them develop their own talents. At the same time he hoped that by developing their talents they might be able to lay the foundations of a German national literature. At the same time he hoped that foreign literatures, especially foreign folk songs, might help the Germans find their own national roots. So with Herder and his concept of "Weltliteratur" we have a first faint forerunner of what I have called literary imperialism.

In contrast to Herder's static and in a way didactic concept, Goethe developed a more dynamic concept of "Weltliteratur" by emphasizing the value of an international (i.e., reciprocal) exchange of literature for a better mutual understanding

---

[7] Johannes Scherr, *Bildersaal der Weltliteratur: Aus dem Literaturschatz der ... ausgewählt, systematisch geordnet, von der ältesten bis auf die neueste Zeit fortgeführt, mit Anmerkungen und einem literarhistorischen Katalog versehen* (Stuttgart: Becker, 1848) VI (translation mine).

[8] Cf. Marek Zybura, *Ludwig Tieck als Übersetzer und Herausgeber: Zur frühromantischen Idee einer "deutschen Weltliteratur"* (Heidelberg: Winter, 1994) 16.

of the nations. Thanks to Goethe's immense influence on literary life in Germany, the term "Weltliteratur" became very popular. Like Scherr, many nineteenth and even some of the twentieth century anthologists have collected their works ostensibly with Goethe's idea of "Weltliteratur" in the back of their minds. Our research, however, has shown that while most of these anthologies refer to Goethe, their architecture follows more or less Herder's conception of "Weltliteratur," for they usually are no more than accumulations of literary texts from many countries. Moreover, they are fairly often introduced by chauvinistic remarks, for instance, that no other people has translated as eagerly and as well as the Germans (Scherr 1848) or that a translation anthology is "ein deutsches Gedichtwerk," a German poetic work of art (Ludwig Goldscheider 1933). [9]

Today the term "Weltliteratur" has lost its conceptual dimension and is used more in the sense that "world literature" is used in the English language: it has become a word rather than a concept. As a word "Weltliteratur" may mean the literature of the whole wide world as one great entity, but it may also mean an evaluation of a work of art: "This text has become part of world literature" means that it is considered as an internationally renowned masterpiece, or, to put it differently, that it has become part of the international literary canon. "Weltliteraturanthologien" published in the second half of the twentieth century usually refer to these two meanings of the *word* "Weltliteratur" instead of reviving the old concepts of Goethe and Herder, although Goethe must be held responsible for having, albeit involuntarily, initiated the now 150-year-old fashion of anthologies of "Weltliteratur."

But whether anthologists followed Goethe, Herder, or their own interpretation of the word "Weltliteratur," or whether they did not think of the term at all and only wanted to present foreign literature, they all made literature from all over the world accessible to German readers, that is, world literature in the first sense of the word mentioned above. And since the selection or non-selection of a text always implies an evaluation, they possibly also present world literature in the second sense of the word as well—at least they are usually offering what they think are masterpieces. It certainly is impressive how deep the editors of "Weltliteraturanthologien" have dug and how many foreign authors they did unearth: After a first

---

[9] Ludwig Goldscheider, *Die schönsten Gedichte der Weltliteratur: Ein Hausbuch der Weltlyrik von den Anfängen bis heute* (Wien, Leipzig: Phaidon, 1933) 470. For a more detailed discussion of Goethe's and Herder's concepts of "Weltliteratur" in German translation anthologies of the nineteenth and early twentieth centuries cf. Birgit Bödeker, "Konzepte von Weltliteratur in deutschsprachigen Versdichtungsanthologien des 19. und frühen 20. Jahrhunderts," Helga Eßmann and Udo Schöning (eds.), *Weltliteratur in deutschen Versanthologien des 19. Jahrhunderts*, Göttinger Beiträge zur Internationalen Übersetzungsforschung 11 (Berlin: Schmidt, 1996) 193–204. Bödeker also lists the literature relevant to Goethe's and Herder's concepts of "Weltliteratur."

careful estimate, close to 6,000 poets from almost 130 countries and nations[10] figure in the roughly 180 German collections of world poetry published between 1848 and 1992.[11] Since these anthologies are only a selection of what has actually been translated into German these numbers are even more impressive.

II

Having said so much about "Weltliteratur" and anthologies of "Weltliteratur" it is now time for a few remarks on what an anthology is. Since the focus of my paper is on German-language anthologies and since I have done my research mainly in a German context, I checked about twenty German definitions of the term only to find out that no two of them correspond.[12] They only agree on an anthology being a collection of texts with but a few of them emphasizing the fact that such a *collection* in truth is a *selection*: an anthology is a collection of selected texts. The selection often starts with a decision on what kinds of texts are going to be included in an anthology. Only one definition demands that an anthology contain texts from just one genre while all the others allow almost any kind of text, either in its full length or as an excerpt: poems, songs, epigrams, aphorisms, sayings, plays, and prose in general. More specifically, they include short stories, novels,

---

[10] The following countries, nations and languages are represented in German "Weltliteraturanthologien" of the nineteenth and twentieth centuries: Afghanistan, Albania, Algeria, Ancient Greece, Arabia, Argentina, Armenia, Australia, Babylonia, Belgium, Belorussia, Bohemia, Bolivia, Bosnia, Brazil, Bulgaria, Burkina Faso, Byzantium, Cameroon, Canada, Caucasia, Chile, China, Colombia, Croatia, Cuba, Czech, Dalmatia, Denmark, Ecuador, Egypt, England, Estonia, Ethiopia, Fang, Finland, France, Georgia (former USSR), Germany, Ghana, Greece, Greenland, Guatemala, "Gypsies," Haiti, Hungary, Iceland, Illyria, India, Indochina, Indonesia, Iraq, Ireland, Israel/Hebrew, Italy, Ivory Coast, Jamaica, Japan, Korea, Kurdistan, Lapland, Latin (Ancient Rome and after), Latvia, Liberia, Lithuania, Madagascar, Malaysia, Mali, Malta, Maori, Martinique, Masai/Kenya, Mexico, Moldavia, Mongolia, Montenegro, Morocco, Netherlands, New Zealand, Nicaragua, Nigeria, Norway, Oceania, Palestine, Paraguay, Persia, Peru, Phillipines, Poland, Portugal, Puerto Rico, Rhato-Romanic/Ladin, Romania, Russia, Samoa, Sao Tomé, Scotland, Senegal, Serbia, Slovakia, Slovenia, Sorbian, South Africa, Spain, St. Lucia, Sudan, Sweden, Switzerland, Syria, Tadzhikistan, Tanzania, Tartarian, Thailand, Turkey, Ukraine, Uruguay, USA, Venezuela, Vietnam, Wales, Yiddish, Zaire/Congo, Zimbabwe.

[11] Members of the *Sonderforschungsbereich* "Die Literarische Übersetzung" at the University of Göttingen are preparing a bibliography of German "Weltliteraturanthologien." It will be published in 1997 together with bibliographies of German-language anthologies of English and American poetry, American short prose, French poetry, Russian poetry, Italian literature, Troubadour poetry, and a bibliography of German-language novel series of the nineteenth century.

[12] Cf. Eßmann, *Übersetzungsanthologien* 29–32.

fairy tales, anecdotes, letters, essays, speeches and philosophical, didactic, edifying, scientific, technical writings.

The definitions also disagree on how many authors may or must be represented: some definitions claim that an anthology must contain at least three or four different authors; others also accept collections of texts by a single author. On yet another important point the different definitions are at variance: should an anthology collect only previously published material, or may it also publish texts for the first time?

These last two criteria—number of authors and publication status—are especially interesting with regard to translation anthologies, for one might ask what to do about a translator's anthology in which one translator has collected his or her translations of several foreign authors: if such translations are published for the first time, can the collection be called an anthology? And is not the translator in a way the author of his/her collection, having chosen, translated, arranged, and possibly even commented on the texts? The only definition that does take up the specific problem of translation anthologies would exclude this example, for here an anthology of translations is defined as "Auswahl und Zusammenstellung von Texten eines oder mehrerer fremdsprachiger Autoren in der Übersetzung von zumindest *vier* Übersetzern" (a selection and compilation of texts by one or more foreign authors, translated by at least *four* translators). [13]

This definition is indeed a stroke of genius, making it unmistakably clear that existing anthology definitions are not exactly helpful to any German researcher who would like to work with anthologies, let alone translation anthologies. The only thing he or she can do is add yet another definition to the host of existing ones, and mine reads as follows: a translation anthology is a collection of selected and mainly translated texts by at least three different foreign or German authors. "Mainly" underlines that it may also contain a certain number of original, that is German, texts. The number of translators involved is completely irrelevant. One might add to the definition that the texts of an anthology are arranged according to a principle chosen or invented by the anthologist. This, however, does not apply to all anthologies. Recent paperback publications of prose anthologies in particular tend to group texts together without any discernible principles. The same is true for multi-volume series (mostly novels and plays), such as the "Reclam Universalbibliothek" with its several thousand volumes, which can also be called anthologies. The latter, however, constitute a special form of publication and as such warrant separate investigation.[14] For the purpose of this paper I will

---

[13] Pforte, "Die deutschsprachige Anthologie" XXV (my emphasis).

[14] At the Sonderforschungsbereich "Die Literarische Übersetzung" we have a project, mainly bibliographical, on series published between 1800 and 1910.

restrict myself to one- or two-volume anthologies. Among these, poetry anthologies are especially interesting because, unlike prose collections, they have been persistently present on the German book market ever since the beginning of the nineteenth century.[15] Thus, most of the following remarks—which can be considered a theory of translation anthologies[16]—pertain to collections of poetry.

III

Since the forms of translation anthologies are defined—as are all forms or types—by features, let me begin by naming some of the most important features that characterize translation anthologies. One can determine these features by asking questions touching on (1) the number of nations represented in the anthology, (2) the printing of the source texts, (3) the anthologist and (4) his/her commentary, (5) the genre, (6) the selection and (7) the arrangement of the anthologized texts. Since these questions shall yield the features that help identify the external form of a collection, it should be possible to answer all these questions without reading the whole anthology—although sometimes this may be inevitable. While these questions were developed from German-language translation anthologies it should also be possible to apply them to translation anthologies in other countries and languages.

(1) Number of nations represented in the anthology: First of all there are *multilateral anthologies*, with "multilateral" indicating that the texts of these collections are translated from many—at least three—different languages representing different nations. Some multilateral collections have amassed as many as fifty nations from different continents, such as Heinrich Solger's school anthology *Im Tempel der Weltlitteratur* (1888).[17] This anthology, of course, is what we would call a "Weltliteraturanthologie" with "Weltliteraturanthologien" constituting one group in the large complex of multilateral anthologies. The multilateral anthologies, in turn, are opposed to *bilateral* ones, which contain texts translated from one lan-

---

[15] One-volume prose anthologies first appeared in the second half of the nineteenth century and became truly popular only in the twentieth century, especially after World War II; this certainly has something to do with the growing importance of short prose. Multi-volume novel and drama series, however, have been published constantly since the beginning of the nineteenth century.

[16] The theory that is going to be presented is based on the observation of corpora of translation anthologies. These observations were made from the point of view of someone who is primarily interested in translation and its cultural impact. Any other point of view—from social history, the book market, etc.—would yield another theory.

[17] Heinrich Solger, *Im Tempel der Weltlitteratur: Eine Sammlung von wertvollen Geisteserzeugnissen aller hervorragenden Länder und Zeiten* (Langensalza: Schulbuchhandlung, 1888).

guage only, such as the first American-German collection *Amerikanische Gedichte* published in 1859 by Friedrich Spielhagen.[18]

(2) Printing of the source texts: A translation anthology can be *monolingual* (only in the target language), *bilingual*, such is the bilateral collection *The Vast Horizons—Die weiten Horizonte: Amerikanische Lyrik 1638 bis 1980* (1985),[19] or even *multilingual*, although experience has shown that multilingual collections are rarely published. "Multilingual" may mean that an anthology is published in the target and several source languages. This is the case with Hans Magnus Enzensberger's famous *Museum der modernen Poesie* (1960, 1980) which presents the source and target texts of sixteen different languages.[20] But it may also mean that there are several source languages, as in *Ohne Haß und Fahne* whose English, French and German poems are printed in their source languages and then translated into the two other languages, thus making this anti-war collection a truly international anthology.[21]

(3) The anthologist: The next distinction to be made is that between an *editor's* and a *translator's anthology*. Most of the multilateral collections are editor's anthologies compiled by one or several editors who select existing translations only (e.g., Solger's *Im Tempel der Weltlitteratur*). Few editors function as translators as well (e.g., Enzensberger in his *Museum der modernen Poesie*). In this case we have a form that lies between an editor's and a translator's anthology. Many of the bilateral collections are translator's anthologies in which (usually) one translator has chosen and translated the texts (e.g., Spielhagen and his *Amerikanische Gedichte*). Since translators can select their texts directly from a foreign literature their anthologies play an important role in the reception of this literature in the target culture. Especially in the field of poetry, many contemporary authors and texts are introduced to German readers through bilateral translator's publications which are often extensively used later on as sources by the editors of multilateral anthologies. As a consequence, multilateral editor's anthologies are usually one step behind the actual development of a source literature, while at the same time they stabilize the canon. In another context we introduced the terms "prospective" and "retro-

---

[18] Friedrich Spielhagen, *Amerikanische Gedichte* (Leipzig: Roßberg'sche Buchhandlung, 1859). Apart from the above mentioned translation anthologies there are also *monoliterary* collections containing untranslated texts of one language/literature/nation.

[19] Teut Andreas Riese, *The Vast Horizons / Die weiten Horizonte: Amerikanische Lyrik 1638 bis 1980* (Hürtgenwald: Preßler, 1985).

[20] Hans Magnus Enzensberger, *Museum der modernen Poesie* (1960; 2nd ed., Frankfurt a.M.: Suhrkamp, 1980).

[21] Wolfgang Deppe, Christopher Middleton, and Herbert Schönherr, *Ohne Haß und Fahne / No Hatred and No Flag / Sans haine et sans drapeau: Kriegsgedichte des 20. Jahrhunderts*, Rowohlts Klassiker 58 (Hamburg: Rowohlt, 1959).

spective" which could be applied to many bilateral or multilateral anthologies respectively.[22]

(4) Commenting texts by the anthologist: Apart from the literary texts which can be considered as the anthology proper, a collection can also contain a motto, a dedication, a preface, an introduction, biographical and other notes, an afterword, or indices (author's index, first line index)—that is, all kinds of texts added by the editor or translator to facilitate or guide the reading and understanding of the anthology.

(5) Genre of the anthologized texts: As indicated above, anthologies (including translation anthologies) are theoretically open to all kinds of texts and genres. Most popular are collections of poetry or short prose, but there are also anthologies that mix all sorts of texts, sometimes including even cartoons or newspaper clippings or—leaving the field of the written word altogether—illustrations, photographs, paintings, etc. In some cases these are integral parts of the anthology proper, occasionally commenting on the literary texts as in Hans Leip's *Das Meer* (1959).[23]

(6) Selection of the texts: While many anthologies try to give an historical survey of the development of one or several literatures, the selection of the texts of other collections is limited to certain areas. These might be defined by literary criteria such as epoch or genre (Romantic poetry, sonnets), but they might also be defined by extra-literary criteria such as literature by women, ethnic minorities, prisoners, or housewives, or literature on special subjects such as love, war, animals, humor, music, religion, the sea, beds—the possibilities are endless. These latter collections can be called "thematic anthologies."

(7) Arrangement of texts: An anthology can also be characterized by its specific arrangement of texts. The major "Weltliteraturanthologien" are usually arranged by nations, and within the national sections, by chronology. The chronological arrangement is likewise very popular with other forms of anthologies, for instance with bilateral ones that intend to present a survey of the literature in question such as the above mentioned *The Vast Horizons*. Other anthologists, especially the editors of thematic collections, arrange their texts thematically, while those who try to be as objective as possible often choose an alphabetical ordering by nations and/or authors, such as Hans Bethge in *Die Lyrik des Auslandes in neurer Zeit* (1907).[24] Anthologies that offer several genres might be arranged by type of text. In some cases, however, the arrangement is not obvious and one has to read the

---

[22] Armin Paul Frank and Helga Eßmann, "Translation Anthologies: A Paradigmatic Medium of International Literary Transfer," *Amerikastudien / American Studies* 35 (1990): 25.

[23] Hans Leip, *Das Meer: Die Landschaft als Erlebnis 1* (München: Kindler, 1957).

[24] Hans Bethge, *Die Lyrik des Auslandes in neuerer Zeit* (Leipzig: Hesse, 1907).

whole anthology to make sense of the text arrangement. This is the case, for instance, with Fritz Adolf Hünich's *Buch der Liebe* (1946), in which the arrangement of the anthologized texts reflects the development of love from its first beginnings to the loss of the loved one.[25] Such anthologies are often very carefully edited and can even be considered as genuine works of art by anthologists.

With the help of this checklist it should be possible to characterize the form of any anthology. At the same time, it should now be clear that the number of different forms is virtually unlimited, especially since new forms can be invented at any time by simply combining the different features in a new way, or by finding new selection criteria (imagine a richly annotated, multilingual, alphabetically arranged anthology of "Sonnets by Thieves on the Use of the Blowtorch").

There are, of course, recurring forms. In the German context "Weltliteraturanthologien" are true evergreens, having been invented in the nineteenth century and still popular in the 1990s. They comprise, as some titles suggest, poems from all times and nations, arranged geographically and chronologically. Equally popular are bilateral poetry anthologies. Organized chronologically, they provide either a survey of recent developments in a chosen literature or of the poetry of one nation over a long period of time; these anthologies are often bilingual and have extensive introductions as well as notes. Thematic anthologies, that is, collections of texts illustrating some extra-literary subject, are usually collected from prose texts or offer a wide variety of texts. And since prose collections are to the twentieth century what poetry anthologies were to the nineteenth century, it becomes evident that thematic anthologies are enjoying increasing popularity.

IV

Unlike the theoretically unlimited number of forms, the number of functions of translation anthologies seems to be easy to survey. When speaking of functions of (translation) anthologies one has to distinguish between several kinds of functions. First of all an editor may assign one or more functions to his/her anthology. These functions may (1) be stated explicitly in an introduction or an afterword; (2) be implicit in the editor's commenting texts as well as in the selection and/or the arrangement of the anthologized texts; or (3) just exist in the editor's mind. These kinds of functions could also be called the editor's intentions or his/her reasons or purposes for collecting an anthology. Another, quite different kind of function would be the actual impact an anthology has on its readers, that is, the real functioning in the reception process, regardless of the editor's intentions. This kind of

---

[25] Fritz Adolf Hünich, *Das Buch der Liebe* (Leipzig: Volk und Buch, 1946).

function, however, is very difficult to determine because it is generally rather complicated to get hold of readers' responses apart from reviews. I shall therefore concentrate on the editors' reasons for publishing a translation anthology by naming the most frequent intentions that lie behind the editing of a collection of translations.

To begin with, it is not always possible to assign a function to an anthology, especially to those collections which do not have an editor's or translator's statement (introduction, etc.). Such statements or at least an indication of the title, such as "Ein Deklamatorium" or "Eine Auswahl für Frauen und Jungfrauen," are needed because otherwise one can only speculate on the purposes of a collection. Only occasionally is it possible to infer that an unannotated anthology has been compiled for young readers or for the use in schools or colleges, for instance when it was published by a publishing house that is specialized in children's literature or on textbooks for schools. Another difficult case is paperback collections of prose texts, many of which do not have an introduction or a discernible structure; quite often one is led to suspect that they are published by a publishing house for the sole reason of profit with perhaps the additional and economically necessary purpose of entertaining the readers.

While these anthologies are often collected a little carelessly, offering texts of authors under contract with the respective publisher—and this kind of anthology must above all be inexpensive for the publisher!—other anthologies are almost perfect reflections of their compilers' personalities. This is especially true for translator's anthologies in which it is often possible to trace the anthologists' predilections even in the translations themselves. Thus, the theatre critic Julius Bab "translates" the first stanza of Stephen Vincent Benét's poem on "Theodore Roosevelt" into a theatre context:

They are calling T.R. a lot of things	Sie schimpften T.R. ja dies und das,
—The men in the private car—	die Herrn auf den feinen Plätzen,
But the day-coach likes exciting folks	doch die Galerie liebt den starken Mann,
And the day-coach likes T.R.	und sie weiß T.R. zu schätzen![26]

Furthermore, Bab, who as a Jew was forced to emigrate to the United States in 1940, liked humor and animals, and this is reflected in his selection of texts for his anthology *Amerikas neuere Lyrik* (1953): Apart from some texts dealing with (the Jewish) religion he primarily selected humorous poems, many of them dealing with animals. Thus he translated some of Ogden Nash's humorous animal poems under the title of "Ogdon Nash's kleiner Zoo" and felt free to add under this

---

[26] Julius Bab, *Amerikas neuere Lyrik: Ausgewählte Nachdichtungen* (Bad Nauheim: Christian-Verlag, 1953) 38.

heading a four-line poem by himself on "Die Maus"—which, of course, cannot be found in Nash's collected poems *Verses from 1929 on* (1959). So in this case we have a typical vanity anthology suited to the self-presentation of its translator. But this anthology also serves as an illustration of what Bab had written in Part II (Poetry) of his critical book on *Amerikas Dichter der Gegenwart* (1951). Although Bab is not the best example it is a fairly common practice to compile anthologies in order to illustrate what was written in critical works or literary histories.[27] Thus, anthologies and literary histories are often complementary to each other and it should have become clear that translation anthologies are not only media of literary transfer but also documents of the reception of one or several foreign literatures by a target language reader, that is, the anthologist.

But not all anthologies are so explicitly personal as Julius Bab's. Most anthologists name other reasons for publishing their collections. A standard reason for collecting a translation anthology is to bring one or several literatures to the attention of the target language readers, which means that the anthologies are used as media of literary transfer. Thus, Kurt Heinrich Hansen states in the afterword to his *Gedichte aus der neuen Welt* (1956):

> Als 1945 die Isolation zu Ende ging, in der wir fast anderthalb Jahrzehnte gelebt hatten, gab es für uns manche geistige und künstlerische Überraschung. Zu diesen Überraschungen gehörte die Entdeckung der modernen angloamerikanischen Poesie. Wir erfuhren zum ersten Mal, daß es in der ersten Jahrhunderthälfte in der angelsächsischen Welt eine ganze Reihe bedeutender Lyriker gegeben hat und gab, die, während der Strom des geistigen Lebens bei uns stockte und schließlich ausgetrocknet war, einen neuen Typ des Gedichts, eine neue Dichtung geschaffen hatten.
>
> (When in 1945 the isolation in which we had lived for almost one and a half decades came to an end, we were handed some intellectual and artistic surprises, one of which was the discovery of modern Anglo-American poetry. For the first time we learned that there had and still existed a number of important Anglo-Saxon lyrical poets in the first half of this century who created a novel kind of poem, a new poetry, while the stream of intellectual life in our world had stagnated and eventually dried out.)[28]

It goes without saying that Hansen's anthology is designed to make its readers share the editor's and translator's astonishment.

---

[27] Better examples are Johannes Scherr and Julius Hart who, besides their anthologies, have published histories of world literature. Cf. Johannes Scherr, *Allgemeine Geschichte der Literatur: Ein Handbuch in zwei Bänden*, 6. neubearb. u. verm. Aufl. (Stuttgart: Conradi, 1880–81). Julius Hart, *Geschichte der Weltlitteratur und des Theaters aller Zeiten und Völker*, 2 vols., Hausschatz des Wissens Abt. X, vols. 15–16 (Neudamm: Neumann, 1894–96).

[28] Kurt Heinrich Hansen, *Gedichte aus der neuen Welt: Amerikanische Lyrik seit 1910*, Piper Bücherei 98 (München: Piper, 1956) 69 (translation mine).

Forms and Functions of German Translation Anthologies

Hansen's statements are a typical post-war reaction. Other German anthologists have published bilateral collections to show German readers the common human nature that connects the former enemy nations. Thus Kurt Erich Meurer in his selections from various nineteenth-century American poets (*Das Goldener Zeitalter*, 1948) tries to emphasize the similarities between American and European culture, and Rolf Göhring states in the same year:

> Es spricht nicht allein englisches Gefühl aus den vorliegenden Versen zu uns. Viele Völker, die in der angloamerikanischen Welt vertreten sind, haben durch ihre Dichter aus ihrer angeborenen inneren Welt zu unserem Herzen gesprochen.
>
> (Not only an English sentiment is speaking to us from the present verses. Many a people who are part of the Anglo-American world have spoken from their native inner world through their poets to our heart.)[29]

In these cases American literature is used to teach Germans a better understanding of Americans and their culture.

Some anthologies are even conceived to *document* the source culture through its literature; these anthologies sometimes have the character of travel literature and are usually richly annotated with explanations of names, titles, customs and so forth.[30]

Other collections intended to introduce foreign literature are compiled and translated by anthologists who think that important foreign texts have never been translated into German; these anthologies are designed to close a translational gap in the target culture. This is the case with Adolf Friedrich Graf von Schack's collection *Anthologie abendländischer und morgenländischer Dichtungen* (1893) which is introduced with the following remarks:

> In diesen beiden Bänden habe ich Uebersetzungen und freie Nachbildungen ausländischer Gedichte zusammengestellt, die sich im Laufe der Zeit in meinem Pulte angehäuft haben. Sämmtliche darin enthaltenen Poesieen sind meines Wissens noch nie übertragen worden, und damit glaube ich meiner Sammlung einen Vorzug vor anderen vindiciren zu können.
>
> (In these two volumes I have compiled translations and free re-creations of foreign poems that have accumulated over the course of time in my desk. As far as I know

---

[29] Rolf Göhring, *Amerikanische Lyrik des 20. Jahrhunderts* (Waibstadt bei Heidelberg: Kemper, 1948) 7 (translation mine).

[30] Such a case is described by Ulrike Jekutsch in her "Die 'Rußlandschwelle': Zur Rezeption russischer Poesie in Deutschland, England und Frankreich in den zwanziger Jahre des 19. Jahrhunderts," Helga Eßmann and Udo Schöning (eds.), *Weltliteratur in deutschen Versanthologien des 19. Jahrhunderts* 151–80.

none of the poems contained in these volumes has ever been translated before, which I believe gives my collection a rightful advantage over others.)[31]

Some anthologists—unconsciously following Herder—even express their hopes that by publishing an anthology they might be offering some good and inspiring examples of literature to German poets and authors. Thus, Julius and Heinrich Hart thought that the German poetry of the 1880s was in a desolate state and that their two big multilateral anthologies, *Buch der Liebe* (1882) and *Orient und Occident* (1885, published by Julius Hart alone), as well as their numerous bilateral ones, such as *England und Amerika* (1885), might stimulate German poets to write good poetry.[32] And in 1921, the still remaining expressionist Claire Goll was convinced that U.S.-American poetry would be able to "rejuvenate" not only German poetry, but also European society:

> Es ist in diesem Buch versucht, das Wesentliche lebender amerikanischer Dichtung zu kristallisieren. Heute ist Europa mehr als je auf die unerschöpflichen Borne jüngerer Länder angewiesen. Es lieh einmal Geld, heute entleiht es neues Blut in Amerika gegen alten Geist. Auch von dort wird ihm Verjüngung kommen. Denn die "Neue Welt" ist nur das Land *einer* Zukunft, das Land der Zukunft aber ist Rußland.
>
> (This book attempts to distill what is essential about contemporary American poetry. Today more than ever Europe depends on the inexhaustible well of younger countries. Once it borrowed money; today it borrows new blood in America against old spirit. From there, too, it will be rejuvenated. For the "New World" is only the land of *one* particular future; the land of the future, however, is Russia.)[33]

Of course she was taking a first step towards this "rejuvenation" by publishing a bilateral translator's anthology which reflects the ideas of German leftist expressionism through the selection of the texts as well as through their translation.

This presentation of American poetry was considered so highly offensive by the German Americanist Friedrich Schönemann and his wife Toni Harten-Hoencke that they felt obliged to correct Goll's image of the United States and its literature by editing another bilateral translator's anthology four years later with the

---

[31] Adolf Friedrich Graf von Schack, *Anthologie abendländischer und morgenländischer Dichtungen in deutschen Nachbildungen*, 2 vols. (Stuttgart: Cotta, 1893) VII (translation mine).

[32] Julius Hart, *Orient und Occident: Eine Blütenlese aus den vorzüglichsten Gedichten der Weltlitteratur* (Minden i.W.: Bruns, 1885) IX–X. Julius Hart, *England und Amerika: Fünf Bücher englischer und amerikanischer Gedichte von den Anfängen bis auf die Gegenwart* (Minden i.W.: Bruns, 1885). Heinrich Hart and Julius Hart. *Das Buch der Liebe: Eine Blütenlese aus der gesammten Liebeslyrik aller Zeiten und Völker* (Leipzig: Wigand, 1882).

[33] Claire Goll, *Die Neue Welt: Eine Anthologie jüngster amerikanischer Lyrik* (Berlin: Fischer, 1921) 10 (Goll's emphasis; translation mine).

standard intention—besides correcting Goll's picture—of providing a survey of American poetry from its beginning to the 1920s.

The remarks on German translation anthologies in this paper offer but a condensed survey of an important and highly complex phenomenon that so far has been almost totally neglected by scholars. It is to be hoped that in the future this interesting form of publication will be given more attention not only in Germany but in other countries as well.

JOHN FELSTINER

Translating as Transference: Paul Celan's Versions of Shakespeare, Dickinson, Mandelshtam, Apollinaire

My intention is to try and find out a little more about Paul Celan as a writer, by examining his translation practice.[1] This may give us an example of "Translating Cultures, Translating Literatures," because not only did Celan bring signal voices from British, American, French, and Russian culture into earshot of postwar Germany, but at the same time he brought to bear on those foreign voices his own cultural legacy, a German mother tongue wounded by abuse, loss, exile. Even in the Czernowitz ghetto and then as a slave laborer, Celan tried making versions of Shakespeare, Sergei Esenin, Verlaine, and others. These versions bear his imprint, and where they matter most to him, they may impinge on, may transmute, their originals. This is a case of what we may call "strong" translation.

Recently an early translation by Paul Celan has come to light. It dates from wartime, around winter 1943. Celan, age 23, was at forced labor, far from a young woman he loved in Czernowitz, Bukovina, when he took up A. E. Housman's tristful quatrains, "The half-moon westers low, my love."[2] His German version resonates along with the English cadence and rhyme, but on one line he makes a startling addition. Housman's "In the field where you do lie" becomes "there where you lie, bereft"—or, literally, "orphaned": *da wo du liegst, verwaist*. Celan's *verwaist* goes beyond the call of duty to the original because, I think, around this time his fervently cherished mother, deported to the Ukraine, was shot by the SS because she was no longer considered fit for work. The poet's own raw orphanhood impinged on this lyric of love and loss. Now it might be thought that Celan's *verwaist* was merely anticipating a rhyme, since he ends his stanza with *du weisst*. But in translation as in any poem, the expedient generates what is essential.

---

[1] Celan's translations and his poems are published in Celan, *Gesammelte Werke*, ed. Beda Allemann and Stefan Reichert, with Rolf Bücher (Frankfurt, 1983). References to this 5-volume edition will occur in the text by volume and page number. On Celan's translations, see Leonard Moore Olschner, *Der feste Buchstab: Erläuterungen zu Paul Celans Gedichtübertragungen* (Göttingen, 1985), and references in Felstiner, *Paul Celan: Poet, Survivor, Jew* (New Haven, 1995).

[2] Celan, "J'ai traduit ...," ed. George Gutu, *Neue Literatur* 41-42/7-8 (1990-91): 152.

165

John Felstiner

The term *verwaist*, as you might expect from an orphan, pressed upon Celan's tongue at later exigent moments. In 1963, translating Shakespeare's sonnet 5, another lyric of love and loss, Celan faced a verse saying that time's "hideous winter" will leave "beauty ... bereft" (5: 325). That word "bereft" prompted in him a surcharged German compound, *sinnverwaist*, "reft of sense," or let us say "orphaned of meaning," since a good few speakers of the German mother tongue, such as Celan, were left "orphaned of meaning." Celan re-encountered one such person, a prewar childhood friend from Czernowitz, toward the end of his life. Visiting Israel in 1969, he wrote her a love poem where the two of them "orphaned into each other," *ineinander verwaisten* (3: 100). Celan's early sorrow was still working on his diction.

Another example of his bent as a translator comes from 1963. When Robert Frost died, Celan translated "The Road Not Taken"—somewhat prosily, but his choice alone spoke volumes, since Frost's lines themselves already befitted an exile who had fled his homeland: "Yet knowing how way leads on to way, / I doubted if I should ever come back."

Celan also undertook "Stopping by Woods on a Snowy Evening," and there several curious changes occur. Watch what happens to the sweep "Of easy wind and downy flake":

> *doch, dies noch: leichten Wind, die Flocken, erdwärts, dicht*
> (yet, this too: easy wind, the snowflakes, earthward, thick)

Twenty years earlier Celan had addressed a winter poem called "Black Flakes" to his mother in the Ukraine (3: 25). Now he does not so much render as rend into pieces Frost's wafting fluent line. And does Celan know what "downy" really means yet still pun with *erdwärts* ("earthward")? Just at the time he was working on Frost, Celan began a short lyric this way: *Mit erdwärts gesungenen Masten*, "With masts sung earthward / the wrecks of heaven sail" (2: 20). Whichever came first, the translation or his own poem, clearly they feed each other.

Now look at Frost's famous ending, followed by Celan's rendering:

> And miles to go before I sleep,
> And miles to go before I sleep.
>
> *Und Meilen, Meilen noch vorm Schlaf.*
> *Und Meilen Wegs noch bis zum Schlaf.*
> (And miles, miles yet before sleep.
> And miles of road yet until sleep.)

Whatever has become of the speaker's "I," something even stranger is happening. Whether Frost's repetition embodies a death wish or its opposite, or mere drowsiness, Celan opts for change, process, possibility. Having answered the claim of repetition already in one line—"miles, miles"—he then shifts "before" to "until," putting off sleep just a shade longer. Translation is, after all, a form of repetition—with a difference. Celan's difference asserts freedom and idiosyncrasy.

What underlay Paul Celan's idiosyncrasy was a typical East European education: Romanian Iron Guard anti-Semitism, Russian occupation, *SS Einsatzkommando 10B*, overnight loss of both parents, nineteen months at forced labor, Soviet takeover, and then exile with literally nothing left but a mother tongue that had turned into the murderers' tongue, passing through what he called "the thousand darknesses of deathbringing speech" (3: 186).

This fatefulness of German made the language in Celan's poems so often ruptured, elliptic, allusive, archaic, technically arcane, rare, or contradictory. And it was his poetry's darknesses—really, its integrity—that carried over into Celan's rendition of poets who stimulated him.

Shakespeare, for instance. For the Bard's quadricentennial in 1964, Celan translated 20 sonnets. Love and loss, time's ravages, beauty, regeneration, and the saving power of verse: these Renaissance themes combusted in the 20th-century survivor's hands. In sonnet 5, Shakespeare's "hideous winter" harshens in Celan's postwar German. "For never-resting time leads summer on," reads the English, whereupon the German says: *Ist Sommer? Sommer war* ("'Tis summer? Summer w a s"). Turning present to past, indicative to interrogative, narrative to dialectic, the fell hand of grammar itself seems at work. "Summer" abuts "Summer"—*Ist Sommer? Sommer war*—forcing a question of transience and of translation itself. The high time of lyric fullness is gone, and Celan's chiasm—"'Tis summer? Summer w a s"—suggests that after the catastrophe, his German version must bear inversely on Shakespeare.

More than any other author, Celan esteemed Shakespeare, whose fluency provoked contraries in his German—the English verse suffering a sea change into something very strange. In sonnet 79, as George Steiner remarks,[3] the poet-lover already sounds like a zealous translator:

> Yet what of thee thy poet doth invent
> He robs thee of, and pays it thee again.

Then after those lines, Shakespeare's balanced phrasing,

> ... beauty doth he give,
> And found it in thy cheek: he can afford
> No praise to thee but what in thee doth live,

---

[3] George Steiner, *After Babel: Aspects of Language and Translation* (New York, 1975) 389.

surges with exaggerated stress in Celan's version:

> ... *Er kann dir Schönheit geben:*
> *sie stammt von dir—er raubte, abermals.*
> *Er rühmt und preist: er tauchte in dein Leben.* (5: 341)
>
> (...To thee he can give beauty:
> it stems from thee—he plundered, once again.
> He'll praise and prize: he plunged into thy life.)

The doubled thrust of "plundered, once again," echoed in "plunged," the adding of "prize" to "praise," plus new stops in German, all display translation's reflexive and possessive force.

In Celan's papers, a Shakespeare translation may appear on one side of a sheet and the draft of a poem on the other. Yet he was writing anything but sonnets then. Here is some of his own verse from late 1963, rendered word for word:

> *Die in der senk-*
> *rechten, schmalen*
> *Tagschlucht nach oben*
> *stakende Fähre:*
>
> *sie setzt*
> *Wundgelesenes über.* (2: 24)
>
> (The in the vert-
> ical, narrow
> day-gorge upwards
> poling ferry:
>
> it puts
> wound-readings across.)

Celan often spoke of translation as a kind of ferrying, and here the ferry "puts" something "across," *sie setzt / Wundgelesenes über*—roughly the same verb as "translate," *übersetzen*. What's put across is *Wundgelesenes*, something read (or gleaned) by way of a wound. Only a wounded reading will arduously rise, as if from one language into another, toward daylight.

One more test case from Shakespeare. Just after the war, translating "If this be error and upon me prov'd," Celan for "error" had used *Irrtum*, the fitting cognate.[4] But in the 1960s he was afflicted by a groundless plagiarism charge, and German Neo-Nazism exacerbated his pain. After being hospitalized for severe depression, he was working at Shakespeare, and returning to sonnet 116 he

---

[4] Beda Allemann and Rolf Bücher, "Paul Celan: Talmacirea sonetelor lui Shakespeare 2," *Manuscriptum* 13/4 (1982): 170.

Translating as Transference: Paul Celan's Versions

changed *Irrtum* ("error") to *Wahn* ("madness")—a plausible change, but one personally fraught (5: 353).

Given Celan's relation to Housman, Frost, Shakespeare and others, I've thought of relating the word "translation" to "transference." This thought arose from reading Freud's 1914 essay "Memory, Repetition and Working Through," which throws light on a poet such as Celan's long postwar attempt to work through compulsive repetition of past trauma toward authoritative memory. I noticed that the term Freud adopted for "transference" was *Übertragung*, which is also the formal word for literary translation (*übertragen*—literally "to carry across"—seems to me closer to "translate" than is *übersetzen*, "to put across"). Although the psychoanalytic phenomenon of transference does not adequately suggest Celan's complex creative activity as a translator, we can still see the orphaned, exiled poet transfusing his unhealed pain into Dickinson's, Mandelshtam's, Apollinaire's verse.

Although Celan did not engage so fiercely with Emily Dickinson as with Shakespeare, her fascination with death and her skepticism about heaven still brought out an excess of translational energy in him. Witness the middle stanza of "I reason, Earth is short":

> I reason, we could die—
> the best Vitality
> Cannot excel decay,
> But, what of that?

Where Dickinson is anything but verbose or abstract, Celan still finds terser, more concrete things to say:

> *Ich denk: Sieh zu, man stirbt,*
> *der Saft, der in dir wirkt,*
> *auch ihm gilt dies: Verdirb—*
> *ja und?* (5: 395)
>
> (I think: Look here, we die,
> the sap that works in thee,
> it too knows this: Decay—
> so what?)

Cannily keeping the off-rhymes (or call them slant rhymes—"Tell all the Truth but tell it slant," Dickinson said), and cleaving to the original meter, Celan still forces a colon where there was none, prompting an imperative "Look here" to the reader or to the poet herself or *him*self. And Dickinson's discreet conditional "we could die" transmutes into blank fact.

What is lost in translation here releases what is gained. Dropping Dickinson's deft word "best," Celan makes Vitality concrete ("the sap"), active ("that works"),

169

and intimate ("in thee"). Then he breaks her already brief line "Cannot excel decay" with an abrupt colon: *auch ihm gilt dies:* Here as in all his most engaged acts of translation, Celan cuts in decisively, the caesura visibly, audibly marking his stake in Frost, Shakespeare, Dickinson, and his literal sense that a verse line today must admit rupture. I think caesuras gave Celan a physical sign of every breach affecting him. And he was struck by Hölderlin's idea of the caesura as a critical moment in classical drama, which tallies with Celan's own key term *Atemwende* from his "Meridian" speech, the "breath-turn" of revolutionary recognition (3: 195). A late poem has him "plow away at / the king's caesura / like that one / at Pindar" (3: 108). Like Hölderlin laboring at Pindar's fragments to infuse Greek spirit into German, Celan feels wedged between Hebraic and German spiritual sources. That "king's caesura" suggests a messianic cutting point, and yet *Königszäsur* also encodes *KZ*, short for *Konzentrationslager*. So we can see the new caesura in Dickinson's line as the signature of her translator Paul Celan.

After the colon, then, rather than her noun "decay," Celan's bluff imperative *Verdirb* tells the lifeblood: "Decay." The only time his own poetry uses that word *Verderben*, which also means "ruin," "destruction," he has in mind what it cost him to be a writer:

> *Welches der Worte du sprichst—*
> *du dankst*
> *dem Verderben.* (1: 129)
>
> (Whichever word you speak—
> you owe
> to destruction.)

to *Verderben*. No wonder Dickinson's shrug, however ironic—"But, what of that?"—turns clipped, brutal: *ja und?* ("so what?").

You will notice, incidentally, that I have not seized a certain occasion here. For Dickinson's "decay" Celan has used *Verderben*: thus when that verb occurs in his own verse, it is tempting to flip back and call it "decay." I first got this idea in translating Pablo Neruda's *Alturas de Macchu Picchu*, wondering what to make of a moment in which he is scraping the *entraña* of the ancient earth to touch humankind.[5] *Entraña* is entrail, inmost part, heart—not quite right. Then I looked at Neruda's own translation of William Blake and found him using *entraña* for Blake's "womb"! So back at Macchu Picchu I had him "scrape in the womb." But such inside tips are not always safe. Whichever word Paul Celan spoke, he owed—not to decay but to destruction.

---

[5] John Felstiner, *Translating Neruda: The Way to Macchu Picchu* (Stanford, 1980) 231.

Translating as Transference: Paul Celan's Versions

We have, incidentally, around Samuel Beckett, a marvelous instance of how the translating of a text can feed back onto its original. My late friend Elmar Tophoven, Beckett's German translator, once told me that in discussing the translation of *En attendant Godot*, Beckett was puzzled over what to do with Estragon's remark, *Ce qu'on est bien, par terre!* ("It's a bit of OK, on the earth!"). Tophoven came up with this: *Man ist gut aufgehoben bei Mutter Erde.* ("We're comfortable on Mother Earth"). Beckett liked this, and when he translated his play into English, Gogo's *Ce qu'on est bien, par terre!* became simply "Sweet mother earth!"

Tophoven, who succeeded Celan teaching at the École Normale Supérieure, once happened to use the verb *einsetzen* with his colleague, saying he would "speak up for" him in some situation. Celan cringed at *einsetzen* for its connection with *Einsatzkommando*, and asked Elmar never to use the word again.

Celan's insistence that his German language was underwritten by the loss of European Jewry shows up even when he translates Marianne Moore, of all people. He chose her poem "What Are Years?," where "All are naked, none is safe," and also "A Grave," with its "ocean in which dropped things are bound to sink"—he calls this their *Untergang*, their "downfall." And even Andrew Marvell's "coy" mistress Celan calls *stumme*, "mute" (5: 369-73, 377).

Above all, Celan encountered an alter ego in the brilliant Osip Mandelshtam. Each poet had grown up close to his mother and because of his father harbored early ambivalence toward Judaism. The Russian was pushed toward a suicide attempt, accused of plagiarism, and hounded to an exile's death by Stalin. For a while, Celan even believed that Mandelshtam had returned from Siberia and (like Celan's parents) been killed by Hitler's troops.

For almost a year in 1958–59, in a shock of recognition, Celan translated Mandelshtam and composed little of his own. Bringing this kindredly alien and in 1958 scarcely known voice into the Bundesrepublik was more important than his own verse. Celan first chose Mandelshtam's 1916 elegy at his mother's funeral. The Russian begins: "Eta noč' nepopravima" ("This night is not remediable"); in German: *Diese Nacht: nicht gutzumachen* (5: 95). Celan is veering this elegy toward the night his own mother was taken away, for *nicht gutzumachen* ("not to be made good") refutes postwar Germany's *Wiedergutmachung* ("making good again"), the reparations recently agreed to for Jewish survivors.

At the end, Mandelshtam's translator takes possession of the elegy's "I." The Russian says:

John Felstiner

> *I nad mater'ju zveneli*
> *Golosa izrail'tjan*
>
> (And over my mother rang out
> voices of the Israelites)

Celan translates:

> *Judenstimmen, die nicht schwiegen,*
> *Mutter, wie es schallt.*
>
> (Jewish voices, not gone silent,
> Mother, they resound.)

Altering Mandelshtam's standoffishly named "Israelites" to "Jews," Celan also adds an entirely new thought: they have "not gone silent." Then where Mandelshtam mentions his mother in the past, Celan in the present tells his own mother how Jewish voices resound. That present tense and direct address bear the translator's imprint.

When Osip Mandelshtam's Voronezh exile poems came out in 1962, Celan took them on. He also started a long poem of his own by musing to himself:

> ... *ein Weg*
> *nach Rußland steigt dir ins Herz,*
> ...
> *der Name Ossip kommt auf dich zu, du erzählst ihm,*
> *was er schon weiß, er nimmt es, er nimmt es dir ab, mit Händen,*
> *du löst ihm den Arm von der Schulter, den rechten, den linken,*
> *du heftest die deinen an ihre Stelle, ...* (1: 284)
>
> (... a path
> to Russia rises into your heart,
> ...
> the name Osip comes toward you, you tell him
> what he already knows, he takes it, he takes it off you with hands,
> you undo the arm from his shoulder, the right one, the left,
> you fasten your own in their place ...)

This fantastic exchange makes for blood brotherhood, a translator's intimate, aggressive act of dismembering and remembering.

No other figure compelled Celan the way Mandelshtam did. "Cyrillic...I rode over the Seine, / rode it over the Rhine" (1: 197). Yet he translated mostly from French: Baudelaire, Nerval, Mallarmé, Verlaine, Rimbaud, Valéry, the Surrealists, Robert Desnos, Supervielle, Michaux, and a 1944 farce by Picasso, which itself had been a gesture of resistance. When Alain Resnais made the first death-camp documentary, *Night and Fog* (1956), Celan purposefully translated its script, only to see both Germanys balk at distributing the film. In 1957, for instance, he heard that Göttingen's city fathers were speaking out against students seeing *Night and*

Translating as Transference: Paul Celan's Versions

Fog. It's not surprising that this particular translation job infiltrated his own writing. Where the film focuses for a moment on the yard of Block Eleven at Auschwitz whose black shooting wall is "shielded against the ricochet of bullets," Celan translates this with *Kugelfang,* "bullet trap" (4: 87). Then in 1958 that word juts up at the end of his "*Engführung,*" where the reader is led to a "bullet trap on / the crumbled wall" (1: 203). Likewise the film speaks of prisoners "bludgeoned awake" at 5 a.m.— *wachgeknüppelt,* Celan says (4: 83). He did not forget using the term *Knüppel* for "bludgeon" when a decade later, visiting Heidegger's Black Forest retreat, he wrote of *Knüppel- / pfade,* "half-trod log-paths" (2: 255). With Heidegger, Celan could only go halfway along the paths of the German language. Thus in his rendition of *Night and Fog*'s closing sentence, as the camera pans in color over the present-day remains of Auschwitz, we can overhear Celan's own voice resounding: "we who look at these ruins and sincerely believe that race-madness was buried in them forever, ... that it all belongs to only *one* time and only *one* country, we who overlook what's happening around us and do not hear that the scream never falls silent"; *on crie sans fin—der Schrei nicht verstummt.*

Clearly Celan needed kindred texts. In 1957 he translated René Char's wartime Maquis notebooks, and when the German offprint appeared, Char sent a copy to his translator, inscribing it: *à Paul Celan, à qui je pensais,* "To Paul Celan, whom I was thinking of"—an uncanny and ideal tribute, as if the 1940s *Résistant* against the Nazis had anticipated his postwar translator, his German-speaking translator!

In the rare case when Celan dealt with a less kindred text, he sometimes made free with it. Attempting the first German translation of Paul Valéry's pure exercise *La Jeune Parque,* which Rilke had maintained was "untranslatable...(if only someone could convince us otherwise!)," Celan took up the challenge.[6] Valéry's opening line runs, *Qui pleure là, sinon le vent simple, à cette heure / Seule.* Celan breaks this line into six fragments: *Wer, so der Wind nicht, er nur, weint hier, zur Stunde, die / allein ist,* thus stamping the rendition as his own (4: 115).

Of all the French poets Paul Celan translated, he shows the most acute affinity with Guillaume Apollinaire, who was fascinated by (among other things) the Wandering Jew and who died of a war wound in 1918. Where Apollinaire mourns a lost love under the sign of autumn, Celan sharpens that mourning, since he lost his parents in autumn 1943. Take this, from "Signe" (Sign):

---

[6] Rainer Maria Rilke and André Gide, *Correspondance: 1909–1926,* ed. Renée Lang (Paris, 1952) 153.

John Felstiner

> *Mon Automne éternelle ô ma saison mentale*
> *Les mains des amantes d'antan jonchent ton sol*
>
> (My eternal Autumn oh my mind's season
> The hands of yesteryear's lovers strew your soil)
>
> *Du ewige, du Herbstzeit, du der Gedanken Jahr:*
> *die Hände, die mich liebten, du häufst sie ohne Zahl.* (4: 783)
>
> (You eternal, you Autumn-time, you year of thoughts:
> the hands, which loved me, you heap them without number.)

Keeping within the frame of rhymed hexameters, Celan breaks up Apollinaire's fluent opening, confronting the "mind's season" head-on as *du*. He then replaces *mentale* with *Gedanken* ("thoughts"), thus calling up *gedenken* ("bear in mind"), just as his *Herbstzeit* ("Autumn-time") and *Jahr* ("year") together evoke the Yiddish *Yortseit*, the yearly commemoration of a parent's death. Celan turns the female lovers (*amantes*) into "hands that loved me"; now they can include his mother's. And he activates autumn: "you heap" those hands.

Celan did not fail to translate Apollinaire's "Schinderhannes," his satire on an 18th-century German brigand notoriously cruel to Jews. This ditty brought out a new voice in Celan, a light tone masking anger. His version (and my version) ends like this:

> *Denn heut, wenns dunkel wird am Rheine,*
> *bring ich den reichen Juden um.*
> *Hell glänzt, wenn harzige Fackeln scheinen,*
> *als Gulden jede Maienblum!*
>
> *So hält man Tafel rund im Kreise*
> *und f...t und lacht beim Abendschmaus,*
> *und wird ganz schwach, nach deutscher Weise,*
> *und geht und bläst ein Leben aus.* (4: 789)
>
> (Today when dusk falls on the Rhine,
> That rich Jew will be mine to slay.
> When resin torches brightly shine,
> florins are ours like flowers in May!
>
> The gang sits down to eat awhile,
> farts, laughs, digs in with fork and knife,
> then softens up, in German style,
> and goes and snuffs out one more life.)

Several years later Celan took up Apollinaire again, choosing "Les Colchiques" (Autumn Crocus). Before the first line has gone by, his translation declares its parti pris, erasing the key word "but" from this "poisonous but pretty" flower:

Translating as Transference: Paul Celan's Versions

Le pré est vénéneux mais joli en automne.
(The meadow is poisonous but pretty in autumn.)

Der Herbst lässt seine Wiese so schön, so giftig blühen. (4: 793)
(Autumn makes its meadow bloom so beautiful, so poisonous.)

For Celan, what is beautiful *is* poisonous: the issue had arisen in his notorious "Deathfugue" (1944), where the commandant shouts "play death more sweetly."

Celan returned to Apollinaire, in a sense, one last time. He was living alone at 6 Avenue Émile Zola, just across the quay from Pont Mirabeau. Why Pont Mirabeau? Years before he had quoted Apollinaire's poem of that title—a song of transiency, loss, and night—and had written these lines:

> *Von der Brücken-*
> *quader, von der*
> *er ins Leben hinüber-*
> *prallte, flügge*
> *von Wunden,—vom*
> *Pont Mirabeau.* (1: 288)

> (From the bridge-
> stone, from which
> he bounded over in-
> to life, fledged
> by wounds,—from the
> Pont Mirabeau.)

In April 1970 Celan went from the bridge into the Seine River and though a strong swimmer, drowned unobserved. His last letter, to that childhood "orphaned" friend in Israel, had quoted Kafka about finding happiness "only if I can raise the world into the Pure, the True, the Immutable." Celan was still making kindred spirits speak for him. A biography of Hölderlin was found on his desk, open to an underlined passage about the great poet's last demented years: "Sometimes this genius goes dark and sinks down into the bitter well of his heart."[7] Yet Celan had not, I noticed one cold night in Normandy while working through his library, underlined the rest of that sentence in the Hölderlin biography. Though Celan did not underline it, I will close now by underlining it for him: "*but mostly his apocalyptic star glitters wondrously.*"

---

[7] Wilhelm Michel, *Das Leben Friedrich Hölderlins* (1940; Frankfurt, 1967) 516.

BRIGITTE SCHULTZE

Highways, Byways, and Blind Alleys in Translating Drama: Historical and Systematic Aspects of a Cultural Technique

I

Translation scholars and translators of dramatic texts find themselves at a disadvantage in comparison with philologists and translators dealing with poetry and narrative fiction:[1] literature dealing with theoretical premises and practical aspects of translating poetry[2] and prose fiction would certainly fill several meters in a bookshelf. In contrast, discussions of theoretical premises of drama translation and of translatory strategies based on such premises would fit into one small volume.[3]

If I am not mistaken, this state of affairs, first of all, has to be attributed to the fact that translation of poetry and prose must take into account the aesthetic codes and functioning of one medium only: the written text (i.e., literature). Drama translation, in contrast, implies simultaneous transfer into two forms of communication: monomedial literature (reading) and polymedial theatre (performance). To quote Raymond van den Broeck, it is the *"dual* nature of the theatrical text," the coexistence of "both a literary and performance text,"[4] which complicates the task of working out theoretical positions. Suffice it to recall that a translator's anticipation of a series of potential performance texts implies a host of imponderables, among them the cultural competence of target side audiences in relation to the source culture. If we accept the idea that drama translation is an operation

---

[1] Cf. SCHULTZE, "In Search of a Theory" 267–268; VAN DEN BROECK 97.

[2] A specific case is given, when poetry is meant to be read in private and also to be declaimed in public, i.e., 'performed', as e.g., some of Majakovskij's and E.E. Cumming's poetry.

[3] Most of the books and articles (approximately 900 items) collected in the bibliography *Probleme der Dramenübersetzung 1960–1988* (1991) contain translation criticism of single translated plays and also case studies of a limited corpus of translated texts; the amount of scholarly work devoted to theoretical problems is rather small.

[4] VAN DEN BROECK 98; cf. AALTONEN, *Gallous Stories* 12; SCHULTZE, "In Search of a Theory" 267–274.

analogous to the transposition of written drama into performance, we have to point out the fact that theatrological research dealing with the transposition of written drama into performance is still far from a breakthrough. Therefore, philologists and translators in search of a sound theoretical framework for drama translation have to do the job of theatrologists before they can move on to the specific questions of translation studies. Furthermore, theatrology has not yet made available a widely accepted metalanguage suitable for a discussion of the whole operation of transposing written drama into performance. These and further facts and circumstances make the task of outlining a theory of translating drama even more complicated and challenging.[5]

However, if more scholars interested in the theoretical premises of translating drama took the trouble of evaluating a larger number of scholarly work on translating drama, they would certainly find out that altogether there has already been impressive progress in this field of research. Among the scholars who have contributed in more recent times is Sirkku Aaltonen from Finland. Sirkku Aaltonen identifies the impact of exterior and interior communication, contextualization, deviation from linguistic norm, and many other features of drama. In her comparative study[6] of two Finnish translations of Synge's *The Playboy of the Western World*, Aaltonen views cultural difference as a key position in translating drama. This perspective may have been prompted by the high degree of cultural difference in the given case study. Cultural difference, however, is not specific to dramatic texts; it may occur in all types of fiction, even in non-fictional texts. Therefore, scholars have to search for key positions, which pertain to the very nature of drama. Such a key concept has been developed and described by the Bulgarian philologist and translator Sophia Totzeva. In her doctoral dissertation as well as in a number of articles, she examines an especially large portion of theoretical work on drama and also of scholarly contributions to a theory of translating drama. As do a number of other scholars, Totzeva starts from the idea that translating drama is an operation largely analogous to the transposition of written drama into performance. She chooses "Theatrical Potential"[7] as a key position in translation theory.[8] This term highlights the capacity of dramatic texts to generate 'theatre texts.' This concept and term is meant to replace a number of concepts not appropriate to scholarly debate: "effectiveness on the stage" (see below), "theatricality" and also the Slavic "sceničnost'"—to give the Russian variant. The

---

[5] Susan BASSNETT ("Ways Through the Labyrinth"), who tried to formulate a sort of theoretical approach to translating drama in the 1980s, has, as she told me, given up hope of ever gaining access to this "labyrinth."

[6] AALTONEN, *Gallous Stories*, 1993.

[7] Cf. SCHULTZE, "In Search of a Theory" 267–268, 270.

[8] Cf. TOTZEVA, *Das Theatrale Potential*.

concept of Theatrical Potential ("Theatrales Potential") is developed in connection with such fundamentals as the dual nature of drama, the coexistence of exterior and interior communication, and the twofold reference of dramatic texts, i.e., reference to both oral and literary communication. This concept also starts from, and underscores, the complex set of contextualizations which constitute a kind of operating platform in any process of generating theatrical meaning. Totzeva's concept of Theatrical Potential also describes a complex set of codes and textual markers which are especially connected with situative and pragmatic context and with oral communication: grammatical and semantic gaps, repetitive structures, deviation from lexical norms and many others (see below). And since *the* theatrical meaning of a given text does not exist, Theatrical Potential is by no means a normative concept: Drama is conceived as an extremely open and complex medium of communication—more precisely as two open and complex media of communication. Sophia Totzeva's study has to be considered as one of the "highways" in the discussion at hand.

My paper will concentrate on three topics: first I shall present what I consider rather hapless attempts at outlining a theory of drama translation or at formulating what may be called a theoretical approach to translating drama; next I shall discuss some characteristic trends within the history of drama translation; and in the third and final section of this paper I will deal with the key category Theatrical Potential.

Before touring the highways, byways and blind alleys of translating drama, I shall recall some of the fundamental poetological aspects of drama. As David Birch's circumspective survey *The Language of Drama* seems to be highly suitable for recalling essentials, it may be helpful to start by quoting Birch:

> No text is ever completed. It is always meanings in process. Similarly, no matter how thorough and detailed the performance processes may be, a production does not complete those processes, it simply creates a new text for a particular time, place and reception (12).

> Meaning should not be restricted simply to what words mean, but to the many levels of meaning involved in language as action; in the social and institutional transactions and interactions of people involved in communication. Most of these meanings never find their way into a dictionary—they are meanings involving body movement, facial expressions, voice quality, speed of delivery (24).

> To consider a drama text as 'the play' and to assume that it is a single entity rather than a multiplicity of potential performances is to ignore 'the context of circumstance'; is to reduce any critical practice to pointlessness (30).[9]

---

[9] Cf. BIRCH 12–53.

Brigitte Schultze

From these and similar statements it follows that translators ought to render as much of a play's contextualizations, openness and ambiguity in the target text as possible. It also follows that translatory strategies which aim at completing grammatical or semantic gaps are detrimental to the very nature of drama. By mentioning meaning which is not contained in the words themselves, Birch, albeit implicitly, indicates both the importance of non-dialogue text (in German "Nebentext" or "extradialogischer Text") and the relation between dialogue and non-dialogue text.

It may also be helpful to highlight two basic features connected with the dual nature of drama: the co-presence of interior and exterior communication and the fact that dramatic language refers to two different codes and traditions—to oral communication and to literature. In other words, language in drama is linked both with spontaneous, situative speech and with the conventions and traditions of aesthetic communication. The co-presence of exterior and interior communication may confront translators with normative decisions.[10] Sometimes translators have to decide whether they are going to render the point of view of the characters in a play or the point of view which readers or an audience may arrive at. The fact that dramatic language is linked with oral communication and also with literature may be a case of specific concern when a drama chosen for translation originates in a different historical period. In such instances, translators may decide to reduce some of the 'literary' features of the play and incorporate elements of spontaneous oral communication of their day. These preliminary considerations may be helpful in the following assessment of some of the theoretical attempts to understand drama translating.

II

First, I shall examine some concepts and terms which mainly, though not exclusively, have their origin in theatrical practice. Theatrical practice has contributed a number of summarizing or collective terms to the debate, among them the catchwords "translating for the theatre" and "effectiveness on the stage." The formula "translating for the theatre" often indicates that a translator or student of translation theory is not aware of the dual character of drama.[11]

An example taken from Witkacy's antimimetic play *Gyubal Wahazar* (1921) may illustrate the relevance of this point. The Polish dramatist uses linguistic

---

[10] FRANK/SCHULTZE 107–109.

[11] HAAG 1984; KRUGER 1986; the headline of VAN DEN BROECK's article (1986) is somewhat misleading since the author in fact discusses the dual nature of drama.

collage, primarily macaronic style, in all of his plays; in addition to Polish, there is also English, French, Latin and other vocabulary—both in dialogue and in non-dialogue texts. Of course, such heterogeneous linguistic textures, when occurring in non-dialogue text, can only be noticed and enjoyed by readers of the play; a theatre audience will be unaware of them. Let us now look at a piece of non-dialogue text which contains such a macaronic element. For the sake of convenience, the Polish 'portion' is given in English. Several characters are entering a room: "The whole crew, *y compris* four hangmen apart from WAHAZAR." The French formula *y compris*, "among them," "including," stresses the four hangmen within the crew and also the fact that WAHAZAR belongs to this group. This should help readers with their interpretation. Two German translators, who—so it seems—understand their job as "translating for the theatre," just skip the formula *y compris*. Thus the formula "translating for the theatre" may indeed cause fundamental misunderstandings.[12] It may lead to translating only for the use of theatres, at the cost of that portion of drama which can only be taken in by readers.

The summary term "effectiveness on the stage" suffers from the fact that this effectiveness can neither be clarified nor measured. The effectiveness of French High Tragedy will certainly be different from the effectiveness of melodrama or monodrama in verse.

Theatre practice is also the donor of the terminological triad "speakability," "playability" and "spontaneous comprehension."[13] By focusing on performance, this terminological triad, not unlike the formula "effectiveness on the stage," neglects that there is also a literary text in its own right. (Here again, the information *y compris* would be considered a *quantité négligeable*.) By concentrating on the actor's role in creating theatrical meaning, the triad disregards the importance of nonverbal sign systems in a performance.

Moreover, every single term implies somewhat dubious 'ideals.' The dubious nature of "speakability" can easily be demonstrated by recalling the role of 'hard words' in English plays: those in Osborne's *Look Back in Anger*—"pusillanimous," "sycophantic" and others,[14]—ought to be translated by words equally hard to pronounce and equally hard to understand.[15] By the way, the Russian and the

---

[12] Cf. SCHULTZE, "Stanisław Ignacy Witkiewicz's 'Drama-Theater'" 482.

[13] Cf. SCHULTZE, "Theorie der Dramenübersetzung" 5–17; SCHULTZE, "In Search of a Theory" 268–270.

[14] OSBORNE 21–22, 49.

[15] Hans Sahl, the translator of Osborne's play into German, imports the hard word "pusillanimous" as is and adds a piece of what may be called metatranslation: "Also das Wort heißt: 'Pusillanimous.' Geschrieben: p-u-s-i-l-l-a-n-i-m-o-u-s, Adjektiv. Es bedeutet: Mangel an

French variants of "speakability" lead even further up a blind alley: "bien en bouche" and "udoboproiznosimost'," meaning "convenient pronunciation."[16] Taken seriously, such categories may lead to banalization[17] and to a reduction of theatrical meaning.

The blurred nature of the coined term "playability" is also obvious. It may suffice to recall how much information can be conveyed by silence which may be marked in a text (e.g., by an ellipsis), but which may also have to be 'detected' by actors with a reading competence for dramatic texts. Of course, the term "playability" ignores the fact that there are numerous plays in which the actors' movements, gestures, facial expressions, etc. are not controlled by dialogue, i.e., in which dialogue and body action are totally independent of one another or even played off against one another (see below).

Even the formula "playable speakability" ("spielbare Sprachlichkeit"[18]) which, having consulted the stage manager Ansgar Haag,[19] Mary Snell-Hornby proposes as a key term in discussing drama translations, has not led to any breakthroughs in research. It has to be pointed out that this formula, like the terminological triad, is rather blurred and anything but precise. Like the categories discussed above, this term also implies normative positions in relation to drama translation. "Playable speakability," to give an example, does not envisage the type of medieval or baroque drama in which dramatis personae have to step forward (to the apron, the forestage) and recite their texts; nor does it envisage types of theatrical performance in which fragments of text are played off against body action, totally independent of the verbal patterns that are recited by the characters. "Spontaneous comprehension,"[20] like "playability," focuses on dialogue to an extent incompatible with a large portion of texts for the theatre—and which is anything but compatible with present-day theatre practice. After all, there many plays in which human words, though articulated by the actors, have to be taken in as mere murmur. This triad, which favors "translating for the theatre," thus tends to neglect the true, dual, nature of drama, suggesting translatory strategies which will lead to a reduction of incentives for a performance. It cannot be disputed, however, that the terminological triad is applicable in theatre practice. During

---

Charakterfestigkeit, Kleinmut, Engherzigkeit, Bösartigkeit, Feigheit. Vom Lateinischen 'pusillus,' sehr klein, und 'animus,' der Geist" (OSBORNE, *Blick zurück im Zorn* 31).

[16] SCHULTZE, "Theorie der Dramenübersetzung" 14; SCHULTZE, "In Search of a Theory" 268.

[17] PAVIS 30; cf. SCHULTZE, "Theorie der Dramenübersetzung" 14.

[18] SNELL-HORNBY 104–108; cf. AALTONEN, *Gallous Stories* 21.

[19] HAAG 218–224.

[20] Cf. AALTONEN, *Gallous Stories* 21; SCHULTZE, "Theorie der Dramenübersetzung" 14.

rehearsals, the given situation will tell actors and stage managers what exactly is meant by a particular term.

Leaving theatre practice aside, I shall now discuss two attempts at dealing with translation theory, which may be identified as the fruits of mainly brainwork. The first case is Patrice Pavis' concept of "verbo-corps"[21] (1987 and later); the second one is Ulrike Essler-Raghunath's approach to drama translation (1990)[22] based on Hans J. Vermeer's "theory of scopos" ("Skopos-Theorie"[23]).

Pavis' attempt at outlining theoretical foundations of drama translation differs from most of the other proposals of this kind: his theoretical model contains the complete series of "realizations" of drama (in German "Konkretisationen")—from the initial stage of the inception of a play in the author's mind, even in his subconsciousness, to the written drama (source text), to the subsequent translation and, finally, to the moment of reception by a target side audience. Moreover, Pavis' proposal is supported by a number of theories, among them semiotics and psychoanalysis. The key concept, "verbo-corps," assumes a sort of union between language and gesture, which is seen as language- and culture-specific. According to Pavis, this pivot of theatricality is grounded in the author's subconsciousness. In order to grasp this culture-specific "verbo-corps," the translator—in a sort of hypothetical operation—has to reconstruct the source side union of language and gesture. This "magma" of the play, then, has to be preserved throughout the whole series of textual and theatrical realizations. Pavis' highly speculative theoretical model of drama translation, so it seems, has not been developed further by other scholars. It leaves a gap between theory and translatory practice which cannot be closed.[24] It may be helpful to recall that the idea of monolithic cultural units is increasingly rejected and refuted by cultural anthropologists; in contrast to earlier positions, cultures are seen as dynamic processes of balancing out 'the own and the foreign.'

While Patrice Pavis' framework rests on the widely accepted structuralist approach, Ulrike Essler-Raghunath's theoretical basis seems to be insufficient. The author, also a translator of two modern English plays, Tariq Ali's *Indian Nights* and Howard Brenton's *Greenland* into German, tried to apply Vermeer's "theory of scopos" to drama translation. It may be therefore helpful to recall Vermeer's central theoretical positions. According to Vermeer, the text to be translated is "an

---

[21] PAVIS 25–44; cf. SCHULTZE, "Theorie der Dramenübersetzung" 14–15; AALTONEN, *Gallous Stories* 21.

[22] ESSLER-RAGHUNATH 251–266.

[23] VERMEER 69–151.

[24] During a workshop organized by the Göttingen Center for the Study of Literary Translations, Patrice Pavis admitted the rather "speculative nature" of his model of drama translation; he also stated that this model is "extremely far away from the practical job of translating drama."

element of communicative action in a given situation" ("kommunikatives Handlungselement in Situation"). The translatory process is determined by a given "purpose" ("scopos").[25] Vermeer considers his concept "valid for *all* sorts of texts" (emphasis H.J.V.).[26] However, it remains unclear whether or not this implies, to quote van den Broeck, "both a literary and performance text." A further basic category introduced here is that of "effect" (in German "Wirkung"): "effect" in the source text has to be "kept constant"[27] in the target text. Yet again, we encounter the somewhat ambiguous term "effect," which can neither be measured nor evaluated. For Essler-Raghunath "the scopos, effectiveness on the stage, is already given."[28] Feeling that "effectiveness on the stage" needs further specification, Essler-Raghunath resorts to the terms "speakability" and "playability." She regrets that both terms have not yet been clarified theoretically. She continues, suggesting that the "ideal scopos might be the translation for one specific performance."[29] The author thus favors a type of drama translation, which may be called 'one-way-translation.'[30]

At this point, it may be helpful to recall Birch's position: Birch rightly emphasizes that there is a multitude of literary texts and of performance texts in any drama. Therefore, 'one-way-translation,' i.e., the type of translation which is the result of one specific *mise en scène*, might be seen as an interesting, instructive experiment rather than an "ideal."

As one of the author's own translations, that of Brenton's *Greenland*, is a comedy, Essler-Raghunath extends the "theory of scopos" to the case of translating comedy. This leads to the introduction of a "sub-scopos" ("to make the audience laugh") and also to a hierarchical order of "scopoi":

1. Achievement of effectiveness on the stage (All embracing scopos)
2. Maintaining comic effect (1. sub-scopos) ...
3. Maintaining realiae (2. sub-scopos).[31]

Here again, a proposal concerning theory of drama translation seems to overlook the problems connected with the measurability of "effect." Moreover, the given triad of "purpose" in translatory process falls short of what deserves to be taken as a sound theoretical approach to translating drama. Instead of "maintaining effec-

---

[25] VERMEER 31.
[26] VERMEER 56.
[27] VERMEER 67.
[28] ESSLER-RAGHUNATH 253.
[29] ESSLER-RAGHUNATH 253.
[30] Cf. SCHULTZE, "Theorie der Dramenübersetzung" 6, 11.
[31] ESSLER-RAGHUNATH 260.

tiveness on the stage," the aim clearly ought to be finding out about the Theatrical Potential contained in a given play. Instead of "maintaining of comic effect," the aim ought to be ascertaining the specific contextualizations[32] and types of comic devices which function in a given play. Summing up, it should be noted that an approach to translating drama based on the category "effect" does not meet the requirements of scholarly work on the cultural technique "translating drama."

As mentioned above, the complex set of contextualizations and of the other translatory device called "Theatrical Potential"—which will be discussed in the last section of this paper—may be seen as a novel approach to our topic. Before discussing a number of items subsumed under the term 'Theatrical Potential,' I shall examine two trends in the history of drama translation: the coexistence of two variants of translated drama, i.e., the coexistence of drama for readers and drama for performances,[33] and the application of 'rules of thumb'[34] in translatory transfer—mainly of comedies, but also of melodrama.

III

Both trends to be discussed here are characteristic of the second half of the 19th century in particular, yet they can also be found in translations which originated in the second half of the 18th and in the first half of the 19th centuries. Of course, it has to be noted that there have always been translators who—either intuitively or consciously—succeeded in rendering 'two texts in one,' i.e., in translating "both a literary and performance text."[35] However, according to comparative analysis of drama translations, such achievements were relatively rare during the 18th and 19th centuries, became more frequent in the first half of the 20th century, and have constituted a new trend since the late 1960s.

First, I shall examine 'double-tracked' drama translation. In this case, translations for readers used to be complete translations with translatory deviations

---

[32] Cf. NASH 34–37 and others. Nash's study, which highlights the role of contextualization in bringing about different types of humor, offers help in spotting witty and other comic structures. I am obliged to Sophia Totzeva, who drew my attention to this title.

[33] Cf. SCHULTZE, "In Search of a Theory" 268–269; SCHULTZE, "Russisch-deutsche und polnisch-deutsche Dramenübersetzung" 525–528; SCHULTZE, "Probleme mit der intrigenlosen Komödie" 221–223, 226.

[34] BASSNETT, "Translating for the Theatre" 78–79; AALTONEN, "Rewriting the Exotic" 139.

[35] Kenneth E. LARSON ("Wieland's Shakespeare" 229–251) demonstrates that Wieland's Shakespeare translation of *King Lear*, though rendered in prose, succeeds in preserving basic elements of Shakespearean Theatrical Potential—syntactic rhythms, rhetoric, deviations from lexical norms etc.

mainly occurring on a microstructural level. By contrast, versions meant for performance used to be adapted to the conventions and traditions of the target culture—more precisely, to target theatre culture. For example, out of seven German translations of Gogol's *Revizor* ("The Inspector General") which appeared between 1854 and 1901, four are abbreviated adaptions, while three are complete translations with only microtextual deviations.[36] One of the rather frequent trends in 'translations for readers' is "expansion":[37] Translators seem to freely fill in grammatical and semantic gaps and add pieces of information which future readers might need. This tendency to complete what seems to be incomplete and to explain what appears to ask for an explanation is often indicative of the fact that translators of 'reading versions' are not very conscious of Theatrical Potential in general. Frequently, inversions are changed into regular word order, linguistic sub-codes are replaced by literary language, etc. Though the production of translations for readers is especially characteristic of the 19th century,[38] translations primarily intended for readers are published to this day.[39]

Translations, more often adaptations for stage use, employ different strategies of abbreviation and adaptation. For example, for many decades, up to the beginning of the 20th century, in German and Austrian theatres, comedies had to have a playing time of two or two-and-a-half hours. Consequently, foreign comedies (English, French and others) had to be shortened considerably. Often, five act plays were turned into three act plays on German speaking stages.[40]

If my observations are correct, the use of 'rules of thumb' in translating drama is especially frequent in adapted comedies and in adapted melodrama. Though, as we have seen, the comprehensive term "effectiveness on the stage" is not suitable for scholarly work on problems of drama translation, there are grounds to assume that many translators had certain ideas about "effectiveness on the stage." Especially in connection with a growing routine of translating foreign comedies for a booming theatre, translators seem to have applied rules of thumb that were useful in quick translation and adaptation of foreign comedies. Instead of transferring the unique patterns and codes of Theatrical Potential contained in a given text, they made use of a tested set of translatory strategies. Among these strategies are many characteristics of spontaneous oral communication—inversion, colloqui-

---

[36] SCHULTZE, "Probleme mit der intrigenlosen Komödie" 190, 227–228, 232–233.

[37] TOTZEVA, "Zum Umgang mit der Expansion" 22–33; SCHULTZE, "Probleme mit der intrigenlosen Komödie" 229, 232; in his translation of Wyspiański's *Wesele* ("The Wedding") "for intelligent readers of English" (p. 10), Gerard T. Kapolka adds a number of lines, obviously, in order to be able to complete pieces of information.

[38] Cf. SCHULTZE, "Das kanonische Bühnenwerk" 381.

[39] Cf. note 35; SCHULTZE, "Das kanonische Bühnenwerk" 369–403.

[40] SCHULTZE, "Probleme mit der intrigenlosen Komödie" 255, 263.

Highways, Byways, and Blind Alleys in Translating Drama

alisms, enumeration of incoherent details, stereotype exclamations and many others. Theatre critics, especially in the second half of the 19th century, seem to have had a close eye for such elements—no matter whether they were taken from the given source text or not. For example, one of the first German translations of Griboedov's *Gore ot uma* ("Woe from Wit") is welcomed by a critic with these words: "We cannot judge the value of the translation, since we are not in a position to compare it with the original. However, it [the translation, B.S.] reads easily and fluently."[41] The critic's remark is quite to the point: Griboedov's satire is rendered as a very elegant and witty verse comedy. However, the device of Theatrical Potential employed by the translator has almost nothing to do with the specific aesthetic codes of the source text.

During the first decades of the twentieth century, translators more and more got away from translating by rule of thumb. There was a definite tendency to produce complete translations which adhered to the poetic and theatrical codes of the source texts. Theatres tended to use adaptations already on the market or produce adaptations on the basis of complete translations. Only after the Second World War, especially since the late 1960s, have translators seemed to be more conscious of the dual nature of drama, of the networks of contextualization that function in every play, of Theatrical Potential which is different in every drama. To name some of the basic components of Theatrical Potential: the coexistence of exterior and interior communication, the dual reference of language in drama (both to literature and to oral communication), repetitive structures (e.g., so-called "*Ansatzwörter*," that is, recurring words to which dual or even triple meaning is attached), presuppositions, inversions, grammatical and semantic gaps, deviations from norms within the lexical field (slang and other variants of linguistic subcode, foreign words), the relation between dialogue and non-dialogue text.[42] Some of the components of Theatrical Potential will now be briefly examined and illustrated by examples.

IV

The relevance of a translator's opting for either interior or exterior communication can be illustrated by one of the climactic moments in Gogol's *Revizor* ("The Inspector General"). Towards the end of the tragicomedy (act V, scene 8), in the

---

[41] SCHULTZE, "Russisch-deutsche und Polnisch-deutsche Dramenübersetzung" 526.

[42] I owe the concept of "*Ansatzwort*" to Sophia Totzeva. For a profound discussion of this element of Theatrical Potential see her published dissertation *Das Theatrale Potential des dramatischen Textes*.

so-called dénouement, the character Artemij Filipovič accuses the devil of having induced the dignitaries of the Russian provincial town to take the fop and gambler Chlestakov for an "extraordinary personality." The crucial phrase is: "Čert poputal." As the Russian verb "poputat'" carries a twofold semantic load, translators have to choose between (1) "the devil confused / irritated [us]" and (2) "the devil seduced [us]." The first translatory solution represents the contextual plane of interior communication. Though the duped dignitaries of the provincial town have gained some insight into the situation at hand, they persist in a state of 'existential blindness,' i.e., they are incapable of understanding the fundamental wrongs in their way of life. They only feel they have been "confused" by the devil. In contrast, readers and theatre audiences may arrive at a different result: that the devil himself—playing the role of an invisible intriguer in a comedy otherwise without any intrigue[43]—concocted the whole scheme. At this point, it may be helpful to recall that for Gogol the devil was 'reality,' no matter how intensely he tried to get away from his (largely culture-specific) dualism. The biblical motive of seduction by the devil functions as an aid to interpreting the whole play: *Revizor* abounds with hints to the devil. There are about 50 direct namings of the evil force and about one hundred allusions to the devil; many of the allusions can only be deciphered by those who are acquainted with the codes of Russian folklore.[44]

Of course, the verb "poputat'" confronts translators with a normative decision. No other language I know of can express 'confusion/irritation' and 'seduction' (with religious overtones) with one and the same word. Translators therefore have to opt for either interior or exterior communication. The first option supports situative context and pragmatic meaning of the action occurring in the play, whereas the second option supports the very meaning of Gogol's tragicomedy, especially meaning contained in the deep structures. In most translations I have examined (English, French, German) translators opt for interior communication. For example, throughout the 19th century, German translators preferred the context of what is going on in the play, i.e., interior communication. One of the most prolific Russian-German translators of the 20th century, however, Johannes von Guenther, opts for exterior communication; he chooses the verbal expression "verführt" (seduced).[45] Since this verb appears more than once in von Guenther's translation, its specific semantic weight may be noticed by readers and audiences.

---

[43] SCHULTZE, "Probleme mit der intrigenlosen Komödie" 187–239.

[44] HAMMERSCHMID/RIEMEKASTEN 269–302, especially 270.

[45] HAMMERSCHMID/RIEMEKASTEN 296; SCHULTZE, "Russisch-deutsche und polnisch-deutsche Dramenübersetzung" 520–521.

It should be noted that the moment of dénouement examined here is omitted in D.J. Campbell's English translation and adaptation of Gogol's play.[46] This omission is in line with Campbell's translatory strategy and interpretation: different from Gogol's obsessions, the devil in this translation mainly figures as a curse—not as an invisible agent in the events of the play.

The dual context of dramatic language—oral communication with its markers of spontaneity and situation, and literature with its time-bound aesthetic codes—is a permanent challenge for translators. Of course this is a field in which 'period-specific' features of Theatrical Potential are especially evident. Suffice it to recall periods of drama history, classicism, expressionism and others, in which language is characterized by a high degree of aesthetic formation, and other periods, naturalism and the last decades of our century, in which dramatic language tends to be close to oral communication. Comparative analysis of translated plays shows that highly 'literary' and nonmimetic dramatic language, when translated one hundred years later is often brought closer to the codes of present day oral communication; a certain number of period-specific markers are eliminated. To give an example, four out of five foreign (American, German and Russian) translators of Witkacy's antimimetic play *Gyubal Whazar* (1921) reduced a certain amount of 'marked language' and brought the verbal texture closer to oral and theatrical codes of the time when the translations were produced—the 1970s and the 1980s.[47] The translators, so it seems, unanimously tried to make Witkacy's ingenious dramatic parable of dictatorship and totalitarianism accessible and acceptable to present-day readers and audiences. In this instance, the American translation by Daniel Gerould is especially rich in colloquialisms and in slang.

Isotopic structures ("Isotopien"), produced either by recurrent lexical material (words or phrases) or by words belonging to a semantic field, also belong to the basic components of Theatrical Potential. They play an important role in producing coherence in drama. Occasionally, single sequences, scenes or acts are characterized by specific isotopic patterns. In the last decades of the 20th century translators have tended to be well aware of this feature and its functioning in the production of theatrical meaning.

Within these isotopic structures occur repetitive words—*Ansatzwörter*, i.e., context-supporting words—which play a more specific role in creating theatrical meaning. By referring to two or more different contexts, *Ansatzwörter* carry dual or even triple meaning. Very often, signals of controversy and conflict are attached to these structural items. The process of contextualization which is cued by *Ansatzwörter* may include both dialogue and non-dialogue text. This will be illus-

---

[46] GOGOL, *The Government Inspector* 104.
[47] SCHULTZE, "Stanislaw Ignacy Witkiewiczs Dramen" 488.

trated by an example[48] taken from Dürrenmatt's tragicomedy *Der Besuch der alten Dame* ("The Visit of the Old Lady"). The title of Patrick Bowles' translation is *The Visit*. The passage is taken from the third act: ILL's shop is crowded with several inhabitants of the small town Güllen, among them the TEACHER and MAN ONE (DER ERSTE), who has just bought an axe in ILL's shop. Two reporters have come in who want to interview ILL and take photographs of him. The FIRST REPORTER wishes that the selling of the axe to MAN ONE (the butcher) be repeated so he can take a photograph of this action:

PRESSEMANN I	... Am besten: Verkaufen Sie das Beil.
ILL zögernd	Das Beil?
PRESSEMANN I	Dem Metzger. Er hat es ja schon in der Hand. Geben Sie das Mordinstrument mal her, guter Mann. *Er nimmt dem Ersten das Beil aus der Hand. ... Er arrangiert die Stellung.*
...	
PRESSEMANN II	... strahlen vor Glück, strahlen, strahlen ...
...	
DER ZWEITE	Klug, äußerst klug, keinen Unsinn zu schwatzen.[49]

The English translation of this passage runs as follows:

FIRST REPORTER	...—I've got it: we'll take you selling an axe.
ILL (*hesitant*)	An axe?
FIRST REPORTER	To the butcher. You gotta have realism for punch. Give me that homicidal weapon here.
	...
(*He arranges the shot*)	
...	
SECOND REPORTER	... you're radiant with happiness ... happily radiant.
...	
MAN TWO	Very smart, you didn't shoot your mouth.[50]

This translation confirms a trend which I have discovered in many American translations of German, Russian, Polish and other plays: the strengthening of

---

[48] Sophia Totzeva allowed me to use this example which is also used in her monograph.
[49] DÜRRENMATT, *Der Besuch der alten Dame* 100–101.
[50] DÜRRENMATT, *The Visit* 126.

linguistic sub-codes (slang), or at the very least an addition of colloquialisms.[51] Often, single words or phrases entirely unmarked in the source text are marked in the target text. This "interference" (in German "Störung") within the verbal texture will also generate Theatrical Potential, unless it occurs too frequently as to be considered a deviation from the norm any longer. If my view is correct, this trend can be explained with reference to American theatre traditions.

In the case at hand, the phrases "you gotta have" and "you didn't shoot your mouth" are not inspired by the source text. The first phrase was added by the translator, the second is modeled after the source text. However, the German phrase "keinen Unsinn zu schwatzen" does not have the slightest tinge of slang, it actually sounds somewhat homely—in this instance even with ironic, menacing undertones.

The repetitive (isotopic) structures based on the words "axe," "butcher" and "radiant" ("Axt," "Metzger," "strahlen") are fully rendered in the target text. The pattern suggested by "axe" and "butcher" is part and parcel of contextualization. On the one hand, "axe," "butcher" and also "homicidal weapon" belong to situative context; on the other hand, they refer to CLAIRE ZACHANASSIAN's murder threat, which is upsetting ILL and turns out to be an instrument of open and hidden terror for almost everybody in the community. What is remarkable about this translation is that in the passage quoted, Bowles introduces *Ansatzwörter* for the whole play: the translator introduces the words *shoot* and *shot*, both of which support contextualization and textual coherence throughout the play. The German equivalents are "schießen," "feuern," "Feuer," etc. One of these items is inserted in non-dialogue text, the other one in dialogue: the German phrase "Er arrangiert die Stellung" ("He arranges the position") refers firstly to the taking of pictures; it may also be interpreted as a hint to the loading of a gun. In introducing the *Ansatzwort* "shot," the translator strengthens the play's coherence and overall meaning. The fact that this translatory operation takes place within non-dialogue text indicates that Bowles is well aware of the dual nature of drama: only readers will know of this additional piece of information. In the second instance, the *Ansatzwort* is added to dialogue: "you didn't shoot your mouth." This translatory operation serves two contexts, the situation at hand and the overall situation of revenge, menace and terror. We may safely assume that the translatory operations examined here were carried out intentionally. This is a competent handling of the cultural technique of translating drama.

The last item of Theatrical Potential to be discussed here is grammatical gaps, that is, variants of ellipsis. The types of gaps occurring most frequently are

---

[51] Cf. SCHULTZE, "Stanisław Ignacy Witkiewicz's Dramen" 486, 488; SCHULTZE, "A Case of Delayed Cultural Transfer."

omissions of copula, personal pronouns and verbs. It is important to note that this observation pertains to English and German but not necessarily to every language. A completely different situation is encountered in the Slavic languages, where the use of personal pronouns in connection with verbs is facultative, and the use of copula is facultative as well—Russian being an exception in that it does not possess the copula.[52] Such grammatical gaps point to the link between drama and oral communication. For persons involved in an act of communication, grammatical gaps can easily be closed with the help of pragmatic and situative context. As a rule, this is also the case in dramatic texts. Of course, when occurring in drama, grammatical gaps open up opportunities for gesture and other forms of nonverbal communication.

Regardless of the connection between dramatic texts and oral communication, there are translations in which copulas, verbs, personal pronouns, etc. absent in the source text are systematically inserted into the target text.[53] Such attempts at grammatical completeness are especially frequent in drama translations for readers. As mentioned above, throughout the 19th century, drama translations intended to be reading matter bear such features. Obviously, actors and stage managers are anything but satisfied with closed textual structures. When used for performances, such translations are 'opened up' again, i.e., actors and stage managers often eliminate a certain number of copula, verbs, personal pronouns and other *genera verbi*.[54] Prompters' copies are quite illustrative of this case.

Even translators who seem to be well aware of the role and importance of grammatical and semantic gaps in drama tend to be somewhat cautious in reproducing this feature of Theatrical Potential in their translations. Such caution may be illustrated by an example taken from Campbell's translation and adaptation of Gogol's *Revizor* (here: *The Government Inspector*) into English: When CHLESTAKOV and the MAYOR (in Russian GORODNIČIJ) confront each another for the first time (act I, scene 8), both being scared to death on account of presumably impending punishment, CHLESTAKOV takes to putting on airs: "Ja prjamo k ministru!"[55] ("I straight to [the] Minister!"). In order to be able to

---

[52] Cf. SCHULTZE, "Stanisław Ignacy Witkiewiczs Dramen" 475–480.

[53] I could name a number of translations, among them the anonymous (1917) German translation of Krasiński's *Nie-Boska Komedia* ("Undivine Comedy"), Wilhelm Lange's translation of Gogol's *Revizor* ("The Inspector General") and Paul Kruntorad's German translation of František Langer's comedy *Velbloud uchem jehly* ("A Camel through a Needle's Hole").

[54] Cf. SCHULTZE, "A Case of Delayed Cultural Transfer"; Otto Zoff and Franz Theodor Csokor who adapted the anonymous translation of Krasiński's *Nie-Boska komedia* for the stage 'created' numerous grammatical gaps in their theatre scripts. The fact that these 'secondary' gaps appear in positions different from the source text allows for the assumption that both adaptors did not consult the source text in this instance.

[55] GOGOL, *Revizor* 53.

maintain this ellipsis in the target text, the translator has to mark the gap by a pause: "I ... straight to the Minister!" The pause, which is quite in line with CHLESTAKOV's rash, uncontrolled and also audacious speech and behavior, allows for an actor's inventiveness in facial expression and in body action. Campbell does not risk omission of the verb. His translation is, "I shall go straight to the Minister!"[56] Of course, such translatory options do not impair Theatrical Potential, if they only occur occasionally; they may, however, be detrimental to Theatrical Potential if they constitute a trend in a given translation. There are several concrete examples that demonstrate on a structural level the negative impact of such source-text deviating trends on Theatrical Potential.

In summing up, I wish to emphasize that, especially during the last two or three decades, translators of drama have shown growing understanding of the cultural technique called 'translating drama.' Both the ideas of producing 'two texts in one' and of creating a translation replete with theatrical meaning, that is, a translation which may be used in a number of different productions, are now largely shared by translators of dramatic texts.[57]

Works Cited

AALTONEN, Sirkku. "Rewriting the Exotic. The Manipulation of Otherness in Translated Drama." *Translation—the Vital Link*. XIII FIT World Congress. Proceedings. 1. London: The Chameleon Press Ltd., 1993. 136–148.

—. *Gallous Stories. Two Transplants into Finnish of "The Playboy of the Western World."* Tutkimuksia. 173. Kielitiede. 21. Vaasa: University of Vaasa, 1993.

BASSNETT-MCGUIRE, Susan. "Ways Through the Labyrinth. Strategies and Methods for Translating Theatre Texts." *The Manipulation of Literature. Studies in Literary Translations*. Ed. T. Hermans. New York: St. Martin's Press, 1985. 87–102.

—. "Translating for the Theatre." *Essays in Poetics* 15 (1990): 71–84.

BIRCH, David. *The Language of Drama. Critical Theorie and Practice*. London: Macmillan, 1991.

---

[56] GOGOL, *The Government Inspector* 49.

[57] Cf. WILLET 2; even in France with her strong tradition of producing two versions of foreign drama, a meticulous piece of literature on the one hand and an adaptation on the other hand, the idea of translating 'two texts in one' is gaining more and more acceptance. Patrice Pavis, who wrote a commentary and notes to a new French translation of Chekhov's *Djadja Vanja (Oncle Vania)*, told me that a series of new translations of Chekhov's plays are "meant for readers as well as for performances."

CHEKHOV, Anton Pavlovich [Anton Tchékhov]. *Oncle Vania. Scènes de la vie de campagne en quatre actes*. Traduction Nouvelle et préface de Tonia Galievsky et Bruno Sermonne. Commentaires et notes de Patrice Pavis. Livre de poche. 6251. Paris: Librairie Générale Française, 1986.

DÜRRENMATT, Friedrich. *Der Besuch der alten Dame. Eine tragische Komödie.* Die Arche: Zürich, 1956.

—. *The Visit*. Transl. Patrick Bowles. *Plays and Essays*. The German library. 89. New York: The Continuum Publishing Company, 1982. 71–153.

ESSLER-RAGHUNATH, Ulrike. "Skopos und Bühnenübersetzung. Aspekte der Translation von Theaterstücken." *TEXTconTEXT* 5 (1990): 251–266.

FRANK, Armin Paul, and Brigitte SCHULTZE. "Normen in historisch-deskriptiven Übersetzungsstudien." *Die literarische Übersetzung: Stand und Perspektiven ihrer Erforschung*. Ed. H. Kittel. Göttinger Beiträge zur Internationalen Übersetzungsforschung. 2. Berlin: Erich Schmidt Verlag, 1988. 96–121.

GOGOL, Nikolai V. *The Government Inspector: A Comedy in three Acts*. Transl. and adapted by D.J. Campbell. London: Sylvan Press, 1947.

—. *Revizor. Komedija v 5 d*. Sobranie chudožestvennych proizvedenij v. 5 t. 4. Moskva: IAN SSSR, 1956. 5–122.

HAAG, Ansgar. "Übersetzen fürs Theater: Beispiel William Shakespeare." *Babel* 30 (1984): 218–224.

HAMMERSCHMID, Beata, and Martina RIEMEKASTEN. "Übersetzungsprobleme mit 'Gott' und 'Teufel': Folklore und Metaphysik in den deutschen Übersetzungen und Bearbeitungen von N.V. Gogol's *Revizor*." *Komödie und Tragödie—übersetzt und bearbeitet*. Ed. U. Jekutsch, F. Paul, B. Schultze and H. Turk. Forum Modernes Theater. Vol. 16. Tübingen: Gunter Narr Verlag, 1994. 269–301.

KRUGER, Loren Adrienne. *Translating (for) the Theatre: The Appropriation, Mise en Scène and Reception of Theatre Texts*. Diss. Cornell Univ., 1986.

LARSON, Kenneth E. "Wieland's Shakespeare: A Reappraisal." *Lessing Yearbook* 16 (1984): 229–251.

NASH, Walter. *The Language of Humour*. English language series. 16. London, New York: Longman, 1985.

OSBORNE, John. *Look Back in Anger. A Play in Three Acts*. 5th ed. London: Faber and Faber, 1958.

—. *Blick zurück im Zorn: Theaterstück in drei Akten*. Transl. Hans Sahl. Frankfurt am Main: S. Fischer, n.d.

PAUL, Fritz, and Brigitte SCHULTZE, eds. *Probleme der Dramenübersetzung 1960–1988. Grundzüge und Bibliographie*. Bearbeitet von Ruth Müller-Reineke in Zusammenarbeit mit Brigitte Schultze und Doris Lemmermeier. Forum Modernes Theater. Vol. 7. Tübingen: Gunter Narr Verlag, 1991.

PAVIS, Patrice. "Problems of Translation for the Stage: Interculturalism and Postmodern Theatre." *The Play out of Context. Transferring Plays from Culture to Culture*. Ed. H. Scolnikov, P. Holland. Cambridge: CUP, 1989. 25–44.

SCHULTZE, Brigitte. "Theorie der Dramenübersetzung, 1960 bis heute: Ein Bericht zur Forschungslage." *Forum Modernes Theater* 2 (1987): 5–17.

—. "Stanisław Ignacy Witkiewiczs 'Drama-Theater' als Herausforderung für Übersetzer: *Kurka wodna* deutsch und englisch." *Ars Philologica Slavica*. Ed. V. Setschkareff, P. Rehder and H. Schmid. Sagners Slavistische Sammlung. 15. München: Verlag Otto Sagner, 1988. 396–411.

—. "In Search of a Theory of Drama Translation: Problems of Translating Literature (Reading) and Theatre (Implied Performance)." *Os Estudos literários: (Entre) Ciência e Hermenêutica*. Actas Do I Congresso Da APLC. Associação Portugesa de Literatura Comparada. Lisboa 1990. 267–274.

—. "Probleme mit der intrigenlosen Komödie: Gogol's *Revizor* in den frühen deutschen Übersetzungen und Bearbeitungen." *Europäische Komödie im übersetzerischen Transfer*. Ed. F. Paul, W. Ranke and B. Schultze. Forum Modernes Theater. Vol. 11. Tübingen: Gunter Narr Verlag, 1993. 187–239.

—. "Russisch-deutsche und polnisch-deutsche Dramenübersetzung: Historische und systematische Aspekte des Kulturtransfers." *Zeitschrift für Slawistik* 38 (1993/94): 515–538.

—. "Das kanonische Bühnenwerk bleibt Lektüre. Mickiewiczs *Dziady* (Ahnenfeier) im polnisch-deutschen Kulturtransfer." *Komödie und Tragödie— übersetzt und bearbeitet*. Ed. U. Jekutsch, F. Paul, B. Schultze and H. Turk. Forum Modernes Theater. Vol. 16. Tübingen: Gunter Narr Verlag, 1994. 369–403.

—. "A Case of Delayed Cultural Transfer: Stanisław Wyspiański's *Wesele* (The Wedding, 1901) in English Translation (1990)." *New Comparison* 19.1 (1995): 71-78.

SNELL-HORNBY, Mary. "Sprechbare Sprache—Spielbarer Text: Zur Problematik der Bühnenübersetzung." *Modes of Interpretation*. Ed. R.J.Watts, U. Weidman. Tübingen: Gunter Narr Verlag, 1984. 101–116.

TOTZEVA, Sophia [Sofija Toceva]. *Das theatrale Potential des dramatischen Textes: Ein Beitrag zur Theorie von Drama und Dramenübersetzung*. Forum Modernes Theater. Vol. 19. Tübingen: Gunter Narr Verlag, 1995.

—. "Zum Umgang mit der Expansion bei der Übersetzung dramatischer Texte." *Zeitschrift für Slawistik* 39 (1995): 23-33.

VAN DEN BROECK, Raymond. "Translation for the Theatre." *Linguistica Antverpiensia* 20 (1986): 96-110.

VERMEER, Hans J. *Skopos und Translationsauftrag*. Part. 2. Heidelberg, 1989.

WILLET, John. "Translation, Transmission, Transportation." *Transformations in Modern European Drama*. Ed. I. Donaldson. Canberra: Australian National University, 1983. 1–13.

WYSPIAŃSKI, Stanisław. *The Wedding*. Transl. Gerard T. Kapolka. Ann Arbor: Ardis, 1990.

THOMAS FREELAND

Heiner Müller's *Mommsen's Block* and the Languages of the Stage

> Fragments of a vessel which are to be glued together must match one another in the smallest details, although they need not be like one another. In the same way a translation, instead of resembling the meaning of the original, must lovingly and in detail incorporate the original's mode of signification, thus making both the original and the translation recognizable as fragments of a greater language, just as fragments are part of a vessel.
>
> *Walter Benjamin*, "The Task of the Translator"

This paper originated as a kind of performance text. Its revision for this anthology has raised, once more, the fundamental problem it set out to address: the applicability of a model based on translation to describe the process through which a *written* work becomes a *staged* performance. The original presentation of this paper incorporated performance, both live (the reading of the paper itself, augmented by cast members from the stage production of *Mommsen's Block*) and video-recorded. This multi-media approach made it possible to abridge any theoretical account the paper may have offered by demonstrating the process outright. The presence of actors (who started off their performance by pretending to be academics at a conference, disputing a question of historical interpretation) could be folded into what was already a staged spectacle. The paper's contribution to this spectacle, in turn, was to describe some of the problems attendant upon creating just such a performance.

Moving now, however, from that initial, multilayered presentation to the very different, single medium of an essay cannot but force a reassessment of employing a translation model to account for this very movement—from text to performance/presentation to text yet again. In this context 'translation' functions not so much as a neat explanatory mechanism as it does rather as a broader way of characterizing the semic economy of the text-performance-text system as a whole. The 'breadth' of this characterization denotes a certain slippage between 'translation' and *transformation*. What originally served as the operative metaphor in my account has become the problem itself: does 'translation' adequately address the differential between 'text' and 'performance?' What follows, accordingly, will therefore take the form of an 'essay' in the very literal sense of being an *attempt*, more an outline of a problem than a fully-realized solution.

In her study of the politics of performance, *Unmarked*, Peggy Phelan argues that "[p]erformance's only life is in the present. Performance cannot be saved, recorded, documented, or otherwise participate in the circulation of representations *of* representations: once it does so, it becomes something other than performance" (146). From this view, there appears to be an irreducible gap separating a text from its performance, and a performance from its subsequent recording or description. As noted above, the original presentation of this paper combined performance and something "other": live performance (which began the presentation) was juxtaposed with video footage and verbal description in order to discuss the problems I had to address when 'translating' a written text into a stage performance. The written work in question is *Mommsen's Block*, a recent text by the noted (and recently deceased) German dramatist Heiner Müller, which I staged in November 1994 at Stanford as *Mommsen's Block/Benjamin's Angel*. The reason for the alteration in the title will become clear in time, as the explanatory scheme shifts more explicitly from 'translation' to 'transformation.' Although interesting difficulties did arise in the course of the primary translation of Müller's German into English, what I wish to address here is the process of turning this relatively stable literary artifact into a living theatrical experience.

Phelan's argument goes to the heart of the ontological distinction to be drawn between what Müller wrote and what the audiences in the theatre saw last autumn. An individual reader controls the pace at which she encounters a text; anything unclear at first glance may be gone over again as many times as the reader might wish. Even before hypertext so dramatically streamlined the process people were known to skip around in books, jumping to the end to find out whether or not the butler actually did it, bypassing dull or perhaps excessively exciting passages and so on, even jumping from one work to another altogether, actively fragmenting texts in a play of cross-reference. A reader may go through an entire text at a sitting, or take it a little at a time. The temporal aspect of the reader's experience is thus highly fluid, and subject to the reader's individual control. This is not so in the case of a live performance. In performance each member of the audience encounters the work at the same rate. They may avert their eyes at the scary parts or doze off during the slower parts, but they cannot skip over them. Nor can they go back for another look at any scene.

Moreover, the verbal element constitutes but one aspect of the performance; the setting, costuming, lighting, music and sound-effects—not to mention the acting—must be taken into account as well. The acting onstage mediates the act of the audience's reading, *enacting* the script as a real-time event. The words on the page assume a physical *presence* as actions on the stage—not merely insofar as they may be taken to *indicate* (or instigate) specific actions, but more directly, inasmuch as the very enunciation of words onstage itself constitutes a form of action. Simply by being heard the text is made manifest as a physical occurrence. A performance thus amounts to a field of possible *experiences*, which perforce must occur in their own sustained *present* (the suspended present of narrative time). Each actor, and every individual member of the audience represents an additional variable brought into play. Stanton Garner (in his book *Bodied Spaces*) suggests speaking not of *presence* in the theatre but rather of an ongoing process of *presencing*, continually re-establishing itself before the audience's eyes and ears (46–7). In this enactment the text is not simply read to the audience, but problematized before them, called into question. The written text, the *script*, may provide a catalyst or a framework for performance, but in even the most minimalist production it can be but one variable in a more complex equation. As the *source*, the verbal master-plan, it carries a tremendous signifying burden, but the communicative power of words on the stage cannot be reduced to their function as signs.

On the level of the linguistic translation, *Mommsen's Block* already presents a challenge: Müller uses very little punctuation, making parenthetical statements and subordinate clauses often difficult to identify. The text quotes from and alludes to several other works, among them Theodor Mommsen's own writings, a letter from Nietzsche to Peter Gast, the *Aeneid*, the *Cantos* of Ezra Pound, and more. In one section Müller writes in a strongly idiomatic German, leaving the translator to search for expressions that correspond in both general meaning and specific feeling.

The even greater challenge, however, lies in the fact that *Mommsen's Block* does not appear to have been written for performance. There are no indications whatsoever of how one would go about staging it. A primary task for the production, therefore, was the transformation of the work into a *performance* text. In practical terms (and the theatre must needs be practical in its apprehension of texts) this amounted to a *con-textualizing* of Müller's writing. How was this work, itself basically a seven-page-long poem, to assume active, physical form on the stage? How was its literary figuration to be realized in images occurring in "real" time and space? How should it be "framed?"

Theatre, it bears emphasizing, is at least as much a *visual* as it is an *auditory* experience. The audience *sees* as well as *hears* a text on the stage. Images set down in the writing must be brought out in the staging. To the extent that one can subject everything in the stage space to an analytic of representation, the more attractive "translation" becomes as a way to characterize the relationship between a performance and the text that is its source. Everything is constructed out of one or another kind of *language*. The immediate affinity between reading and performance in the theatre suggests a way to expand (to corporealize) the conception of language in such a model. To *read* a text in the theatre automatically means to read it *aloud*; the text becomes a pre-text for the activity of speaking. The text thus gives rise to itself as an *event*—for any actor performing a text onstage, even an actor doing no more than simply speaking the words, is *doing something*. This event unfolds for an audience to *witness*: they, too, are doing something. The audience must undertake to assess all the information coming at them in various forms from the stage, carrying out their own reading. My task as director and designer was to bring all the signifying apparatus of the theatre to bear on conveying this information to the audience. The result can be viewed as an "imagining" of the text, its projection into the collectively-generated "what-if" space-time of the stage. The performance demonstrates my and the actors' reading (with the additional connotation of *interpretation*) of the text. The intertexts I wove into Müller's writing serve both to contextualize, to orient the piece, and as well to point up the nature of the performance as *a* reading of the text, a network of associations bearing obviously or obliquely on the script. They echo the many allusions woven by Müller into his own text.

To illustrate this process of "imagining" I shall describe the development of two images from the production, in the first instance an image initially textual (Walter Benjamin's "Angel of History") and in the second an image originally visual, which then proved to have a direct relation to the script (the famous 1895 photograph of a train wreck in Paris).

With *Mommsen's Block* I was faced with a dense and syntactically fragmented text that dealt with issues and ideas with which I could not be assured that my audience was conversant. In order to contextualize the piece I seized upon the well-exercised passage in Walter Benjamin's *Theses on the Philosophy of History* in which Benjamin discusses the Paul Klee painting "Angelus Novus" as an allegorical image of his conception of the idea of historical progress. The influence of Benjamin's thought on Müller's writing has been well documented—in fact, Müller wrote his own updated version of the "Angel" passage, which I also spliced into the show—so I felt that the Benjamin quote would serve to set the tone for the performance as a whole. I also wished to address the recent pop-cultural explosion of angel images—in everything from television sit-coms to the film *Wings of Desire*—so various kinds of angels appeared throughout the piece. Benjamin's angel, then, started off the performance; we also had Müller's adaptation of that text, as well as a poem he later wrote as a post-1989 follow-up; in addition I took a section from Kafka's diaries describing a dream-visitation of an angel, and finally a few lines from Rilke's "Seventh Duino Elegy."

Heiner Müller's Mommsen's Block

The point of all this splicing was to find verbal anchors for visual metaphors to give the different philosophies of history in the piece physical form. On this interpretive point turns much of Müller's speculation about Mommsen's writer's block. It was also important that these images resonate with Müller's Benjaminian philosophy of history. Benjamin's angel-of-history image combines ideas of the mounting disasters of "progress" with the apparent absence (or perpetual deferment) of divine intervention. Historical understanding, on this view, amounts to a process of sifting through the wreckage. At the same time the angel, as an *angel*—a messenger from God—also suggests the possibility of redemption, of a divine perspective and summation that at least retroactively can invest the disasters of history with meaning.

Picture 1 shows this moment of the show. The actor playing the angel stands before a screen, upon which Klee's painting is projected. Two other actors (dressed to suggest they are workers of some kind) hold a large book open in front of a powerful electric fan. The pages of the book come flying out of their binding, swirling around the angel and scattering across the stage, as a recording of the Benjamin passage is played over the speaker-system.

Another image that proved especially useful for the production was the train wreck mentioned above (pictures 2A and 2B). I came across it by chance while preparing the text for rehearsal and was struck by its strange appropriateness to the way I envisioned depicting "progress" and "modernity" in the show. I later found an interview with Heiner Müller specifically addressing the influence of Benjamin's ideas on his writing. In this interview Müller mentions Benjamin's commentary on Marx's statement that "revolutions are the locomotives of world history." Benjamin suggested that perhaps the situation is quite different; perhaps revolutions represent the human race, which is riding in this 'train of history,' reaching for the emergency brake. Müller then asks the interviewer whether he had ever seen that picture of the locomotive crashed through the wall of the train station, resting on its nose on the street below. This picture, for Müller, epitomized Benjamin's view of history. Such a serendipitous encounter provided all the proof I could wish for that I had, indeed, come across an apposite image. Upon entering the theatre the audience was met with this train-wreck picture, and at the end of the show it reappeared, this time accompanied first by the Marx quote, and then by Benjamin's comment. Here again, the idea was to interweave Müller's text with striking visual images that reinforced and commented on the verbal portions of the performance. The shifting backdrop of rear-projected slides throughout the show itself constituted a level of imagistic translation. Here again, however, the notion of translation is extended (not to say attenuated) into transformation, into *transmutation*.

Thomas Freeland

These processes, then (of creating visual images, of arranging the actors' speech and movement, etc.), raise the question whether any analogy can be drawn between the work of theatrical production and linguistic translation. The close affinity in English between "translation" and "interpretation" becomes important in this regard. Translating the script was only the first step in the *mise-en-scène*, the "putting-on-stage." With the addition of selections from other texts, the arrangement of the constantly changing "stage picture," and the overall arrangement of the performance as a field of *experience* for the audience, other semic systems are brought into play, in ways that at times help to clarify, and at other times to complicate or interrogate the ways in which meanings are generated out of the text. Theatrical staging volatilizes Müller's text in an overdeterminate *combinatoire* of shifting variables. No one of the varied languages of the stage can lay sole claim to carrying *the* translation of *Mommsen's Block*; Müller's text is *one* source of material, which along with a group of actors, a set of pictures, a director-designer, a stage-manager and so on, underwent a production-process, a *transformation*, resulting in (or evidenced by) a performance. In the original presentation of this paper I illustrated the complexity of this process by pausing at this point to show a videorecording of the section of Müller's text with which I had begun the presentation. I wanted to demonstrate the multifariousness of the field of possible relations between text and performance, to give the audience a feel for the range of "imaginings" (i.e., stagings) that can come out of one text.

In the Stanford production this segment was designed as an extended allusion to Wim Wenders' *Wings of Desire,* to offer another view of angels and their relationship to the disasters of human history. To reinforce the association the music used in this section came from the film's soundtrack. Familiarity with that film, however, could not be made a prerequisite to understanding that section of the performance. As happens with literary allusion, an audience member familiar with the reference simply had another set of associations to draw upon in assessing the work.

Probably the most striking difference between reading *Mommsen's Block* on one's own and seeing it on the stage is hearing the words produced by several different voices. Müller provides no indication of divisions of dialogue (except for one short section at the end), and yet the script's narrative structure is highly fragmentary and contentious with itself. By assigning particular lines, and parts of lines to different individual actors and combinations of actors, I sought to give this textual polyphony a physical form. The repetition of certain sections worked to the same end; in the segment shown on video in the original presentation the opening section was presented once as a fairly coherent whole, and then repeated in a more dispersed choral mode. Likewise, Benjamin's angel, from whom the performance partly took its title, also makes another appearance, the second time being performed by the entire ensemble. Instabilities in the script itself were seized as opportunities to underscore the provisionality of the meanings produced in the stage action. The section of text borrowed from Kafka became the scene of a collision of texts: while four actors performed the Kafka text two others offered quotations from Rilke, and the remaining two actors softly recited the same Rilke passages in the original German. Here in one theatrical moment the disparate voices of competing theories about Mommsen, and about the writing of history in general, are invoked at once. Here, too, the range of possible experiences is dramatized; each individual in the audience, depending on where they sat, and what they chose to pay attention to, would have a markedly different impression of the stage action. (Picture 3 shows the Kafka section. The projection in the background shows the Winged Victory statue being hoisted back into place in the course of the postwar restoration of the Brandenburg Gate in Berlin.)

Throughout the process of staging this piece, the challenge remained to find concrete activities for the actors that still conveyed something beyond their immediate appearance. A director cannot simply tell an actor to perform "history," or "progress;" a situation must be established, specific images must be found for the actors to present. These images, in turn, provide a basis of common experience to which the members of the audience may then bring their individual associations and interpretive faculties.

There is also the question of the cultural and historical context in which *Mommsen's Block* was written. The text first appeared in 1993, and takes the events of 1989 as its backdrop. The phantom fourth volume of Mommsen's *Roman History* serves as a spectral palimpsest for the works Müller cannot write in a newly reunified Germany. For a writer who for so long was so closely identified with divisions in German cultural consciousness and historical experience, reunification amounts to a form of internal exile. The closing segment of *Mommsen's Block* captures Müller's dilemma vividly. It is all the more striking for being by far the most "realistic" dialogue in the piece—it is, in fact, the only part of the script divided by Müller into dialogue form.

The concluding section of *Mommsen's Block* presents two stockbrokers dining at the table next to Müller's (from whose individual viewpoint the entire poem has been narrated) in a Berlin restaurant. The two engage in a cryptic exchange of high-finance jargon, apparently discussing the professional misfortunes of some hapless colleague. Müller expressly contrasts the parochial narrowness of their discourse with the magisterial scope of Mommsen's lectures, finding in the gulf between them a growing understanding of Mommsen's writer's block:

> Animal noises Who would want to write that down
> With passion Hate doesn't pay Contempt is running
> empty

Thomas Freeland

> I understood for the first time your writer's block
> Comrade Professor at the time of the Roman Caesars (9)

The idea of *translation* as a model for the process of staging texts thus helps shed some light on the various signifying means the theatre brings to bear in the course of its work. A common feature of much avant-garde performance in recent years is a suspicion of a stable, coherent text as a clear blueprint for stage action. Samuel Beckett demonstrated throughout his body of work that words are not always necessary to staging, and that when they are present they are ultimately only additional materials to be refashioned by the theatrical enterprise. And as with all translation, if one encounters a version that one feels does some disservice to the original, one can always undertake a translation of one's own. The theatre, in its very nature, is always beginning anew.

Works Cited

BENJAMIN, Walter. "The Task of the Translator." Benjamin. *Illuminations*. Trans. Harry Zohn. New York: Harcourt, Brace, 1968.

GARNER, Stanton. *Bodied Spaces*. Ithaca: Cornell University Press, 1994.

MÜLLER, Heiner. "Mommsens Block." *Drucksache* 1, ed. Berliner Ensemble (January 1993): 2–9. Translated for the Stanford production as *Mommsen's Block* by Thomas Freeland (unpublished).

PHELAN, Peggy. *Unmarked*. London: Routledge, 1993.

Heiner Müller's Mommsen's Block

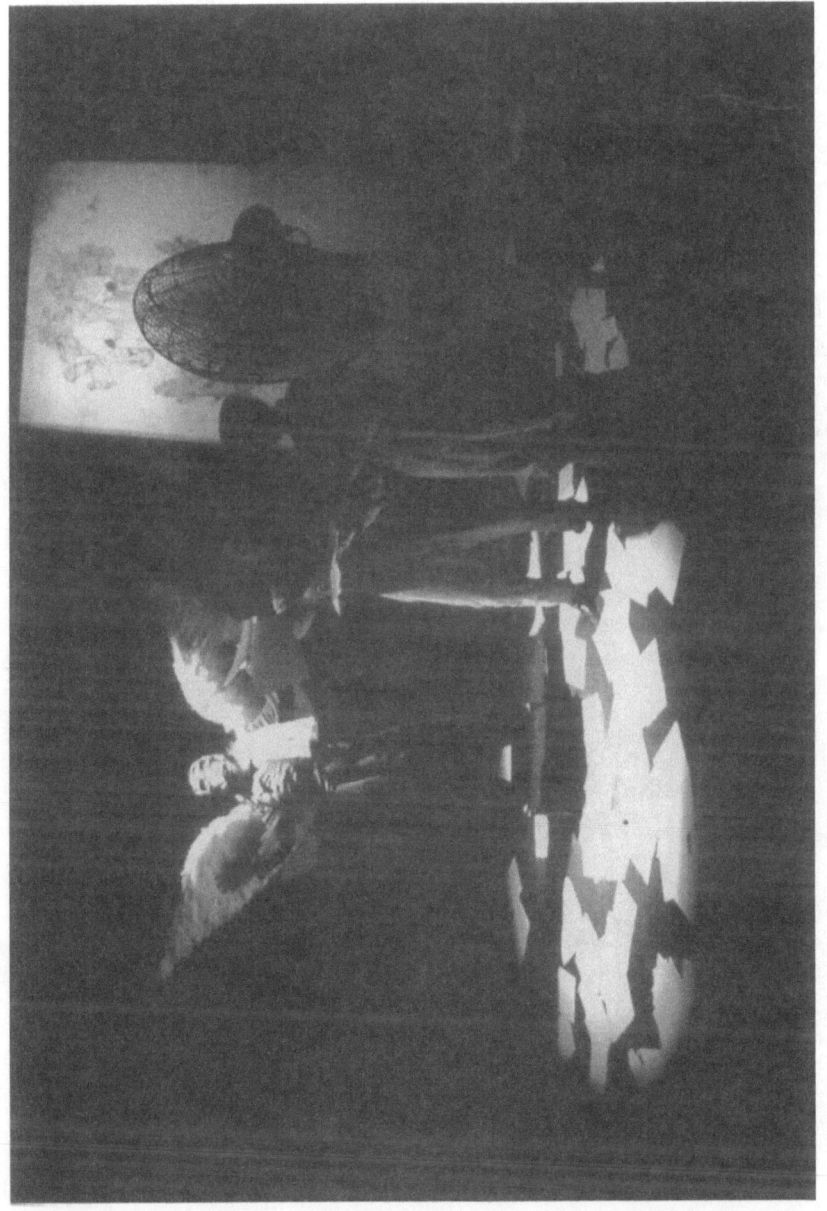

Picture 1 (Photo by Alexander Stewart)

Picture 2, part A (Photo montage by Freeland)

Heiner Müller's Mommsen's Block

Picture 2, part B (Photo montage by Freeland)

Picture 3 (Photo by Alexander Stewart)

Contributors

Prof. Ernst Behler†, Department of Comparative Literature, University of Washington, Seattle, WA 98195, U.S.A.

Dr. Helga Eßmann, SFB 529 (Internationalität nationaler Literaturen), Georg-August-Universität, Humboldtallee 17, 37073 Göttingen, Germany

Prof. John Felstiner, Department of English, Stanford University, Stanford, CA 94305, U.S.A. (felstine@leland.stanford.edu)

Prof. Armin Paul Frank, Seminar für Englische Philologie & SFB 529, Georg-August-Universität Göttingen, Humboldtallee 13, 37073 Göttingen, Germany

Thomas Freeland, Department of Drama, Stanford University, Stanford, CA 94305, U.S.A. (thomas@leland.stanford.edu)

Prof. Liselotte Gumpel, University of Minnesota, P.O. Box 650, Morris, MN 56267, U.S.A. (gumpell@caa.mrs.umn.edu)

Prof. Cyrus Hamlin, Department of Germanic Languages, Yale University, P.O. Box 208210, New Haven, CT 06520-8210, U.S.A. (cyrus.hamlin@yale.edu)

Michael Irmscher, Department of German Studies, Stanford University, Stanford, CA 94305-2030, U.S.A. (irmscher@leland.stanford.edu)

Dr. Harald Kittel, Seminar für Englische Philologie, Georg-August-Universität Göttingen, Humboldtallee 13, 37073 Göttingen, Germany

Prof. Kurt Mueller-Vollmer, Department of German Studies, Stanford University, Stanford, CA 94305-2030, U.S.A. (kmv@leland.stanford.edu)

Prof. Rainer Schulte, Translation Center, The University of Texas at Dallas, Richardson, TX 75083-0688, U.S.A. (schulte@utdallas.edu)

Prof. Brigitte Schultze, Institut für Slawistik, Johannes Gutenberg Universität Mainz, Saarstraße 21, 55099 Mainz, Germany

Index of Authors*

Aaltonen, Sikku 178
Alcott, Bronson 116, 117, 122
Ali, Tariq 183
Apollinaire, Guillaume 169, 173, 174, 175
Aristophanes 132–134
Aristotle IX, 48, 55, 56, 58, 72, 135, 139
Auerbach, Berthold 120
Austen, Jane 25

Bab, Julius 159, 160
Bacon, Francis XIV, 33, 43
Bancroft, George 89, 90, 95, 113
Barfield, Owen 61
Bassnett, Susan X, 88
Beardsley, Monroe C. 48, 58, 72
Beauvoir, Simone de 67
Beckett, Samuel 171, 204
Behler, Ernst XV
Benét, Vincent 159
Benjamin, Walter 197, 200, 201, 202
Bethge, Hans 157
Birch, David 179, 180, 184
Bödeker, Birgit 11
Bowen, Francis 102
Bowles, Patrick 190, 191, 194
Bréal, Michel 51, 67
Breme, Lodovico di 91, 92
Brenton, Howard 183, 184

Brokmeyer, Henry 116, 117, 122
Brooks, Charles T. XV, 104, 112, 118–123
Bryant, Williams 25
Busch, Wilhelm 120
Byron, George G. 104

Campbell, D. J. 189, 192–194
Carlyle, Thomas 114, 120
Cassirer, Ernst XIV, 55, 60, 61, 63, 68
Celan, Paul XVI, 76, 165–175
Chai, Leon 86
Channing, William E. 90, 99
Chomsky, Noam 60, 65, 70
Cicero 57, 98
Clarke, James F. 92, 100, 101, 104
Coleridge, Samuel T. 104, 113, 121, 122
Colli, Giorgio XV, 127–130, 142
Constant, Benjamin 99
Cooper, James F. 23, 25–28, 89
Cousin, Victor 99
Croce, Benedetto 81

Dekker, George 25
Denham, Sir John 20
Derrida, Jacques XIV, 61, 62
Dewey, John 116
De Wette, Wilhelm M. 94, 97–100
Dickens, Charles 9
Dickinson, Emily E. 169, 170
Diderot, Denis 133, 134

---

* Please note that the index only lists names of authors who are discussed in the main body of the text.

Dilthey, Wilhem 110
Droysen, Johann G. 82
Dryden, John 20
Dürrenmatt, Friedrich 190

Eckermann, Johann Peter 99
Eichendorff, Joseph v. 53, 77
Eichhorn, Johann 94, 98
Elliott, Emory 23, 82
Emerson. Raph W. XV, 23, 81, 83–86, 89, 90, 91, 94, 98, 100, 101, 103, 104–106, 109–111, 113, 114, 117, 119, 121–123
Enzensberger, Hans M. 156
Essler-Raghunath, Ulrike 183, 184
Eßmann, Helga XVI, 11
Even-Zohar, Itamar XI, 16, 87
Everett, Edward 89, 103

Fichte, Johann G. 97, 99, 102, 111, 113, 121, 122
Felstiner, John XVI
Follen, Charles 97, 113, 119
Foucault, Michel 88
Frank, Armin P. XIII, XIV, XVII, 7, 11
Freeland, Thomas XVII
Frege, Gottlieb 48, 59, 65
Freiligrath, Ferdinand 120
Freud, Sigmund 169
Fries, J. F. 101
Frost, Robert 166, 169, 170
Frothingham, Octavius B. 99
Fuller, Margaret XV, 90–92, 94, 98, 99, 104, 113, 114, 121

Gentzler, Edwin XII, 98
George, Stefan 77, 78
Gerould, Daniel 189
Goethe, Johann W. v. 16, 18, 23, 89, 90, 93, 103–106, 108, 111, 114, 115, 119, 121–123, 132, 134, 151, 152
Goethe-to-God ratio 103, 104
Gogol, Nikolai V. 186–189, 192, 194, 195
Göhring, Rolf 161
Goldscheider, Ludwig 152
Goll, Claire 162, 163
Goodman, Nelson 47, 49
Griboedov, Alexander 187
Grillparzer, Franz 120
Grimm, Jacob 52
Gryphius, Andreas 93
Guenther, Johann v. 188
Guizot, François 99
Gumpel, Liselotte XIV

Haag, Ansgar 182
Hamlin, Cyrus XV
Hansen, Kurt H. 160, 161
Hardenberg, Friedrich v. → Novalis
Harris, William T. XV, 112, 115–118, 121–123
Hart, Heinrich 162
Hart, Julius 160, 162
Hawthorne, Nathaniel 27
Haym, Rudolf 110
Hedge, Frederic H. XV, 91, 92, 98, 102, 103, 112–116, 121–126, 123
Hegel, Friedrich W. 93, 97, 111, 114, 121–123
Heidegger, Martin 62, 101, 173
Heine, Heinrich 3
Herder, Johann G. v. 15, 16, 89, 90, 91, 94, 95, 97, 99, 143, 103, 138, 151, 152, 162
Hermans, Theo XII, 6, 7
Hölderlin, Friedrich XV, 109, 110, 111, 170, 175

Index

Hollingdale, R. J. 131, 132
Holmes, James S. 87
Hölty, Ludwig 99
Horace 136
Housman, A. E. 165
Humboldt, Alexander v. 107, 108
Humboldt, Wilhem v. XIV, 51, 62, 88, 93
Hünich, Fritz A. 158

Ingarden, Roman XIV, 67–76, 78
Irving, Washington 89

Jabès, Edmond 31, 32
Jacobi, Friedrich H. 98, 99
James, William 116
Jaspers, Karl 141
Jean Paul → Paul, Jean
Jefferson, Thomas 107, 108
Jesus 96
Johnson, Mark 54
Jouffroy, Théodore 99

Kafka, Franz 175, 200, 203
Kant, Immanuel 18, 47, 49, 50, 51, 63, 67, 68, 97, 100, 102, 103, 106, 111, 113, 116, 117, 121, 122, 138
Kaufmann, Walter 131, 132, 136, 142
Kittel, Harald XIII, 22
Koller, Werner XI, 20
Körner, Theodor 99, 119
Kotzebue, August v. 23

Lakoff, George 54
Lambert, José XII
Lefevere, André X, 88
Leip, Hans 157
Lessing, Gotthold E. 133, 134
Levý, Jirí 3

Lieber, Francis 93, 101
Locke, John 85, 102
Longfellow, Henry W. 104
Lowth, Robert 15

Machiavelli, Niccolò 133, 134
Mandelshtam, Osip 169, 171, 172
Marsh, James 90–92, 95
Marx, Karl 201
Mauthner, Fritz 141
Melville, Herman 21, 37
Menzel, Wolfgang 99
Meurer, Kurt E. 161
Montinari, Mazzino XV, 127–130, 142
Mueller-Vollmer, Kurt XIV, XV, XVII, 28
Müller, Heiner XVII, 198–203
Mundt, Theodor 109, 110, 111

Nash, Odgen 159, 160
Neruda, Pablo 170
Nida, Eugene A. 16, 20, 86
Niebuhr, Barthold 93
Nietzsche, Friedrich XV, XVI, 47, 50, 51, 53, 71, 110, 113, 125–146, 199
Novalis 99, 105, 106

Osborne, John J. 181

Parker, Theodore 86, 90, 92, 95–98, 101, 104, 119
Paul, Jean 99, 109, 119, 120, 122
Paul, Fritz 11
Pavis, Patrice 183, 194
Paz, Octavio 32, 35
Peirce, Charles S. 116
Perkins, David 82
Petronius, Gaius 132, 133
Plato 133, 134

Index

Poe, Edgar A. 22
Pound, Ezra 26

Quintilian 57

Resnais, Alain 172
Richards, Ivor A. 78
Richter, Jean P. → Paul, Jean
Ricoeur, Paul 60
Rilke, Rainer M. 38
Ripley, George 89, 90–92, 97–99, 104, 119
Rousseau, Jean J. 61
Royce, Josiah 116
Rückert, Friedrich 119, 120
Ryle, Gilbert 56

Sachs, Hans 120
Sallust 135
Saussure, Ferdinand de 48, 51, 59, 65
Schack, Adolf F. v. 161
Schelling, Friedrich W. 92, 93, 97, 99–101, 111, 113, 121, 122
Scherr, Johannes 150, 152, 160
Schiller, Friedrich 108, 119, 120
Schlechta, Karl 127
Schlegel, August W. 91, 93, 144
Schlegel, Friedrich 96, 103, 109
Schleiermacher, Friedrich 83, 85, 86, 93, 94, 96–99, 100, 101
Schopenhauer, 93
Schulte, Rainer XIV
Schultze, Brigitte XVI, 11
Scott, Sir Walter 23, 25–27
Shakespeare, William 3, 58, 72, 165–170
Shelley, Percy B. 104
Snell-Hornby, Mary XI, 182
Solger, Heinrich 155, 156

Spielhagen, Friedrich 156
St. Jerome 19, 29
Stackelberg, Jürgen v. 20
Staël, Madame de 86, 91, 103, 104–106
Stevens, Wallace 18
Strindberg, August 9
Synge, John M. 178

Taber, C. 86
Thoreau, Henry D. 91, 122, 123
Ticknor, George 89, 91
Totzeva, Sophia 178, 179, 187
Toury, Gideon XI
Trilling, Lionell 22
Turk, Horst 11

Uhland, Ludwig 99, 109, 119

Valéry, Paul 172, 173
Van den Broeck, Raymond XII, 177, 184
Venuti, Lawrence X
Vermeer, Hans J. 183, 184
Voltaire 133, 134

Washington, George 26
Webster, Noah 24
Wenders, Wim 202
Wieland, Christoph M. 151
Williams, William C. 34
Witkacy, Stanisław 180, 189
Wittgenstein, Ludwig 62
Wollschläger, Hans 22
Wordsworth, William 18, 25, 104
Witkiewiczs, Stanisław → Witkacy

The authorized representative in the EU for product safety and compliance is:
Mare Nostrum Group
B.V Doelen 72
4831 GR Breda
The Netherlands

www.ingramcontent.com/pod-product-compliance
Lightning Source LLC
Chambersburg PA
CBHW021808220426
43662CB00006B/232